Advance Praise for
The Ultimate New York Diet

"The Victoria's Secret show is the most challenging appearance for any model. Just eight weeks after giving birth, David had my body lingerie-and-runway ready for the show. His program works fast—and, more important, the results last."

—*Heidi Klum*

"For many years David has helped me to look and feel my best. Now, roughly one year after the birth of my first child, his guidance has never been more relevant. More than anything I've tried before, David's comprehensive approach has transformed not only my body, but also how I feel inside my body. More than just a quick fix, his New York Plan has truly changed my life, giving me the strength, knowledge, and confidence to be my best self."

—*Liv Tyler*

"David is incredible. For David, no one is beyond looking their best. No one is too old or too large. I have many close friends who go to him, people who the public might think have gorgeous bodies. A couple of months after training with David, I can tell you that they are much more gorgeous than before."

—*Ellen Barkin*

"David Kirsch has an unbelievable way of individualizing a comprehensive exercise plan for achieving better health and physical strength. His charismatic and energizing personality are evident in his latest book, where exercise becomes the pillar for the motivation and willpower to seek overall health."

—*Connie Gutterson, R.D., Ph.D.,*
author of The Sonoma Diet

"Too often, patients feel that they must make a trade-off between losing weight and staying healthy. David's plan does not require this trade-off, and it's for this reason that I endorse it wholeheartedly."

—*Mehmet C. Oz, M.D.,*
Professor and Vice Chairman of Surgery, Columbia University,
and coauthor of You: The Owner's Manual

"David is an artist and a craftsman, able to transform the human body with intelligence, expertise, commitment, and love. I am endlessly grateful for the input David has had on my body and in my life."

—*Kerry Washington*

THE ULTIMATE

NEW YORK

DIET

THE ULTIMATE
NEW YORK
DIET

The Fastest Way to a Trimmer You!

DAVID KIRSCH

New York   Chicago   San Francisco   Lisbon   London   Madrid   Mexico City
Milan   New Delhi   San Juan   Seoul   Singapore   Sydney   Toronto

The **McGraw·Hill** Companies

Library of Congress Cataloging-in-Publication Data

Kirsch, David.
    The ultimate New York diet / by David Kirsch ; exercise photographs by Shonna
Valeska.
        p.   cm.
    Includes bibliographical references.
    ISBN 0-07-147582-6
    1. Reducing diets.   I. Title

RM222.2.K54257   2006
613.2'5—dc22   2006016665

1 2 3 4 5 6 7 8 9 10 11 12 13 14 15   DOC/DOC 0 9 8 7 6

ISBN-13: 978-0-07-147582-2
ISBN-10:   0-07-147582-6

Interior design by Think Design Group, LLC

McGraw-Hill books are available at special quantity discounts to use as premiums
and sales promotions, or for use in corporate training programs. For more information,
please write to the Director of Special Sales, Professional Publishing, McGraw-Hill, Two
Penn Plaza, New York, NY 10121-2298. Or contact your local bookstore.

This book is for educational purposes. It is not intended as a substitute for individual
fitness, health, and medical advice. Please consult a qualified health care professional
for individual health and medical advice. Neither McGraw-Hill nor the author shall have
any responsibility for any adverse effects that arise directly or indirectly as a result of
the information provided in this book.

This book is printed on acid-free paper.

To Mom and Dad—
I'm so proud of you both!

Contents

Foreword

As director of the Cardiovascular Institute at Columbia University Medical Center in New York, I usually see patients who, during the course of their lives, were told to lose weight, exercise, and change their diets but, for whatever reasons, couldn't pull it off. Over the years, as their cholesterol, blood sugar, blood pressure, waist circumference, and other heart disease risk factors crept upward, they dieted, purchased gym memberships, and signed up for the fitness fad of the month. Sometimes they lost weight, only to gain it back soon after.

So, instead of enjoying their best years cruising through life, they ended up on the operating table awaiting an angioplasty or a coronary bypass. It wasn't how they wanted things to end up. They had good intentions, but they just couldn't turn their intentions into results. They couldn't make the leap from wanting to eat well and exercise to actually doing so day in and day out.

Thus, it was with great interest that I heard about a unique wellness program created by David Kirsch. His clients who followed this program had dropped astounding amounts of weight, kept it off, and, most important, improved their overall health. Through Kirsch's guidance, they had stopped smoking, given up coffee, broken addictions to sugar, and ended bouts of emotional eating. In addition to fitting into clothes many sizes smaller than when they started Kirsch's program, they also reported other benefits. They felt calmer, more energetic, more focused, and more at peace with their bodies. One of Kirsch's clients saw his total cholesterol drop from a high of 243 to a low of 168 after just two weeks on Kirsch's program. These results stunned his doctor, who had tried and failed to lower the man's cholesterol levels with medication. Another client was told by his doctor that his blood pressure was high enough to give him a stroke. After a few months on Kirsch's plan, his blood pressure had normalized, without medication.

I wondered, "What is this guy doing with these people? How does he enable such powerful transformations?"

This is what I have since learned. During his 20 years in working with various clients, Kirsch has not only prescribed tried-and-true techniques but also has looked at each person as a unique individual. With each client, he has explored unique barriers to weight loss. When someone skipped a workout, he wanted to know why. When someone binged on ice cream, he wanted answers. When someone skipped meals, he explored the excuses. He didn't chastise or try to motivate with guilt. Rather, he peeled away their bad habits, exposing their weaknesses. Then he gave them the strategies they needed to overcome those weaknesses.

"Every day I want my clients to experience the benefits of making healthy life choices from vitamins, food, and exercise," Kirsch says. "Getting the combination of those choices just right is something I try to do for everyone at the Madison Square Club."

In this way, slowly, over 20 years, Kirsch eventually developed the plan laid out in this book. The entire book encompasses a phrase that Kirsch seems to say multiple times a day every day: "And your point is?" Kirsch has heard as many excuses as I have over the years for missed workouts and culinary overindulgences. It doesn't matter the excuse, he always responds, "And your point is?" To Kirsch, there are no excuses for poor health, and he's worked hard to help his clients overcome their excuses.

As a result, Kirsch has created an excuse-proof system for shaping up the body—and the mind. I've seen it and read it, and I can confidently tell you that it's a plan designed for real people—people with real jobs, real families, and real lives. It's also designed for people with real taste buds. Whatever your excuses for not losing weight in the past—a too-busy career, kids who need your attention, a sweet tooth, a body that hates to exercise—Kirsch has heard it all before and designed the plan to accommodate you.

Don't misunderstand me. His program is not easy. Kirsch is known for his grueling workouts and strict eating plan. From London to Germany and throughout the world, Kirsch has worked hard to develop and spread the word of the Ultimate New York Diet, and it encompasses everything that he's known for, including his intensity. It requires a commitment. To succeed on Kirsch's plan, you must sweat and you must eat differently. There's no way around that. Throughout this book, however, Kirsch offers his best advice—the same advice he whispers to his clients—for making those changes. You must do the work, but he helps you to find the strength and willpower to get it done.

Perhaps most interesting and most unique, the program works fast and the results last. Program participants see real results within days and stunning results within just two weeks. The Ultimate New York Diet is a rapid-weight-loss diet, one that promises to help you lose up to 14 pounds and five inches in your waist within the first two weeks of the plan. David's reasoning is that losing weight fast helps spark the motivation needed to go the distance. Too often, he reasons, when weight comes off too slowly, people get fed up with their new way of eating and abandon it altogether—only to gain everything back.

I usually don't endorse such diets. Unlike other rapid-weight-loss diets, however, the Ultimate New York Diet is not a starvation diet, a food-deprivation diet, a no-exercise diet, nor an unhealthy diet. This plan is about healthful foods. It prescribes three meals and two snacks a day—meals that consist of lean protein, lots of nutrient-rich vegetables, and nutritious grains, with plenty of fiber.

Too often, patients feel that they must make a trade-off between losing weight and staying healthy. Many popular diets are short on nutrients, vegetables, and fiber and/or heavy on artery-clogging saturated fats and trans-fatty acids. Kirsch's plan does not require this trade-off, and it's for this reason that I endorse it wholeheartedly. As a cardiac surgeon, I simply could not endorse a weight-loss plan that was not also heart healthy. On Kirsch's plan, you'll not only get into those tight jeans you keep in the back of your closet, but you'll be healthy enough to wear them for many years to come. It's a win-win.

Mehmet C. Oz, M.D.

Professor and Vice Chairman of Surgery, Columbia University
Coauthor of *You: The Owner's Manual* (HarperCollins, 2005)
Senior Medical Consultant, Discovery Health Channel

Acknowledgments

When I look back at my life, I have so much to be grateful for. First and foremost, I have the most amazing, loving, and supportive family—parents, sisters, brothers, and extended family. As is often the case, I take those closest to me the most for granted. I would be truly remiss if I failed to tell them how much I love and appreciate them and how much fuller my life is because of them.

To the supporters of *Sound Mind, Sound Body* and *The Ultimate New York Body Plan*, I thank you for your comments, critiques, suggestions, and praise, as they helped form the basis of this book. My clients, friends, trainers, and workers at the Madison Square Club continue to be a source of pride, inspiration, and love. I am very proud of the club I created over 16 years ago and am grateful for your loyalty and dedication through the years.

I am blessed and surrounded by some of the most talented people all over the world who advise, counsel, and support me.

I must give special mention to Marcy for her friendship and support. In the six years I have known her, my life has changed immeasurably and much of that I owe to her. I am eternally grateful. To my friend Desiree, whose counsel, friendship, love, and support I value and return in kind. To Heidi and Darren, for never being afraid to tell me what I need to hear—I love you guys! To lovely Sue, who single-handedly made *The Ultimate New York Body Plan* a bestseller in the United Kingdom. The real bonus for me is our lifelong friendship. To my friend Christian, who, along with his team, tirelessly promoted my book and made it a bestseller in Germany. To Julie, for her intelligence and generosity of spirit and Nina, my friend and counselor, for her sage wisdom—I send you my love and many thanks. To my friend Sam, for being the creative genius behind my brand and for always being there when I need him to be. To my assistant, Amanda, for never looking at the clock—thanks for your support, dedication, and loyalty.

To "my girls" Heidi, Liv, Linda, Karolina, Kerry, and Ellen—the sexiest New Yorker I know! You all make getting up early in the morning so easy. I love and adore you all!

To my *New York Times* bestselling authors whose support and generosity are so aptly represented in their endorsement of this book—Dr. Mehmet Oz and Connie Gutterson—my undying gratitude. Dr. Oz is a world-renowned cardiologist who happened to be my dad's cardiac surgeon, for which my family and I will be eternally grateful.

To everyone at McGraw-Hill, my second family, especially Phillip, Keith, Judith, Isabella, Lynda, Deb, Julia, Tom, and Lydia, I am proud to be a part of your team and look forward to great successes with you in the future. To my friend Alisa, for once again effortlessly and tirelessly performing her brilliance, and to Shonna for her beautiful photographs—thank you, thank you.

I would be remiss if I didn't personally and publicly tell my sister and friend Bonnie how much I love and appreciate her. Her tireless effort, love, and support have not gone unnoticed. I would be lost without you!

To my nieces, Samantha and Cara, whose unconditional love and support make every day sunnier for me.

Last but not least, I want to thank and dedicate this book to my parents. To my dad, who, thanks to the brilliance of Dr. Oz, has gotten through a very difficult year and still runs and exercises regularly, proving that one can really conquer most anything with strength and courage. To my mom, who in many respects was the inspiration and driving force behind this book, which is all about hope and possibility. At 69 years young, my mother represents and embraces my strongest belief: *One is never too old and it is never too late.* If you believe in yourself, anything is possible.

I thank you all for giving me the opportunity to share my passion and knowledge with you.

Introduction

Welcome to the Ultimate New York Diet, the revolutionary eating, exercising, and thinking plan that enables you to shed fat fast, keep it off long term, and improve your health in the process. You can expect to lose up to 14 pounds, five inches in your waist, and a heavy (no pun intended) percentage of body fat during the first two weeks of the plan alone.

Such results are truly amazing, but they are not what set this program apart from the others you will find on the bookstore shelf (perhaps ones you are considering buying right at this very moment). During my more than 20 years as a personal trainer and wellness coach, I've counseled some of the busiest, brightest, and most beautiful clients. They all generally share one thing in common. Before walking into my fitness center, they had tried just about every lose-weight-fast gimmick in the universe, including those shelved in bookstores as well as those available on the Web. Based on their experiences, I can tell you that just about all diets do one of two things:

- Some diets take off pounds extremely quickly but fail to give you the tools needed to keep off the weight. These diets tend to cause fast losses of water and muscle weight, which slows your metabolism. Once you break the diet, the fat makes a fast comeback.
- Other diets stress a moderate approach of no more than two pounds a week of weight loss, claiming that losing weight any more quickly sets you up for the yo-yo effect.

What if you could have the best of both worlds? What if you could lose 14 pounds and 5 percent of your body fat in just two weeks? Let's say five inches of this fat would come from the place you want to shed it most: your tummy. And let's say you could do all of this while simultaneously improving your health, feeling more energetic and less hungry, and, most important, speeding your metabolism. You'd also keep the weight off long term—with absolutely no dreaded yo-yo effect.

To take things a step further, let's say you could get these impressive results with a fabulously simple, convenient, and delicious meal plan, one that lets you eat out—that's right, *eat out*—nearly every meal if that's your prerogative. Finally, let's say this meal plan gave you the tools you need to follow the "diet" for the rest of your life, enabling it to become a part of your overall lifestyle.

With the Ultimate New York Diet, you can have all of this and more. Based on the needs and lifestyles of the many New Yorkers that I counsel day in and day out, this incredibly simple, easy, and effective plan works for the busiest of dieters.

The Big Apple

The phrase "in a New York minute" struck a cord while I was writing this book. Everything about my lifestyle—the fast walking, fast talking, very deliberate manner—all describe a person on the go, someone with a mission or a purpose. Indeed, New York represents a lot more than just a geographic location.

When many non–New Yorkers think of New York, they tend to think of the fashion district, of the glam of Madison Avenue, of the city that houses some of the world's most beautiful, most slender, and most expensively dressed women. Those all exist, but people may not realize that the ultrathin, glamorous woman who has come to embody all things New York is actually an anomaly.

Indeed, just as New York is known for its high fashion and posh stores, it's also known for something much less glamorous. According to an annual ranking of cities by *Men's Fitness* magazine, New York is the eighth-fattest city in the United States.

Surprised? I'm not. After spending more than 20 years helping New York's rich and famous develop the bodies, minds, and lives of their dreams, I've learned a few things about New York and its many temptations. Among other things, New York is the restaurant capital of the world. On every block of every section of the city, you'll find restaurants serving up all sorts of fat-cell-friendly fare, from bagels and lox to Italian biscotti to French pastries and everything in between. Have a craving? You need not even get off your couch. A nearby restaurant will deliver your sugary, fatty, calorie-laden treat to your doorstep. This fact was brought home to me when my friend Sam was doing my two-week program (phase 1 of the plan laid out in this book). He had gotten through the first few days without incident, and then he hit a wall. He had been sequestering himself at home to avoid being tempted by all of New York's culinary offerings. By day five, however, he went for a walk and his senses were assaulted with the smells of hot dogs, pizza, and pretzels. All of New York looked edible.

Sam overcame his mini "food meltdown" and ended up losing 14 pounds and more than three inches in his waist during his first two weeks on the plan, but his experience made me realize that weight loss isn't only about knowing what to eat and what not to eat. It's also about learning how to coax yourself to actually do it. It has been almost 18 months since Sam successfully completed the program, and I am proud to say that he carries with him the knowledge and the waistline to prove that the plan works and is maintainable. Sam is the typical New Yorker on the go. He eats most, if not all, of his meals in restaurants, and he has been able to apply all that he has learned as he deftly navigates through these menus.

In addition to temptations of the culinary kind, New Yorkers can easily spend their days and nights in just two positions: sitting and lying down. Need your laundry done? A service will pick it up and drop it off. Dog needs to go out? Call a professional dog walker. I know hair stylists, manicurists, trainers, makeup artists, and personal shoppers, to name just a few, who make house and office calls.

As if all of that weren't enough, New York houses a type of busyness and fast pace that seems to make the city literally buzz. With the average one-room apartment renting for more than $2,000 a month and selling for more than $300,000, you *need* to work 80 hours a week just to pay the rent or the mortgage. This type of stress encourages poor eating habits and even poorer exercise habits.

As Frank Sinatra once sang, if you can make it here, you can make it anywhere. The good news is that—even when you are surrounded by the fast-paced frenzy of New York—you *can* make it. You can create the body of your dreams. You can eat well, get fit, lose weight, and develop an inner sense of calm and confidence. And it's true whether you live in New York or not. I know because I've helped countless clients do just that.

In the coming weeks, you will challenge your body and mind with new foods, new movements, and an entirely new philosophy on life. As a result, you'll experience dramatic results.

Yes, even *you.* If somewhere in the back of your mind you're thinking, "not me, the one with the slow metabolism, the one with the overpowering cravings, the one who has no time to prepare food or to exercise," I have two words for you: *yes, you.* You *can* control your cravings rather than having them control you. You *can* maintain a demanding career, family, and social life and still find time to exercise and eat well. You *can* get a handle on the demons that in the past have led you to self-sabotage. You *can* fit into that dress, that pair of jeans, or whatever it is that you still keep in the back of your closet just in case you ever lose the weight.

Yes, you can burn off the fat, firm up the flab, and feel better about your body and yourself. I know because I've been helping people to do just that for the past 20 years. I know because people just like you—people who had tried every diet, fitness plan, and weight-loss supplement—come to me every day for answers. I know because I've seen friends, clients, and even family members (such as my mom) transform their bodies and their lives with this plan. They all had plenty of excuses for not doing it. They were busy. They liked to eat out. They had young children. They liked to socialize. They, however, through the guidance of the program you will soon embark upon, were able to turn those excuses into strengths. They succeeded, and you will, too.

My Personal Journey

I started writing this book immediately after finishing my previous book, *The Ultimate New York Body Plan*. It represents a continuation of thought process, but this book is a lot more than just The Ultimate New York Body Plan, Part II. During the writing process, people often asked me what this book was about and how it differed from *The Ultimate New York Body Plan*. My previous book was born out of my experience on the television show "Extreme Makeover." It showcased a strict two-week meal plan and intense two-week exercise regimen. The 90-minute-a-day workouts plus the very low-carbohydrate and low-fat diet offered incredibly swift results, allowing readers to lose two dress sizes and up to 14 pounds in just two weeks.

Because of its intense nature, I never imagined that *The Ultimate New York Body Plan* would enjoy the success it did. Through the worldwide success of that book, I became an absolute believer in the power and the importance of rapid weight loss.

The Ultimate New York Diet grew out of the successful feedback and informative e-mails I received from graduates of *The Ultimate New York Body Plan*. Soon after the book was published, I realized that in order to maintain their impressive results, readers needed a follow-up manual, one that helped them apply the principles of the Body Plan for *life*. Thus, the Diet was born.

The Diet picks up where the Body Plan ends, with some overlap. In addition to a two-week meal plan that teaches you to abide by my A, B, C, D, E, and F of nutrition, you also will find six more weeks of meals that help you learn how to maintain your results for a lifetime. These subsequent weeks will show you how to work some carbs and other A, B, C, D, E, and Fs (see Chapter 2) back into your life, without going overboard. The Diet's comprehensive eight-week Eating Plan is broken down into three phases and takes you from the initial (and extreme) two weeks of nutrition to phase 2, where you are allowed a little more healthy carbohydrate latitude, to phase 3, one that includes weekly cheat meals, among other things. It is in these two latter phases of the plan that you "start living your life," incorporating the lessons learned during the initial two weeks and applying them to your everyday life. The cookies look and smell good, but are they really worth it? My hope is that, after reading this book, the cookies won't smell as good as they did before, but if they every now and again do, you will have the knowledge and confidence to enjoy the cookies and get right back on the plan.

Throughout the pages of this book, you'll find the practical "how-tos" to deal with challenges that we all face from time to time, including these:

- Living in a "to-go" society
- Finding the time for a "real" workout
- Following the plan in all types of restaurants, from fast food to fine dining
- Surviving the holidays, including cocktails, pigs in blankets, and everything in between
- "Getting back on the horse" when you have strayed
- Incorporating all of these principles and making a lifelong commitment to wellness for you and your family

As the creator of No Excuse training, it was imperative for me to answer the often-asked question, "What do I do if I don't have time to work out 90 minutes per day as prescribed in *The Ultimate New York Body Plan*?" The creation of David's Express Workout Plan is another unique feature of this book, which addresses this very common dilemma. It is great to think we all have 90 minutes a day to work out, but I know that we all have days when a set of push-ups is barely manageable. Using my specially formulated workouts like a doctor's prescription—doing them several times per day throughout the day—you can work out and see effective results even if you have only 10 minutes to spare. The routines are broken down into body parts—often combining things like butt, thighs, and hips or an overall cardiosculpting minisession—just enough to get the heart pumping and the muscles softly singing as you sumo lunge, plié squat, and crab race your way to a new you! Obviously, the more effort you put into the program, the more impressive the results will be.

The Diet is also an honoring process. By dedicating yourself to this plan, you will find the time to reprioritize your life. You will find time for you, the focus of the honoring process. Throughout the book, you will find the mental and physical skills you need to maintain and improve upon your results.

There is something very "New York" about wanting to change your life and successfully transforming it in just two weeks. The reality is that life transformation can often take a lot longer than that. For a truly meaningful transformation, you must delve into the how, why, what, and what for of your life and how you conduct it. This plan is not just about losing a couple of dress sizes, as weight loss is often the easy part. The process of introspection is much more complicated and can and usually does take much more time.

I have seen some clients use this program as the blueprint for a whole new life. My mom at age 69 has decided to tackle not only her many-decades-long battle with weight but many other heady issues as well. Mom has gone from not working out at all to asking (sometimes insisting) to be fit into my schedule for a workout. Mom's struggles—and the struggles of countless others—have become the heart and soul of this book. I have said numerous times that one is never too old to change his or her life. It's never too late to turn things around. So go on, give it a try. What do you have to lose besides body fat? I guarantee the Ultimate New York Diet will transform your life forever!

Welcome to the Ultimate New York Diet

When my clients come to me, they don't want to hear a long speech about how they need to slow down and find some patience. They want to lose weight now, as in today, this hour, this very minute—this New York minute!

I used to fight this mind-set. Like many fitness professionals, I used to preach the benefits of slow, steady weight loss to my clients. I told them that losing weight faster than two pounds a week would only result in lost water and muscle mass, a slower metabolism, and subsequent weight regain. My clients begrudgingly listened and let me talk them into a longer, slower body-transformation program.

This changed when ABC approached me to participate as the fitness and wellness expert for its popular television show "Extreme Makeover." I was asked to help women completely make over their bodies in just 14 to 21 days. So, I modified the traditional nutrition and fitness program that I generally prescribe to my clients. Basically, the plan became much more intense.

The results were amazing, and they got me thinking. What would happen if I offered this fast-results program to others? How would it affect their motivation? How would it affect their long-term success?

So, I did. After working on "Extreme Makeover," I began introducing this faster, more extreme program to additional clients. It changed the way I think about weight loss—and it will soon change the way you do as well.

The New Rapid-Weight-Loss Diet

In my first book, *Sound Mind, Sound Body*, I clearly admonished readers to avoid diets. "*Diet* is a four-letter word," I insisted, conjuring up images of crazy fasts, zero-carb diets, and myriad other incredibly unsafe, short-term means of achieving smaller waists and hips and attempting to shed unwanted pounds. I believed then and still believe now that to maintain a healthy mind, body, and spirit, we all need to embrace an intelligent approach to living. In calling this plan a diet, I have not abandoned that approach. Rather, I've simply redefined my understanding of the word *diet*.

This understanding, of course, has changed over the years. When I wrote my first book five years ago, I equated diets with short-term fixes. I thought of them as an unhealthy way to shed pounds fast. In my second book, I softened a little, saying that a quick fix every now and then—say to get in shape for a wedding, bathing suit season, or, as is often the case with a few of my clients, the Victoria's Secret Fashion Show—was doable and safe. Now, two years and many more clients later, I've embraced the notion of fast weight loss. I now feel it's not only attainable and safe but also the best way to lose weight and keep it off long term.

My reasons are many:

1. I'm aware of the needs and practicalities of people with busy, multitasking lives. As a born and bred New Yorker, I recognize and appreciate the need to have things done "yesterday."

You'll Know You're Kirsched When You Say . . .

At the club, it's not uncommon for me to overhear my clients teasing one another with phrases such as "stop Kirsching me." One of these clients, Nina Joukowsky Koprulu, made up a T-shirt with some of the most commonly uttered phrases regarding the intensity of the Ultimate New York Diet. I thought you would appreciate them.

"Day one: Your scale is obviously wrong!"

"OK, I skipped my coffee, but I also killed the first person I met."

"Hey, I just discovered that there is caffeine in the vitamins and minerals drink; I drank five."

"No chocolate, cheese, or alcohol? Those are my three food groups. What's left?"

"But it's about to be Thanksgiving, Christmas, New Years, Valentine's Day, St. Patrick's Day, Arbor Day . . ."

"No alcohol? What about just straight? Does straight work?"

"Did I accidentally join the army?"

"The new gym clothes I bought last week are too big!"

"How does vanilla shake taste in coffee?"

"Phase 1 was so much fun; let's do it again next week!"

2. When you don't lose weight fast enough, you get discouraged and head back to the Cheez Doodles and Ding Dongs. Rapid weight loss is the best motivator for people who need to shed a lot of weight. Losing weight slowly just makes weight loss that much more frustrating.

3. In training countless clients, I've found that you can lose stunning amounts of weight in record time *without* ruining your health and without damaging your metabolism. This isn't just my personal conviction.

Christine Capulong

I met Christine as part of a Fox News Channel Challenge. I picked six people to transform within two weeks. Christine had been trying to lose weight in order to fit into an unforgiving dress that she had intentionally purchased a few sizes too small to wear to her best friend's wedding. She had succeeded in losing some weight on her own but was struggling to shed enough weight to fit into the dress. When she started the Fox News Channel Challenge, the wedding was just six weeks away, and she felt that she "looked like a sausage" in the dress.

Celeste Dobbins/Celeste Photo Art

Q: **What is your history with weight gain and weight loss?**

A: I've had a weight problem since I was 10 years old, when I was about 15 pounds overweight. By the time I was in high school, I was 50 pounds overweight. I peaked at 60 pounds overweight. I've tried Weight Watchers, Jenny Craig, and various diet centers. I've done hospital-based programs and fat camps. Each time I would lose the weight but hit a plateau. Each time I was hungry—starving—and dreaming about food.

Q: **What was missing that caused you to fail on those diets?**

A: I needed to do this on my own. In the past, I had always relied on prepared food or a camp with a structure so I didn't have to lift a finger. The diet was presented to me on a platter. I didn't have to learn how to eat differently or how to exercise. It was as if I were a marionette, with other people pulling the strings.

Q: **How was this plan different?**

A: This time, I took control of the process. I now feel I can control my

While there are certainly opinions on both sides, many medical researchers agree with this idea, too. Weight-loss researcher James Anderson, M.D., a professor of medicine and clinical nutrition at the University of Kentucky in Lexington, has tested the concept of rapid weight loss numerous times. He has put hundreds of dieters on a "very low-calorie" weight on my own, that I don't have to depend on someone to do it for me. I can do this. Also, for someone who has been on so many diets, I found this one really easy. The food was tasty.

Q: How do you keep yourself on track?

A: I wear jeans that are tight, to give myself some feedback when I eat. I also keep a food journal, writing down what I eat. I weigh myself once a week. Other than that, I'm not anal about this. This is not a diet; it's a lifestyle. I love that you get a cheat day on this plan. It's about moderation, not deprivation.

I've also made the elements of the plan a nonnegotiable part of my lifestyle. I'm an interior designer, and I fly back and forth from New York to San Francisco often. I always carry David's protein powder, almonds, and a hard-boiled egg to eat just in case I can't find any better alternatives during my travels. I also have David's 45-minute cardiosculpting workout memorized. No matter where I am—at home or at a hotel room—I do it.

Q: Did you fit into the dress?

A: I didn't just fit into the dress, I looked great in the dress. I looked as great as the bride. I was so toned that I didn't have to wear waist-slimming nylons or a girdle. It was all me, and that was so cool.

CHRISTINE'S ADVICE FOR YOU: You have to be in the right mind-set to lose weight and keep it off. You need to know not only why you are doing this but also why you've been struggling. Also, if you go off the plan, get right back on. Don't just continue to slip up.

POSTSCRIPT: *Christine's success was so motivating that not long after she completed the program, she brought her sister and friends into the club. She is so pleased with her results and the way she is feeling that she has gotten quite evangelical in spreading the "David Kirsch Wellness" word.*

liquid diet. The participants drank most of their daily 900 calories in the form of high-protein, low-carbohydrate shakes. When he tracked the results of participants over time, he determined that most of the participants kept off all the weight they lost for more than five years (which at this point is as long as the researcher has followed his participants).

Whether you call my plan a diet or—as I prefer—a healthy nutrition plan, the effect is the same. After reading this book and embarking on the Ultimate New York Diet, you will transform your life. You will learn how to eat on the run; prepare quick, delicious, and nutritious meals with few ingredients and little time; and exercise on the go. All told, you'll find the tools you need to create the body of your dreams—and maintain those results for a lifetime.

How It Works

To lose all of the weight you want, you need a diet that you can stick to for the duration, until you reach your goal. If you have only five pounds to lose, that's easy. You could shed five pounds fast in any number of healthy or unhealthy ways. (I hope, however, you prefer and choose the healthy approach!) If you have much more to lose—say 15, 20, 50, 100 pounds, or more—then starving yourself won't cut it. How long can you wake up feeling hungry and go to bed dreaming about food? Can you deprive yourself for weeks and months in order to drop those pounds? Don't feel sheepish about saying no, because few people have the will-power, determination, and lifestyle to do so.

Although the Ultimate New York Diet yields impressive, fast results, it does not do so by leaving you hungry all day and all night long. It doesn't do so at the expense of good health. It doesn't do so at the expense of your personal sanity.

In this rapid-weight-loss diet, you will take steps toward living a better, more complete, more worthwhile life. You will change not only the way you think about nutrition and exercise but also how you think about living. That's the only way to lose weight and keep it off. You must not only change what you eat but also create the optimal lifestyle and psychological habits needed to make that change a permanent one.

To that end, the Ultimate New York Diet yields fast, effective, permanent weight loss because it includes the following principles:

- **A 7-to-7, low-carb eating schedule.** Too many people try to lose weight by eating less. They skip breakfast and lunch and generally starve themselves throughout the day. Then comes dinner. At this meal, they eat more carbs, fat, and overall calories than a normal person eats all day long. After dinner, they generally keep right on eating. It's as if a magnet has sucked them into the kitchen and directly to the refrigerator. This type of eating pattern puts the bulk of calories into your body when your body is least able to process and burn them. It also disturbs your sleep, and, perhaps most important, it slows your metabolism. On the Ultimate New York Diet you will eat regularly spaced meals and snacks starting at 7:00 A.M. and ending at 7:00 P.M. These regular meals will keep your metabolism up and cravings down, enabling faster, easier weight loss.

Your frequent meals will showcase lean protein and fiber-rich vegetables and minimize carbohydrate and fat. You'll learn the importance of this approach both for weight loss and for your health in Chapter 2. In phases 2 and 3 of the plan, you will learn to eat your carbs before 2:00 P.M., when your body is best able to process and burn them. At 7:00 P.M., you'll put a mental lock on the fridge and kitchen.

- **Effective and convenient exercise.** When you diet without exercise, you lose mostly lean tissue rather than fat, slowing your metabolism and increasing your risk of regaining the weight. To help you fit exercise into the busiest of days, I've created David's Express Workouts (aka Workouts in a New York Minute). This 10-minute mix-and-match workout system allows you to sneak in effective bursts of exercise throughout the day, when you have time.
- **Success-promoting supplements.** You'll learn how to use the best your local health food store has to offer to turn down appetite, turn up energy, and speed the metabolism—all while improving your health.

When you add the Ultimate New York Diet's eating, supplementing, and exercising together, you create a dynamite package that peels off the fat in record time. The diet works in three phases. During phase 1, you'll see the most rapid results. In phase 2, you'll continue to lose weight—albeit not as rapidly—as you cement the eating habits you learned during phase 1 into your life. Phase 3 of the meal plan spans four weeks, but it lasts the rest of your life. Throughout the book, you'll find solid advice for making the transition from a temporary diet to a permanent lifestyle. You'll learn how to safely eat out and even indulge on the plan—without gaining weight.

You'll also learn the mental strategies needed to succeed on the plan long term. Finally, you'll find the recipes you need to make it all happen.

To borrow a concept from a great television advertisement for American Express, this is my city and this is my plan. I was born here and live, work, eat, and interact here on a daily basis. I have navigated this city—potholes and all—using the Ultimate New York Diet as my guide. Because of it, I and the followers of the Diet are healthier and happier—mentally, physically, and spiritually.

What You Can Expect

Now, this is where things get really exciting. If you commit yourself to the plan, you will have these great results:

- **Lose weight and keep it off.** You may be tackling this diet because you want to look good for a special occasion, but wouldn't it be great if you continued to look great for months and even years afterward? You can, and you will. The Ultimate New York Diet gives you the tools not only to lose weight but also to keep it off long term. Throughout the pages of this book, you'll find my strategies for incorporating this plan into your life. You'll also read the empowering stories of my clients who did just that and, as a result, have kept off the weight.
- **Give your metabolism a serious kick in the pants.** Before embarking on this plan, many of my clients waged a frustrating existence of eating less only to gain more. After age 35, their metabolisms began slowing down. Usually, by their early to mid-40s, they came to me as frustrated as you might expect. They went on the Ultimate New York Diet and saw their metabolisms make an about-face. As I write this, one client in particular, Virginia Gordon, comes to mind. When she entered menopause, she began gaining weight, ballooning from her usual size 6 to a size 10. "No matter how much I exercised and limited my eating, I couldn't get back into my size 6 pants," she told me. "This program totally shocked my metabolism. I lost 10 pounds in two weeks and kept it off."

- **Boost your mood, energy levels, and overall focus.** On this plan, everything you put in your mouth is something your body needs and wants to use for energy and overall maintenance. As a result, near the end of the first week on the plan, you'll find that you feel better than you have in years. "When I did this program, my husband remarked that I was so on top of everything," says Nina Joukowsky Koprulu, who lost 13 pounds during her first two weeks on the plan. "I am so focused and so efficient." Because of this energy boost, some of my clients have been able to get off coffee for the first time in their lives. They also have reported a sense of calm. Another participant, Sabina Remy, did my program three weeks before her wedding. She mostly wanted to tone up, but she discovered the program yielded many other benefits. Her skin and hair took on a beautiful shine, and, somehow, she felt placidly relaxed about planning her wedding at her husband's family home in France. "We had more than 350 people coming from all over the world. It can be intense to be the center of attention of that many people. There were so many preparations that had to be done to organize a wedding in a foreign country where I didn't speak the language and on someone else's turf, but everything went so smoothly, and I attribute that to the fact that I was so relaxed. I never worried about all of the different things that had to get done. I was always in the moment."
- **Create radiant skin and hair.** Your skin will take on a glow because you are feeding your cells—including the cells in your skin—the nutrients they need to function optimally.
- **Improve your health.** Before embarking on this plan, some of my clients were told their blood pressure was so high they were in danger of having a stroke. Within two weeks on the program, they lowered their pressure to normal levels. Others have seen dramatic drops in total and bad (LDL) cholesterol. Greg Namin saw his triglycerides drop from 900 to 89 and his cholesterol from 243 to 168 within just two weeks. "My dad is a cardiologist. When he heard just how much my triglycerides, blood sugar, and cholesterol dropped within two weeks, his reaction was priceless. I had tried cholesterol-lowering medication in the past, but it didn't do much for me," he said.

Nina Joukowsky Koprulu

I know Nina well. She first came to me when she wanted to lose "those last 10 pounds." She's since signed up for my two-week phase 1 program three times. It's not that she reverts to her old ways after each two-week segment, but rather she realizes she could commit herself even more. I feel blessed that through the process of her training, Nina and I have developed a lifelong friendship.

Q: How did you gain the weight?

A: I've battled excess weight my entire life. I'm one of those people who goes from one extreme to another. I had a baby in my early 40s. After he was born, I gained 60 pounds due to the stress of midlife motherhood. Somewhere around age 45, my body changed. My metabolism slowed down.

Q: You're a lifelong dieter. Why do you think you struggled to lose the last 10?

A: I've always exercised and knew that I had to exercise, but I didn't know what real weight lifting was, and I didn't know how much cardio I would need to do in order to be successful. I always swam, but I just didn't have an understanding of what type of exercise a middle-aged woman needs. I also didn't understand how to eat. I thought fruit was a diet food. I thought that by avoiding protein, I was avoiding calories. To lose weight I would starve myself and I would swim. Before I met David, I had never lifted a weight in my life.

Q: Why did you return to phase 1 three times?

A: Each time I tackled phase 1, I got more in control of my eating and exercise habits. It reinforced those habits. Each time I returned to phase 1, I recommitted myself to the philosophy of the program, and I would lose a few more pounds as a result.

- **Develop the invincibility of a New Yorker.** The Ultimate New York Diet will help you to develop a sense of power, the invincibility that I so often see in my clients. I believe that New Yorkers have learned (for the most part) to turn negatives into positives. We have learned to deal with stress—bad jobs, crazy relationships, rush-hour traffic, and

I'm now in better shape than I was in my 30s. I'm fitter. I feel better, and I can chase a cab or a four-year-old. I now have the physical and mental energy to sustain myself over a very long day. This is the most in control of my weight I have ever been.

Q: How has your diet changed since starting this program?

A: I no longer starve myself. I no longer eat 20 servings of yogurt a day or eat as much fruit as I used to. I stopped drinking diet soda. I also know that I need to eat dinner earlier at night, that if I eat dinner at 9:00 P.M., my body will spend the night digesting my food and I won't sleep well. Also, for me, protein is no longer the bad guy. I am also hooked on David's Meal Replacement Powder and Vitamin/Mineral Super Juice. The latter I have at least three or four times a day. It fuels me with energy throughout the day.

Q: What had to change for you emotionally in order to succeed on this plan?

A: I'm a mother, and my time is stretched over 20 different things or tasks each day. I learned I had to take the time to take care of myself, because I couldn't take care of my family if I wasn't in the top physical and mental condition.

NINA'S ADVICE FOR YOU: Get ready. The sense of accomplishment and gratification you will feel is worth every agonizing moment. You could lose the weight through diet alone, but the exercise solidifies the weight loss.

POSTSCRIPT: *Nina has become a walking billboard for the benefits of the Ultimate New York Diet. Not a Saturday or Sunday morning goes by that I don't see her doing her one hour of cardio—rowing, elliptical, stairs, and treadmill. She is truly an inspiration, and I am very proud of all of her accomplishments.*

so on. In this way, we are tough. Of course not every New Yorker possesses this power, and you don't have to live here to feel it.

In navigating this plan, you will learn the psychological strategies that you need not only to maintain your weight loss but also to better navigate all life's challenges. In this way, you'll develop the New York mind-set and energy that will carry you through any difficult situation.

My Mom's Story

I've worked with many clients of all shapes, sizes, ages, and ethnicities, but nothing prepared me for the emotional and psychological issues I dealt with when I started training my mother, Helen. She had spent years living a relatively sedentary life, coupled with some illnesses, physical ailments, personal tragedies, and a lack of interest.

How was I going to get her off of the couch and motivated? With so much weight to lose (well over 100 pounds), how was I going to keep her feeling positive, focused, and driven? How would I answer the question of whether it was possible to lose 150 pounds at 69 years old? More important, how would I help her find the purpose for losing it at that age at all?

It wasn't easy, and there were definitely some occasional bumps in the road, but the process of training her taught me things about myself (and about her). For example, I have learned that fear can paralyze anyone at any age. Not only is it theoretically more physically challenging to exercise at the age of 69 versus 39, some of the superficial reasons for doing it may not be as relevant. Are we still trying to get that "six-pack" stomach or look great in a bikini? Perhaps, but the compelling reason for wanting to be healthy and well comes from a much deeper place.

At the writing of this book, Mom was only a third of the way to her goal weight. Yet, the effort and time she had put into reaching that goal helped me to fine-tune and shape the Ultimate New York Diet for the better. In fact, this morning she was awakened by some aches and pains throughout her entire body. She was having a tough mental day yesterday, and I treated her to one of my "butt-kicking," sweat-inducing, heart-pounding workouts. When she called me to complain about a pain she was having just about everywhere in her body, I said, "Your muscles are greeting you. They are happy that you are paying attention to them." You see, movement is a good thing, at any age!

Throughout the pages of this book, you'll read about Mom and her struggles. I think you'll find her story quite compelling and motivating, and I'm grateful that she's allowed me to tell it. When I asked Mom whether she would allow me to go public with her struggle with her weight, her answer was so honest and positive that it confirmed why I am so proud of her and why she continues to do so well on the Ultimate New York Diet. I don't think she knew going into the program what was in store for her. Quite selflessly, when I asked her to work with me on the book, she thought that this was all about her helping me on a project—my homework assignment. I have watched with great pride and extreme admiration as she has slowly turned her life around. When I asked her if she minded if people knew how much weight she had to lose, her response was perfect: "It's taken me a long time to put on this weight, and I wasn't private about that so I'm not going to be private about taking it off. I'm down 60 pounds, and I'm shooting for another 100 pounds off!" She's 69 years young and full of hope, full of life. Whatever the outcome here—whether or not Mom loses the additional 100 pounds—one thing is certain: she has changed her life.

The Ultimate New York Diet has empowered Mom to transform her life. What started out as "my homework assignment" has become Mom's mission. To Mom and to all of you out there feeling hopeless about your health and wellness, please remember that it is never too late. If you give me a little effort, I will encourage and teach you to push harder and reach higher. The Ultimate New York Diet will help you make the most of your life.

Heidi Klum's Story

When it comes to unique genetics, Heidi Klum is as different from Mom— and from most of us—as chocolate is from lettuce. Heidi possesses incredible genetics that have allowed her to look amazing while paying very little attention to her diet. Throughout her second pregnancy, she told me that she ate whatever she wanted whenever she wanted. Yet she gained only the usual 35 pounds.

Even though Heidi's metabolism may be the polar opposite of your own, I think you can learn from her story. About one week after Heidi gave birth to her second child, Henry, we were instant messaging each other. All was well with the newly expanded family, and they were all enjoying the new addition as well as coping with the sleep deprivation and added pressures of having a second child in just two years.

I asked Heidi whether she was doing the Victoria's Secret Fashion Show. Yes, she told me, she had every intention of doing the show. Mind you, the show was November 9, barely eight weeks after the birth of her son. She asked if I would help her find somebody to work with her to get her into shape. I asked her how she felt about my coming to Los Angeles for a couple of weeks to work with her and get her on the right track. She gladly and excitedly accepted my offer.

The first step was creating a rigid schedule. Making exercise a ritual isn't any different when you are one of the most famous models in the world. Second order of business—giving Heidi a very rigid and specific food plan. It's not that she wasn't eating well, but rather some of the choices were not ideal for Victoria's Secret lingerie! For example, there would be no more corn on the cob or dairy—one of the food groups she ate from regularly during her pregnancy.

Although she was nursing, she would have to modify her meals and eat frequently throughout the day. I listed the A, B, C, D, E, and Fs to her (you'll learn them in Chapter 2) and explained that, as much as possible, she had to avoid them for those two weeks. One of the first suggestions I made to her was to hard boil one dozen eggs first thing in the morning. I instructed Heidi to pop a hard-boiled egg white into her mouth every time she went into the kitchen. As best as she was able, she was going to eat every three hours and work out one to two times a day every day for two weeks. Heidi started every morning with one of my Protein Meal Replacement Shakes. It gave her high-octane, natural protein; organic, ground flaxseed; and fiber for only 175 calories. She followed that with one of my Vitamin/Mineral Super Juices. We worked out every morning between 8:30 and 9:00 A.M. Then she had her midmorning snack, either the hard-boiled egg whites or an egg white omelet with spinach. Lunch was the biggest meal of the day (very European) and consisted of some sort of grilled protein—lean meat, fish, or chicken with a big salad and steamed vegetables.

Her afternoon snack consisted of a handful of raw almonds and one of my protein shakes or a couple of hard-boiled egg whites. Because she was nursing, we altered the plan to allow some carbohydrates that would not ordinarily be permitted, at least during the first two weeks. Things like lentils, kidney beans, and quinoa were permissible if she had them with lunch.

The combination of exercise plus diet began working its magic fairly quickly as Heidi was down two inches in her waist in the first few days. After a couple of weeks, Heidi was off to Germany for business. There were still 10 days until the show, and these days were going to be critical. I wasn't leaving anything to chance, so I sent her off with the essentials of a good workout—my boot camp DVD, specially made ankle weights, and a custom-made four-pound medicine ball. I also packed my Protein Powder, my Vitamin/Mineral Powder, and my favorite low-carb protein bars for those days when she didn't have time for a proper meal. (See the Resources section at the back of the book for where to find these items if you are interested.)

The next time I saw Heidi was the afternoon of the show. I will never forget when Heidi appeared on the stage for the first time that night. Seal was performing his song "Crazy"; then the lights went up, and Heidi came out on stage to the sound of oohs and aaahhhs. She took away my breath and that of everyone there! She had worked so hard to get back into shape, and I was so proud of her. She looked gorgeous, from the inside out. She radiated beauty, and it filled the room that night.

Please don't just turn the pages and say, "This is Heidi Klum and it can never be me. I am not a supermodel." I'm not saying that we are all meant to be supermodels; we're not. Heidi's beauty is rare and unique to her, but we all have a beauty of our own. We are all born with the strength and ability to strive for and be the best that we can be.

Heidi succeeded not because she is beautiful but rather because she worked and sweated as we all have to. The Ultimate New York Diet has served Heidi and will continue to serve her very well. The things she learned over those few weeks with respect to her stamina, discipline, and fortitude, along with the knowledge of nutrition and exercise that I taught her, will be with her forever. I know that this experience has transformed her life and can transform all of our lives if we let it. We need to believe in ourselves—in the power of our own light—and it is all possible.

Your Story

Now the spotlight comes to you and the road that lies ahead. It's my sincere hope that the Ultimate New York Diet becomes a way of life—a transformative process that reshapes your thinking and your attitudes not only about nutrition but, on a larger scale, about your everyday life choices. The better (cleaner) you eat, the clearer, more rational, and more lucid your thoughts. The more you engage the brain and the body in exercise, the better your "engine" runs. You'll soon learn how self-love and self-acceptance lead to self-empowerment. The choices you make on a daily basis with respect to what you eat, how you exercise, and how you conduct yourself help to determine your "bigger picture." Will you be the best that you are meant to be? Will you have the fortitude, perseverance, and courage to stay the course when the going gets tough?

Based on the people who have completed the Ultimate New York Diet, I know that it has the ability to empower, educate, and enrich you, providing you embrace its principles.

As you embark on this plan, I would like you to reach higher, strive farther, and accept nothing less than the best that you have to offer to yourself first and foremost and then to others. I have never felt stronger in the belief that anything is possible. You are truly amazing—just open yourself up to all of your possibilities. I believe in you. It's time for you to believe in yourself.

David's Principles to Live By

You may not understand the importance of all of the following affirmations today, but by the end of the eight-week program you will. Make the following 10 promises to yourself today, and revisit them often as you navigate the program.

1. I will take charge of my life. Today is the first day of the rest of my life.
2. I will be accountable. I will no longer be a victim of circumstances, my surroundings, or others' influences.
3. I believe in the importance and value of self-empowerment.
4. I believe that everything happens for a reason. Rather than allow myself to feel like a victim of bad circumstances, I will look beyond everyday challenges to figure out why they happen and how I can better control them.
5. I love and accept myself. Among everything else, I rank myself first.
6. I will incorporate good living, healthy eating, and spirituality into my everyday life. I'll make it ritualistic, like brushing my teeth.
7. I am the captain of my own ship called destiny.
8. I make health and wellness my top priority.
9. Failure is not an option for me. If I set attainable goals and reasonable expectations, I will succeed.
10. I live in the present. I do not live with "I should haves" or "I could haves."

The Ultimate New York Eating Plan

Many diet programs (including this one) brag about the number of pounds you can expect to shed in a given period of time. Yet fast results really aren't all that hard to come by. Want to lose weight fast? Just stop eating!

Indeed, you're holding this book in your hands right now because you want more than rapid weight loss. You want that seeming contradiction in terms. You want easy weight loss, and you want the weight to stay off once you lose it. More important, you want to preserve your health—or possibly even improve it in the process. You also don't want to trade in eating out or ordering in for an evening of chopping, stirring, and standing in front of that thing in your kitchen called a stove.

Now, a diet that delivers those benefits—stunning yet lasting weight loss without torture—would be truly revolutionary. Well, hold onto your belt buckle because the revolution is now. You can drop 14 pounds in just two weeks while eating real food in real portions and still enjoying life to the fullest. You can still eat out. You can maintain the energy and brain power you need for your demanding work, social, and family life. You can improve your health in the process, and, yes, you can even keep the weight off.

In the following pages, you'll learn how the Eating Plan of the Ultimate New York Diet will help you accomplish all of those benefits and more. The magic starts with the diet's unique combination of carbohydrates, fats, and proteins in each meal.

The New Low-Carb Diet

I'm not the first wellness coach to recommend low-carb diets for fast weight loss, and I certainly won't be the last. Various incarnations of these diets have been around—in one form or another—for at least 30 years. The low-carb diets of yesteryear, however, promoted carb cutting as a way to encourage ketosis, the process your body uses to convert fats into energy. According to the promoters of these diets, you can eat anything you want, as long as it's low in carbs. Bacon? Bring it on. Cheese sauce? Go right ahead. Prime rib? Dig in!

The Ultimate New York Diet is not one of those diets! It takes only a reasonable amount of common sense to come to the following conclusion about high-fat, low-carb diets—they promote weight loss at the expense of future weight regain and poor health. Consider this study, completed in New Zealand. For it, researchers compared a high-fat, low-carb diet (Atkins) to a high-protein, lower-fat diet (the Zone) and a high-carbohydrate, low-fat diet. All of the participants lost weight. A quarter of the participants who followed the Atkins diet, however, saw a spike in their bad (LDL) cholesterol numbers. Interestingly, about 13 percent of the participants who followed the high-carbohydrate, low-fat diet also experienced an increase in LDL cholesterol. Participants who followed the Zone diet saw no change in their cholesterol levels.

In addition to eroding your heart health, these diets also tend to result in not-so-fun side effects such as headaches, fatigue, and even bad breath. The resulting headaches, lack of energy, and general malaise cause people to move less, which can be counteractive, especially after the weight comes off.

The Ultimate New York Diet falls into a new category of low-carb, low-fat, healthful diets. In addition to encouraging fast weight loss by reducing carbs and increasing protein, the diet also includes lots of fiber, vegetables, and generally wholesome foods. This diet works *primarily* because it increases the amount of protein you eat. That's true, but other components of the diet also help by speeding metabolism, encouraging fat burning, reducing hunger-promoting hormones, boosting mood (which, in turn, reduces your cravings), and creating the optimal internal environment for lean-tissue growth and fat-tissue loss. Possibly most important, it contains the delicious, gourmet flavors you've come to expect from your food—flavors that you need to stick to a new way of eating long term.

When you follow the Ultimate New York Diet, you can expect the following amazing benefits:

- **You'll eat less—because you'll feel satisfied on fewer calories.** Dietary protein affects a number of appetite-regulating hormones that help promote a lasting sensation of fullness after eating. Protein enhances the effects of leptin, a hormone that helps the body register fullness. It also stimulates gut hormones that turn off your brain's appetite center, making you feel full and satisfied sooner than if you ate carbs or fat. Protein also helps to regulate blood sugar and insulin levels, which in turn helps to turn down hunger and appetite. For those reasons, people automatically eat fewer calories when they swap carbs for protein. In a study of 57 people completed in Adelaide, Australia, participants who ate a 34 percent protein diet reported feeling more satisfied and less hungry during the three hours between meals than dieters who followed an 18 percent protein diet. Both diets contained the same number of calories. In another study completed at the University of Washington, participants who ate 30 percent of their calories from protein automatically consumed 441 fewer calories than they did when consuming a 15 percent protein diet.

Protein isn't the only nutrient that the Ultimate New York Diet uses to turn down hunger levels. You'll also eat plenty of fiber in the form of vegetables and nuts during phase 1 and beans, legumes, and whole grains in phases 2 and 3. Fiber works by making you feel full, slowing digestion, and even sucking some fat out of your gut before it can be absorbed into the bloodstream. It also alters the secretion of gut hormones that help promote a sensation of fullness after eating.

- **You'll speed up your metabolism.** Studies published in the *Journal of Clinical Nutrition* and the *New England Journal of Medicine* recently came to this startling conclusion: carb cutting generates twice as much weight loss within six months as fat cutting, even when participants consume the same number of calories. In one small but well-controlled study, study participants followed one of three diets: (1) an 1,800-calorie low-carbohydrate diet, (2) an 1,800-calorie low-fat diet, or (3) a 2,100 calorie low-carbohydrate diet. Participants in the first group, not surprisingly, lost the most weight: 23 pounds. Amazingly, however, the participants who ate 2,100 calories a day—300 daily calories *more* than the low-fat group—lost more weight than participants in the low-fat group!

Most people, when they hear about such research, think that the scientists are cooking the numbers. They're not. There's a real physiological reason why high-protein diets generate more weight loss per calories than high-carbohydrate diets. Certain foods waste more energy during the process of digestion than others. Any time you eat, your body must burn calories in order to break food down, push it through your intestine, and absorb its nutrients, a process known as the thermic effect of food. Researchers now know that your body burns roughly 40 more calories per meal if your meal is high in protein compared to one that's high in carbohydrate or fat.

During digestion, your body wastes just 2 to 3 percent of fat calories as heat, 6 to 8 percent of carbohydrate calories, and a whopping 25 to 30 percent of protein calories. So, for every 100 calories of protein you eat, you waste 30 calories. For every 100 calories of fat, you waste only

3 calories. For every 100 calories of carbs you eat, your body wastes just 8 calories. According to a recent review article written by scientists from the State University of New York Downstate Medical Center in Brooklyn, reducing your carbohydrate calories to just 8 percent of your overall calories (as you will do during phase 1 of this plan) triggers your body to waste an extra 140 calories a day as heat!

This protein-metabolism link may stem from our hunting and gathering days. When our cave-dwelling ancestors ate a lot of protein in the form of wild animal meat, they were feasting and their bodies could afford to waste calories. When they were eating a mostly carbohydrate diet in the form of berries, it generally meant that food was scarce and that their bodies had to conserve calories.

In addition to the increased protein you'll eat on the Ultimate New York Diet, you'll also speed your metabolism in yet another, lesser-known way. If you take a quick glance at the diet, you'll see that every single meal contains an abundance of some type of vegetable, usually a green vegetable. Vegetables are alkalinizing foods. Your blood, bones, and bodily organs all function optimally at a certain pH, which stands for "potential of hydrogen." Your body's pH represents the balance of positively charged ions (acid forming) to negatively charged ions (alkalinizing). When your blood and organs become too acidic (with a low pH), you suffer a host of ill consequences, including a drop in thyroid hormone, which slows your metabolism.

Vegetables help to balance your body's pH, creating the optimal environment inside your cells for fat burning to take place. Of all of the vegetables out there, green vegetables—such as spinach and brussels sprouts—tend to be most alkalinizing to the body, which is why the Ultimate New York Diet contains a lot of green foods.

The Ultimate New York Diet is also rich in salmon and other sources of omega-3 fatty acids. And it includes some monounsaturated fats from nuts and olive oil. Both of these fats coax the cells in your body to waste calories, burning them only to release their energy in the form of heat. When researchers compared a diet rich in maize (corn) oil to those with lots of beef tallow or fish oil, they found that rats that ate the diet rich in fish oil gained less weight than rats on the beef or corn oil diet. Other studies show that replacing saturated and trans fats with unsaturated fats results in weight loss, even when total caloric intake is held constant. Unsaturated fats are also better for your heart. Eating unsaturated fats instead of saturated or trans fats lowers your unhealthy LDL cholesterol and lowers levels of triglycerides (a nasty type of blood fat).

- **You'll preserve muscle mass, preventing weight rebound.** You often hear that rapid weight loss results in rapid losses of muscle mass. Although many nutritionists, trainers, and other fitness professionals spout this tidbit as if it were a fact, it's not completely true. If it were true, it would be destructive because your muscle tissue runs your metabolism. Each pound of muscle you lose results in 35 to 50 fewer calories a day that your body burns for energy. Numerous studies, however, show that increasing the amount of protein in the diet helps preserve muscle mass, even when calorie intake is very, very low.

  In a four-month-long study of 48 women completed at the University of Illinois, women who ate more protein while trying to lose weight preserved muscle mass compared to those who followed a high-carbohydrate diet. Women in the protein plus exercise group, of course, preserved the most muscle mass, but women in the protein only group weren't far behind, and they actually preserved more muscle mass than women who exercised but ate a high-carb diet.

  Research also shows that this preservation of muscle mass helps you to keep the weight off. In a study of 113 overweight men and women, those who ate 18 percent more protein after they lost weight were better able to maintain their weight loss than participants who ate less protein.

- **You'll burn fat rather than store it.** Researchers also know that high-protein foods tend to cause a slow, even rise in blood sugar, whereas some types of carbohydrates spike blood sugar levels. The slower your blood sugar rises, the less insulin your pancreas must secrete to clear the sugar out of your blood. Among other things, insulin triggers fat storage and hunger. The fiber you eat on the plan will also help to keep insulin in check. By reducing insulin surges, the Ultimate New

Why Low-Fat Diets Result in High-Fat Bodies

During the 1990s, high-carbohydrate, low-fat diets were all the rage. At the time, scientists blamed the high amounts of saturated fats in the American diet for our bulging waistlines and skyrocketing rates of heart disease. A plethora of low-fat and nonfat products soon hit the supermarket shelves, from nonfat cookies to baked potato chips. The U.S. government led the charge by releasing its Food Guide Pyramid in 1992, a nutrition plan that placed grains and other carbs at the base. Americans caught on quickly to the new trend and cut back on meat, switched from whole milk to skim, and gave up their Chips Ahoy! for reduced-fat SnackWell's.

As more and more people turned to pasta, rice, bagels, and nonfat snacks, more and more people got fat. Although some people certainly were able to lose weight during these low-fat years, the vast majority of Americans porked out. Perplexed, scientists went back to the drawing board, trying to figure out where things went wrong. After many years of research, scientists have made some interesting discoveries.

One of the reasons nutrition scientists began promoting low-fat, high-carbohydrate diets was because each gram of fat contains nine calories, compared to carbohydrate's four. They reasoned that simply switching from high-fat foods to high-carbohydrate foods would automatically lower the overall caloric intake, thus resulting in weight loss. Well, this didn't happen, for a number of reasons.

First, thanks to the addition of sugar and high-fructose corn syrup, many low-fat, high-carbohydrate foods are not lower in calories than their high-fat counterparts. For instance, to make low-fat cookies taste good, manufacturers added more sugar in place of the fat. From a calorie standpoint, low-fat cookies are just as bad for your waistline as high-fat cookies. Second, most people eat a larger portion size of low-fat foods than they do of high-fat foods, possibly under the false belief that low fat equals low calorie. Think about it. If you were scooping some low-fat ice cream into a bowl, would you scoop out the same amount as you would high-fat ice cream? Probably not. You'd reward yourself for eating the low-fat ice cream by adding an extra scoop, which brings me to my third point. High-carb, low-fat foods are not as satisfying as their original counterparts. In the end, many people consume more calories on a low-fat diet than when on a high-fat diet.

York Diet helps your body to funnel fat away from your fat cells and into muscle and other body cells that burn it for energy.

Lean and Healthy

What about all of those health worries you've heard? Won't eating more protein clog up your arteries, cause kidney stones, and make you want to sleep all day long? Not in the least. In a University of Pennsylvania study that followed dieters for an entire year, participants who followed a low-carb diet experienced a greater improvement in typical heart disease risk factors—such as lower levels of LDL cholesterol and higher levels of HDL (good) cholesterol—than participants who followed a high-carbohydrate diet. Many other studies have yielded similar results, finding that high-protein, low-fat diets—such as the one you'll soon embark on—specifically help to lower triglycerides, a type of blood fat. Although it is not as well known and publicized as cholesterol, you should pay attention to your triglyceride level. Carbohydrates supply the body with glyceride, the molecule to which three fats attach to form triglycerides. When you cut your carb consumption, you reduce your overall triglyceride levels.

Studies also show that going low carb will not only help you shed fat faster while keeping you satisfied but will also help you to reduce insulin levels and shrink your waistline, and a large waistline is also a risk factor for heart disease. Indeed, the Ultimate New York Diet may be particularly helpful if you suffer from low HDL cholesterol coupled with high triglyceride levels and also have insulin resistance, a precursor to diabetes. It's not *not bad* for you; rather, it's *good* for you. Based on this research, the Institute of Medicine has finally concluded that "no clear evidence links low-carbohydrate diets with an increased risk of kidney stones, osteoporosis, cancer, or heart disease." Researchers in the Division of Endocrinology at the SUNY Downstate Medical Center who examined numerous randomized controlled trials concluded that low-carbohydrate diets were either comparable to or even better than the traditional high-carbohydrate diet at reducing weight, blood cholesterol, and other side effects of diabetes. They wrote, "Evidence from various randomized controlled trials in recent years has convinced us that such diets are safe and effective."

Unique Features of the Ultimate New York Eating Plan

Unlike those early low-carbohydrate diets that allowed you to eat anything you wanted, the Ultimate New York Eating Plan helps you preserve your health as you lose the weight. Unique hallmarks of the diet include:

- **The right types of fat in the right amount.** There are many different types of fat, ranging from the artery-clogging saturated fats found in fatty cuts of meat and whole milk to the processed trans fats found in commercially baked goods and margarine (which, by the way, may be worse for your health than butter) to the heart-friendly unsaturated fats found in certain vegetables, nuts, flaxseeds, and fish. The Ultimate New York Eating Plan contains a reasonable amount of fat, most of it the unsaturated variety to stimulate weight loss and improve your health.
- **The right amount of fiber.** Numerous studies show that body weight goes up as fiber consumption goes down. Unfortunately, many popular low-carb diets don't focus on this important nutrient, and most adults eat less than half the amount of fiber they need for optimal health and weight control. On the Ultimate New York Eating Plan, you'll consume fiber in the form of vegetables, legumes, beans, and nuts.
- **The right types of protein.** All of the food you put in your mouth on the Ultimate New York Eating Plan will be as fresh as possible, be as low in fat as possible, and contain as little processing as possible. You'll eat a diet rich in lean protein such as skinless chicken breast and grilled sirloin.
- **The right meals at the right times.** Your body best responds to carbohydrates early in the day, when insulin sensitivity is highest. When you first wake, your body cells are hungry for energy. During early morning and until about 2:00 P.M., these cells are more responsive to the hormone insulin, which acts like a key to unlock these cells and

Helen Kirsch

My mom has struggled with her weight for much of her life. I've at times offered to help her in this quest, but I knew I could help only if she really wanted to change. Over the years I've seen her try Weight Watchers and many other diets. They didn't work for Mom. Although I have tried countless times in the past to get Mom to exercise and eat better, it wasn't until she moved back into New York City that she began this quest in earnest. When she came to me last year and told me she was ready to do something about her weight, I was overjoyed. Soon, our work began.

Q: How did you end up more than 150 pounds above your ideal weight?

A: I lost my sister when she was only 45 years old. My brother died two years later. Later, I was diagnosed with cervical cancer. I couldn't handle these deaths and emotional setbacks, so I turned to food. I think my eating was a silent protest, a way of saying, "You can take these people away from me, but you can't take this away, too." It was my way of saying, "I'm going to do what I want to do."

Q: How did excess weight affect your life?

A: It never did, which is probably why I waited until I was almost 70 to do something about it. I have never felt that a person—any person—is what they look like. I'm a big woman, but I was never uncomfortable in my body. I was never embarrassed to go anywhere. I tried to look as good as possible, but my weight never stopped me from doing anything. I'm a nice person. I'm a good friend, mother, grandmother, and person. If someone has a problem with the fact that I'm heavy, it's their problem, not mine.

Q: What changed in your life to wake you up and get you committed to a wellness program?

A: My husband had quadruple bypass surgery. After more than 50 years of marriage, I had gotten accustomed to him and wasn't ready to have him leave me. At night, I would put a mirror up to his nose to make sure he was alive. It scared me. I realized that I, too, wasn't ready to leave this world. I wanted to be around for my children and grandchildren. I wanted *both* of us to be around. I realized that it was time to cut to the chase and finally do something for myself.

We moved to New York for a couple of months for the surgery and his subsequent recuperation. I did not have a car, so I walked everywhere. I started to lose some weight just as a consequence of the walking. Around that time David came to me and suggested I do his program so he could include me in his next book. I said, "Oh sure," not truly realizing what I was committing myself to.

Q: **At times you've struggled on the Diet and worked to recommit yourself. During those times, what went on inside your head?**

A: My priorities were in the wrong place. I felt like I had other things to take care of that were more important than taking care of me. I also was trying to do this for my son, and I had to realize that was the wrong reason to exercise and change my eating habits. I had to do this for me, first and foremost.

Also, whenever I indulged off the plan, I was trying to comfort my inner child. I was trying to use food to create the warmth and comfort that I remember receiving from my mother many years ago. I learned that food cannot provide that kind of comfort.

Q: **How do your results affect your life?**

A: I got into a jacket recently that I had not worn in two years. It's suede and has no give. Even my shoes are flopping around. People who don't know I'm on a diet say, "Wow you are looking good." When I tell people that I'm going to be 69, they say, "You are not!" This is the first time in my entire life that I've exercised in a gym. I am enjoying it. I am proud of myself.

HELEN'S ADVICE FOR YOU: Focus on one day at a time. If you get through today, that's great. Deal with tomorrow, tomorrow.

POSTSCRIPT: *What can I say that I haven't already said throughout the book? Working with my mom has been a gift from God. Although on some level the roles have changed a bit, Mom is still teaching me life lessons. Our mutual belief in one another has forged a friendship that will last beyond our lifetimes. I hope she inspires all of you as much as she inspires me. I am so proud of all of her accomplishments!*

shuttle in sugar to be burned for energy. Around 2:00 P.M. insulin sensitivity begins to drop, and cells don't respond as well to the hormone. Unless you complete a heavy workout later in the day, the carbs you eat after 2:00 P.M. generally find their way into only one type of cell: your fat cells. Also, new research completed in Switzerland has found that late-evening consumption of carbs interferes with sleep. In the study, participants who ate spaghetti and carrots (a high-carb meal) two to three hours before bedtime had higher body temperatures and heart rates during the night than participants who ate their main carbohydrate meal in the morning. Most people sleep better when their body temperature and heart rate is lower, not higher. For this reason, the Ultimate New York Eating Plan includes high-carbohydrate foods only early in the day.

In addition to timing your carbohydrate intake, the plan spreads all of your calories evenly throughout the day. You'll eat five meals and snacks every day to keep blood sugar levels stable, which will also help improve insulin sensitivity and enable fat burning. This allows you to feed your body every two to three hours, preventing the metabolism slowdown that's common with dieting. Just this simple change can transform a body that hoards fat to one that sheds it. One of my clients, Virginia Gordon, was doing just about everything right when she met me. She was exercising and eating well-balanced meals, but she wasn't eating very often. As a result, she began gaining weight, particularly after menopause. She at first resisted eating every two to three hours because, she said, "I'm going to be a cow if I eat that much." I convinced her to trust me, and soon her frequent eating gave her metabolism the kick she needed to drop the weight. This simple switch also worked for another client, John Kiehne. He already worked out a lot, ate an extremely healthful diet, and generally looked great when he started my program. He was running six miles a day and lifting weights religiously. He was building muscle but couldn't seem to burn off the fat. He simply wanted to take things to the next level, to get, as he said, "cut." When he began eating five times a day rather than only two, his body responded. "Things really kicked in," he said.

- **The right amount of indiscretion.** If there's one thing that I've learned over the years, it's this: people cheat on diets. I give my clients a

Improve Your Endothelial Function

If you don't know what your endothelials are, don't worry. I didn't either until I began doing research for this book. Here's what I learned. The human body contains more than 70,000 miles of blood vessels. The internal layer of each blood vessel is covered by a single layer of endothelial cells. These cells play a central role in many health and disease conditions. Endothelial dysfunction is the earliest measurable functional abnormality of the vessel wall. A study that compared various types of diets determined that diets high in saturated fat tended to impair endothelial function and raise levels of the bad (LDL) cholesterol. Diets high in carbohydrate tended to raise triglycerides, especially in participants who already had low HDL (good) cholesterol. Diets low in carbohydrate and saturated fat and high in monounsaturated fat—such as the Ultimate New York Diet—actually *improved* endothelial function.

meal plan, and I stay on top of them to follow it. Regardless, I invariably find out that they at one time or another snuck in champagne, cookies, or some other guilty pleasure. Because of this, over the years I've searched for a way to build such eating into a meal plan, basically planning cheating into the process. The meal plan you will find in Chapter 7 does just that. In phase 3, you'll find one day each week that allows you to include more high-carbohydrate fare, satisfying that yearning without going overboard. During this weekly cheat meal, you can eat whatever you want. This will help keep your motivation strong for the rest of the week, reduce cravings, and prevent bingeing. If you find yourself craving a particularly naughty food, reserve it for your cheat meal. Once your cheat meal rolls around, eat guiltlessly, but not mindlessly. Research shows that the body will turn up the metabolism and burn off excess calories during occasional indulgences. So you can safely cheat once a week without seeing ill effects on your waistline. That said, cheating any more than one meal a week could have disastrous consequences.

Rita Chamoy

I met Rita when I did the Fox News Channel Challenge. She was one of six participants who tried my program for two weeks, as Fox chronicled their progress. Rita was trying to shed the 30 pounds she couldn't get rid of after her pregnancy three years before. She stood five feet seven inches tall but weighed 164 pounds. She has stuck with the program for months, whittling herself down to 135 pounds. The last we spoke, she was still losing a pound a week.

Q: **Why do you think you struggled to lose your baby weight?**

A: When I was pregnant, I ate a huge quantity of food. My husband never got to eat his meals. I ate mine, and I ate his, too. When we would get a large deep-dish pizza, for example, I would eat three-quarters of it. I ate until 11:00 at night. There was a Cold Stone Creamery around the corner from where I lived at the time, and at 10:00 every night, I would say, "Cold Stone?" and we would get into the car and go. It was crazy. I had no idea how to take care of myself.

Even after my son was born, I continued to eat huge portions. I exercised a lot—every single day. But my eating was my undoing.

Q: **How have your eating habits changed?**

A: I still eat out, but I eat a lot less. The key thing is I stopped eating after 7:00 P.M. If I don't eat dinner by 7:00, I don't eat dinner. I make a point of that. If I feel hungry when I go to bed, I know my body is looking for energy to burn, and it will find that energy in my fat cells. I tolerate it because I know I will weigh less in the morning. Oh, and I don't step foot into Cold Stone Creamery.

Q: **How do you eat out so often and still stay true to the plan?**

A: We do eat out a lot, but now I order different foods and eat smaller portions. Before I would order BBQ chicken sandwiches and pizza. Now I order Asian chicken salads, Cobb

salads without the bacon, and sushi with brown rice. I listen to my body, and when I feel satisfied, I stop eating.

Q: Could you describe your results and how they've changed your life?

A: I used to wear a size 14, and now I wear a size 6. When I wore a size 14, I didn't feel good. My face was big. One day I walked by a construction site near my house and didn't get one catcall. I told my husband, "When those guys don't howl, you know you've got to hit the gym." I was upset for days.

Now that I'm a size 6, it's fantastic. People I've never met come up to me and tell me how great I look. I'm thinner now than I was when I met my husband. Everything fits better, and now, when I'm outside running, random people honk their horns. I like that.

More important, I'm healthier, and as a result, so is my son, Asher. Everything in our fridge is whole grain. I take my son for walks. I play ball with him in the yard. We're not a sedentary family.

Q: How do you maintain your results?

A: When I first moved beyond phase 1 and into the maintenance phases, I had a lot of doubts. I worried that adding foods back in would make the weight come back, but the pounds kept falling off of me. Something about the plan really cranked up my metabolism.

I stick to the basic principles of the plan. The Eating Plan became ingrained in me, and now six months later I know what to eat and how often to eat. I know what's good and what's not good. I still eat what's not good every now and then, but I'm human.

RITA'S ADVICE FOR YOU: If you're a mom like me, then exercise first thing in the morning. If you wait until later, you'll get sidetracked with other tasks. I am up every day at 6:00 A.M. to run—before my son gets out of bed. When my son gets up, my husband watches him until I return. Then, when my son is napping, I do my cardiosculpting routines.

POSTSCRIPT: *As a stay-at-home mom, Rita has learned how to find time to be there for herself and for her family. She has balanced that nicely and continues to inspire and motivate herself to be the best that she can be.*

The A, B, C, D, E, and Fs: What You Won't Be Eating

The Ultimate New York Diet spans three phases, with phase 1 the strictest. During phase 1, you will not eat any foods from the following A, B, C, D, E, and F list. During phase 2, you will add some healthful, high-fiber carbs back into the menu in the form of beans, quinoa, and whole grains. In phase 3, you'll experiment, eating about two daily servings from the following list of caution foods.

A—ALCOHOL

Sedating, relaxing, and appetizing, alcohol lowers your ability to resist the other A, B, C, D, E, and Fs. It also supplies an abundance of calories. A standard mixed drink contains 100 to 250 calories. Made from fermented wheat, barley, grapes, or some other carbohydrate ingredient, alcohol contains 7 calories per gram, compared to 4 calories per gram in most carbs. Although you might think that you can compensate for your glass of wine by eating less for dinner, it rarely works out that way. Often alcohol makes you crave the very foods you are trying to avoid. Your body treats alcohol as a toxin, so your liver processes alcohol calories before all others in an attempt to clean the toxins from your bloodstream. As other calories wait on line, your body shuttles many of them into your fat cells.

For these reasons and more, you will drink no alcohol during phases 1 and 2 of the meal plan, and you'll have it only occasionally during phase 3.

B—BREAD

Bread is filled with empty carbs that spike your blood sugar, sending your body into fat-storage mode and increasing your sensations of hunger. Most types of bread really pack on the calories. For example, most bagels contain more than 400 calories. Just one slice of white bread contains 100 calories. I am also throwing crackers (regular and fat-free) in the forbidden Bs. They deceptively pack a mean punch of carbohydrates and often sodium and, usually, trans fats (a type of synthetic fat that clogs your arteries).

After phases 1 and 2, you may be able to reintroduce certain types of bread products into your dietary repertoire, but only if you can do so without going overboard and only if you keep your bread eating to a once-a-week occurrence. During phase 3 of the plan, you'll be able to eat trans fat–free, whole-grain bread products such as Kashi TLC 7 Grain crackers and 100 percent whole wheat bread, preferably the type from a bakery that contains flax and other seeds. Even whole-grain bread often contains quite a bit of white flour, so reserve bread for your cheat meal, and, even then, minimize it as much as possible. For example, if ordering pizza, order a thin crust. When having a sandwich, order it open-faced with just one slice of bread. When eating out, choose just one piece of bread from the basket and then send the basket away. My mother likes to treat herself to a flat whole-grain bagel once a week. It contains much less "bread" than a regular bagel but still gives her the satisfaction she yearns for. In addition, she does that New York thing and scoops out the middle of the bagel, cutting down on the carbohydrates and calories considerably. You can safely treat yourself to such indulgences, but only if you stop at one.

C—STARCHY CARBS

Want to know why most people are fatter than they were 10 or 20 years ago? Starchy carbs. Research has linked consumption of processed carbs with higher numbers on the scale, and the Centers for Disease Control reports that women eat about 300 more calories a day—mostly in the form of these carbs—than they did in the 1970s.

Highly processed carbohydrates—the type you find in boxes, shrink-wrap, and other packaging in the middle aisles of the grocery store—are made from white flour and white sugar. To create white flour, the processor starts with wheat, an otherwise healthy food. Once you remove the hull and outer covering, however, you're left with just the inside of the grain, which contains no fiber and few, if any, nutrients. It's no better for you than table sugar. The lack of fiber and high number of calories in processed carbohydrates cause them to hit your bloodstream faster than just about any other food you can eat.

Researchers have tested hundreds of foods and ranked them for their speed in spiking blood sugar levels on a scale known as the glycemic index. Foods that rank high on the index, such as table sugar and potatoes, spike blood sugar quickly, causing an overrelease of the hormone insulin. Foods that rank low on the index, such as beans and most vegetables, cause a slow, even rise in blood sugar, which keeps insulin in check. In addition to highly processed carbohydrates, carrots, potatoes, instant rice, and corn all rank high or relatively high on the glycemic index. In addition to making you fat, eating too many high glycemic carbs—and therefore experiencing an overabundance of excessive insulin releases—promotes a process called glycation, which increases the deposit of sugars into connective tissue and other body proteins. These sugar deposits make you feel stiffer as you age. The process happens more rapidly if you have diabetes, prediabetes, a metabolic disorder, or insulin insensitivity.

For all of those reasons, you will eat only very little overall carbohydrate during phase 1, the first two weeks of the plan. During phase 2, you'll work some wholesome carbs back in the form of quinoa, lentils, and beans. Phase 3 allows for more indiscretion, but, if you're smart, you'll always keep processed and starchy carbs to a minimum.

COFFEE

Another C that you will be avoiding (save the occasional cup) is coffee. I would much rather have you drink a cup of green tea instead of coffee because it is full of healthy polyphenols, among other things.

D—DAIRY

When one of my clients, Rita Chamoy, was nursing her baby boy, she tried to consume five servings of dairy a day, thinking all of the milk, yogurt, and cheese would boost her own milk production. All it did, however, was prevent her from losing the 60 pounds she had gained during her pregnancy. Many people don't realize that dairy products contain high amounts of a sugar called lactose. Not only that, most people are sensitive to this sugar and can't digest it well. It leads to bloating, which is the last thing you want when you want to look your best. On the other hand, dairy products are high in the mineral calcium, which is an important component of fat burning. To make sure you consume enough calcium in your diet while on this plan, you'll take a calcium supplement and consume nondairy sources of calcium such as broccoli and almonds.

On phase 1, you'll consume no dairy at all. On phases 2 and 3, you'll still keep it to a minimum. Choose organic low- and nonfat versions of

My Take on Sugar Substitutes

In my previous books, I have admonished readers about the use of artificial sweeteners such as aspartame. In my mind, these sweeteners served as a crutch that kept sugar cravings going strong. I also didn't feel these sweeteners were particularly healthy, as recent research seems to have confirmed in the case of aspartame and cancer. Since those books, two sweeteners have caught my attention. One, sucralose (called Splenda), is a sweetener made from sugar. Because of the process used to remove the calories from it, your body does not process Splenda the same way it processes sugar, keeping blood sugar levels stable. Another, Stevia, is an herbal product sold in health food stores. So far, these sweeteners seem to be safe. If you have a sweet tooth and simply can't wean yourself off sugar, I suggest you use them. That said, too much of anything can be bad for you. So use them, but try to use them sparingly.

milk and yogurt. Use these mostly in recipes rather than as true meal servings. For example, use plain nonfat yogurt in place of mayo.

E—EXTRA SWEETS

Any sweet food, including some sugar substitutes, can lead to carbohydrate cravings. The Institute of Medicine recommends you consume no more than 25 percent of your total calories from added sugar, but they are simply trying to keep sugar cane–producing countries and the corn industry in business. Personally, I recommend you try to consume none of it, if possible.

I'm not talking about the sugars that occur naturally in foods such as fruit. I'm talking about sugars that are added during processing. On the food label, these sugars often appear as "corn syrup" and "high-fructose corn syrup." This synthetic sugar starts off as fructose. Manufacturers add glucose. The body rapidly absorbs this synthetic fructose-glucose combo, which sets the stage for weight gain.

Soda, which is full of high-fructose corn syrup, is particularly evil for the waistline. In a Harvard study, women who increased their soda

Virginia Gordon

When I met Virginia, I immediately thought, "Here is a quintessential type A New Yorker." She is highly motivated, focused, overworked, and overstressed. At the time, she was balancing family and work with taking care of herself, and, often, the "taking care of herself" took a backseat to all of her other responsibilities. She wanted to look and feel sexy again. She wanted to prove to herself and to her doubting husband that she was up to the challenge of the Ultimate New York Diet. She not only succeeded, she exceeded her goals and expectations.

tried Weight Watchers, Jenny Craig, even acupuncture, but I couldn't take off the 15 pounds I gained after menopause.

Q: **When did you begin your battle with your weight?**

A: I've always worked out and have always been in good shape. When I went through menopause, however, I started gaining weight. Before I knew it, I was a size 10. It seemed as if no matter how much I exercised or how little I ate, I couldn't get back to my premenopause size 6. I exercised every day. I did yoga, Pilates, rollerblading, cycling, Precor machines, you name it. I lifted weights three times a week. I was an avid exerciser. I skipped meals. I

Q: **What did you do differently on this program that enabled you to turn things around?**

A: I started eating every three hours. Before this program, I would stop eating in order to lose weight, but I always ended up gaining weight because I was slowing my metabolism down in the process. Also, on David's plan, I exercised differently from the way I had in the past. His workouts were much more intense. That intensity really kicked up my metabolism. Also, David has these unique exercises. Just one of his moves would work eight areas of my body at once, whereas the moves I had been doing targeted only one area of my body at a time.

Q: **How did your mind-set change in order to be successful on this plan?**

A: Eating every three hours did change my metabolism, and the weight came off, but pulling it off took some discipline for me. I'm a New Yorker, and I'm always in a rush. I also had a mind-set that eating every three hours would turn me into a cow, so I had to consciously work on changing that way of thinking. I carry almonds with me everywhere. If all else fails, I have some almonds just to get something in me. I always have a bottle of water with me. I always have one of David's protein shakes with me, too.

Q: **How did your rapid results help you stay successful?**

A: On this program, you see results within three days. On the first day, you might think, "Oh my God, what did I get myself into," but by day three you are already seeing a different body. When I experienced these results, I was actually really angry because I had tried so many other diets that didn't work. I spent all of these years doing all of these crazy diets when what I really needed to do was so simple.

The results span well beyond my body, too. Not only are my muscles in better shape, but my skin has a glow. After menopause, my skin lost some of its elasticity and became dull. Now it's glowing.

VIRGINIA'S ADVICE FOR YOU: Hang in there. The first day of the plan, you're going to think, "What have I gotten myself into?" On the second day, you will think, "OK, maybe this is doable." By the third day, you'll see results and you'll have the determination to move forward.

POSTSCRIPT: *It has been more than a year since Virginia completed the program, and I'm proud to say that she still follows the plan's principles very closely. The lessons she learned about the proper combination of exercise and nutrition have served her well and converted her into a happy and healthy New Yorker.*

consumption from one or fewer soft drinks a week to one or more a day gained an average of 10 pounds over four years. What about diet sodas? Although these drinks may not contain calories, they may cause you to overeat calories from other sources as research shows that people who drink them allow themselves to overeat other calories later in the day. Also, most diet sodas contain the artificial sweetener aspartame, which preliminary rat studies have linked to an increase in malignant tumors and other cancers.

Foods high in sugar and fat also leave you feeling drained, which puts a damper on your exercise efforts. Sugar spikes blood sugar, while fat is hard for the body to digest. Your body pours its reserves into your digestive tract to digest the fat—and away from your working muscles. Soon, your pancreas oversecretes insulin, causing blood sugar to plummet. End result: you curl up in a corner under your desk.

Finally, sugars erode your immunity. Disease-causing bacteria feed on the sugar you eat, especially the refined type in candy. Refined sugars also increase your risk of breast cancer.

During phases 1 and 2 of the plan, you will avoid all sources of added sugar, high-fructose corn syrup, and most sugar substitutes. That means no fruit juice, no diet or regular soda, no NutraSweet, no honey, and no molasses. If you crave a sweet taste, then try an herbal tea such as peppermint or vanilla flavor. During phase 3, you can indulge in small servings of sweets—and I really do stress the word *small*—during your cheat meal.

F—FRUIT AND MOST FATS

Nina Joukowsky Koprulu, one of my clients, used to think of fruit as a "diet food." Yes, fruit is good for your heart and is loaded with vitamins, fiber, and other healthful nutrients, but it's not necessarily good for your waistline, as Nina learned the hard way. When she reached middle age, she found herself gaining weight rather than losing, even though she was exercising more and eating less. When she cut back on her generous plate of fruit each morning, she reversed the problem.

Fruit contains high amounts of fructose, a sugar. Dried fruit is the worst offender in this category. The drying process depletes water-soluble nutrients such as vitamin C and potassium from fruit. Dried fruit also contains four times as much sugar and calories per ounce compared to its fresh cousins. During phase 1 of the eating plan, you'll cut all fruits from your dietary repertoire. In phases 2 and 3, you'll be able to reintroduce some types of fruit back into your diet. During these weeks, you'll choose the lower-carb and -calorie varieties such as blueberries, strawberries, cantaloupe, kiwi, apples, and pears. Stay away from sweet, tropical fruits such as papaya, mango, and pineapple.

As for fat, you'll nearly eliminate the artery-clogging saturated and trans fats and focus exclusively on certain types of unsaturated fats and omega-3 fatty acids. You'll eat no fatty cuts of red meat, pork, bacon, or other types of fatty meats. Instead, all of your protein will be lean: skinless chicken breast, egg whites, fresh roasted turkey breast, turkey bacon, wild salmon, fresh tuna, halibut, striped bass, and lean sirloin, to name a few. Nuts are good and satisfying, and the plan prescribes snacking on raw almonds. Not only will you be getting a great supply of fiber (which will help keep you more regular), almonds have the highest concentration of vitamin E of any food. You can also use up to a teaspoon of olive oil a day, as a dressing for your salad. For phase 1, you will generally stay away from additional unsaturated fats such as avocados, olives, peanut butter, and egg yolks. Although some of these foods are healthy, they all contain high amounts of calories.

Ultimate New York Diet Staples: What You *Will* Be Eating

When it comes to shedding fat fast, I find that it helps to focus your efforts on what you *can* eat rather than on what you can't. So although you certainly need to know your A, B, C, D, E, and Fs, don't obsess over them. Instead, pay attention to adding the following fat-fighting foods into your daily arsenal. As you focus on addition, the subtraction will seem much less distracting.

PHASE 1 STAPLES

It will be necessary for you to make a list of the following staples and ensure they are readily available to you throughout the day. The more prepared you are to enter phase 1, the greater the likelihood of success.

If this is the "battle of the bulge," be sure to enter into battle fully armed and ready to roll.

Organic Low-Starch Vegetables. The U.S. government now recommends you eat four and a half cups of vegetables (and fruit) a day. Most people consume much, much less. Packed with appetite-suppressing fiber, most vegetables contain just 40 calories per serving, making them a dieter's dream. Vegetables also help to balance your body's pH, promoting the optimal internal environment for fat burning.

Try to eat organic whenever possible, and when you have to buy conventionally grown produce, wash it well before eating. Some research shows that pesticide toxins can inhibit hormonal activity in the body, leading to weight gain. One animal study showed the pesticide dieldrin doubles body-fat levels in mice. These toxins interfere with fat-burning hormones such as epinephrine and norepinephrine (also a brain chemical). They also interfere with thyroid function, which also lowers metabolic rate. Finally, these toxins may even lower levels of the brain chemicals norepinephine and dopamine, making you feel tired and listless. In addition to filling your lunch and dinner plate with veggies, look to them as a convenient snacking alternative. If you feel a craving for one of the A, B, C, D, E, or Fs coming on, first turn to a raw veggie such as broccoli. After eating half a cup of broccoli or another green veggie, your craving may still get the best of you, but you'll probably eat much less of that chocolate chip cookie than you would have if you hadn't dampened your appetite with the broccoli.

Cauliflower. Cauliflower counts as a vegetable, which I've already mentioned, but I'd like to talk about it separately because it's so good for you, especially if you eat it as a substitute for baked or mashed potatoes. One cup of mashed cauliflower supplies only 29 calories compared to 133 calories of mashed potato, and it also delivers three times as much vitamin C and folate. This and other cruciferous veggies (broccoli, brussels sprouts, and cabbage) contain phytochemicals that help prevent cancer. Eat it raw or steamed and smashed as an alternative to mashed potatoes.

Fresh and Canned Wild Salmon (and Other Types of Fish). Salmon contains high amounts of omega-3 fatty acids, a type of fat that speeds

Flush and Cleanse!

Chances are that you haven't been living in a hermetically sealed bubble your entire life. If you are like most people, you've spent years breathing in toxic air and eating toxins on your food. Your body has stored away these toxins in your fat cells. One of the unfortunate side effects of weight loss is this: as your fat cells release their fat, they also release these toxins into your bloodstream. To enable your body to deal with these toxins, I suggest you drink plenty of filtered water each day—at least eight eight-ounce glasses. This will help your liver to flush these toxins out of your blood. For this reason, the Ultimate New York Diet is rich in soluble fiber, which will also help to flush these toxins out of the body. In Chapter 3, you'll learn of a series of supplements that I recommend to further enable this process.

metabolism and promotes fat burning. Don't make the mistake, however, of buying the farm-raised variety. Because of the fish chow often fed to farm-raised salmon, this variety can not only be lower in this important fat than its wild cousins but it can also be high in PCB (polychlorinated biphenyl), a carcinogen.

Compared to other types of fish, wild salmon is generally low in mercury, a heavy metal that, in high amounts, can cause neurological problems and can be particularly dangerous to women in childbearing years. One in 12 women has too much mercury in her blood, causing aches, fatigue, and other flulike symptoms. According to Purdue University research, canned salmon contains less than a quarter of the mercury found in certain types of canned tuna. If you do not like salmon or are not able to locate it in the grocery store, studies have shown that chunk light tuna is lower in mercury than the fancier, generally more expensive solid white albacore.

Salmon is also a rich source of the mineral calcium, which aids fat burning. In addition to salmon, you'll notice that the Ultimate New York Diet menus include other types of fish and shellfish as they are rich sources of protein but relatively low in calories. Sardines are also a good choice, as is crab, which is surprisingly low in mercury and other toxins but relatively high in omega-3s. The menus do not showcase orange roughy, red snapper, and swordfish, which are all relatively low in omega-3s and high in mercury.

Chicken Breast. Although not technically a power food in its own right, chicken breast allows you to eat protein without all the saturated fat. Just make sure to remove the skin. It's also incredibly convenient, which is why I've included lots of it in the food plan.

Nuts. I strongly suggest you eat eight or so raw almonds every day—during every phase of the plan. Almonds and other nuts, including walnuts, contain sterols and sterolins. These essential components of cell membranes boost immunity and balance hormonal function. Beta sitosterol in particular helps your body convert linoleic acid into arachidonic acid to promote muscle growth. Remember: more muscle equals a faster metabolism. When researchers at Loma Linda University in California supplemented the diets of obese participants with 85 grams of almonds a day, the participants lost weight, shrank their waist circumference, and improved their insulin sensitivity.

Again, in addition to aiding your weight-loss efforts, nuts are also good for your health, as various studies show that twice-weekly consumption of nuts helps reduce total cholesterol levels. Avoid Brazil nuts and macadamia nuts as they are higher in saturated fat and calories and don't have as much vitamin E.

Mushrooms. According to research completed at the University of Illinois at Urbana-Champaign, mushrooms contain beta glucan and chitin, two types of fiber that absorb fat and shuttle it out of the blood, lowering heart disease risk and reducing your caloric intake. When you eat mushrooms, you are essentially eating negative calories because they are filled with water, are low in calories themselves, and give you fiber that sucks other calories out of your gut before they can be absorbed into your bloodstream. Certain types of mushrooms are high in the minerals selenium and potassium as well.

Celery. Celery houses plenty of potassium, a mineral that helps lower blood pressure and regulate water balance. Most people eat only half as much potassium as they need. Other foods high in potassium include potatoes and bananas, but these foods contain way too many carbs for rapid weight loss. Also, you can munch down four medium celery stalks and take in only 24 calories. Plus, the crunch will help prevent you from eating other crunchy and high-carb and -calorie fare. Finally, ingesting celery will help you lose weight because you actually expend more calories digesting its high-fiber and low-calorie content than you're taking in.

Egg Whites. In my egg recipes, you'll see that you'll be making scrambled eggs and frittatas with just one yolk and the rest whites. The one yolk provides the right amount of fat—and some taste and texture—without too much calories and cholesterol.

Asparagus. Asparagus is one of the few good vegetable sources of vitamin E. It also contains glutathione, an antioxidant that may prevent cancer. Asparagus is also a natural diuretic, which is ideal for women around their menstrual cycle.

Spices. Throughout the recipes, you'll find red pepper flakes, chopped jalapeños, and Tabasco sauce used to spice up your meals. In addition to making food taste delicious, these hot spices help to turn down hunger. In one study, people who consumed a gram of hot red pepper ate 15 percent fewer calories than people who had none.

PHASE 2 AND 3 STAPLES

Well, you've made it through phase 1 of the program. During phase 2, you will ease up a bit on the restrictions, incorporating things such as lentils, red beans, chickpeas, and sweet potatoes. Remember that your body will be very sensitive to the carbs, so slowly integrate them back into your diet.

Beans. Did you know that black beans contain more antioxidants than oranges, grapes, or cranberries? Most people don't. Beans also contain solid amounts of protein, the B vitamin folate, calcium, and fiber—all nutrients that help promote sensations of fullness, control insulin levels, and promote fat burning. In addition to aiding your weight-loss efforts, beans are also good for your overall health. A study published in the *International Journal of Cancer* that compared the diets and health outcomes of 90,630 women determined that women who ate one-half cup of beans and other legumes twice a week were 24 percent less likely to develop breast cancer than women who ate legumes less often.

Berries. Remember when I said you wouldn't be eating much fruit on the Ultimate New York Diet? Well, during phases 2 and 3, berries—strawberries, blackberries, blueberries, cranberries, and the like—are an exception. Sixteen extra-large strawberries contain only 100 calories, which is probably why studies show that people who include berries in their diets tend to weigh less than people who don't eat berries. These low-sugar, low-calorie, high-water-content fruits all rank high in antioxidant capacity. Antioxidants help to keep your cells healthy. Healthy cells contribute to a healthy metabolism. Cranberries, blackberries, blueberries, and strawberries also contain a substance called anthocyanidins, a flavonoid that bolsters the immune system.

Sweet Potatoes. Just one of these packs more than twice your daily needs of vitamin A, a third of vitamin C, as well as iron, potassium, folate, vitamin B_6, and fiber—all for only 103 calories (compared to 133 calories of a baked potato).

Lentils. Along with beans, lentils may also reduce breast cancer risk. Based on the research conducted on 90,630 women participating in the health study mentioned earlier, women who ate one-half cup of legumes twice weekly were 24 percent less likely to develop breast cancer than women who consumed them once a month.

Apples. When you are on the run—as almost all of my clients are—you need a healthful food that you can toss in a briefcase or jacket pocket and eat on the run. Apples supply that need. They also eat clean. Unlike some other types of fruit (juicy oranges come to mind), you generally don't feel sticky after eating an apple. They also promote weight loss. Apples contain a substance called polyphenols, a powerful type of antioxidant that helps protect your cells, improving metabolism. One small apple contains the antioxidant power of 1,500 milligrams of vitamin C.

Quinoa (keen-wah). This grainlike seed delivers significant amounts of 20 different amino acids (all of the essential ones). Usually only animal protein can make this claim, as most veggies and grains are short on one or more of the essential amino acids. Your body needs these essentials to help repair tissues, especially if you are exercising intensely. As an added bonus, quinoa is much lower in calories than meat and contains magnesium, with a half cup supplying 50 percent of your daily needs for this mineral.

The Phases of the New York Diet

You'll tackle the New York Diet in three phases:

- **Phase 1** will last two weeks (or longer if you'd like) and will definitely set you on the right track.
- **Phase 2** will last two weeks and will gradually ease you into the middle part of the program, where restrictions begin to ease up.
- **Phase 3** (aka the "life" part of the plan) will intelligently guide you on a lifetime wellness path.

PHASE 1

This is your weight-loss phase. During this phase you'll eat no foods from your A, B, C, D, E, and F list and very little overall carbohydrate. Your meals will consist of lean protein—usually in the form of egg whites, chicken, turkey, or fish—and lots of veggies. (For you vegetarians out there, don't fret. Many vegetarians have been able to substitute the animal protein for acceptable sources of protein such as quinoa, tofu, and tempeh—all to great effect.) This extremely low-carb phase will accomplish two goals. For the carboholics among you, it will help you to break your psychological addiction to carbs. During your two weeks without carbs, I encourage you to find other outlets for those times when you usually turn to carbs. If you tend to eat when under stress or when tired, consider a brief relaxation session or a 10-minute exercise bout, for example. If you must eat to relieve stress, satisfy the texture you crave without piling on the carbs and calories. Want some crunch? Turn to celery. Want something warm and mushy? You might try my turkey chili or my cauliflower mash with sautéed garlic.

Phase 1 of the plan follows a formula. If you find you need to stray from the plan—say you are traveling and can't cook your own meals—worry not. As long as you stick to the formula, you can go out to eat and still be successful on the plan. I have heard from many clients who have been able to religiously follow the plan and still have business dinners, eat with their families, and so on. Follow these pointers:

- **Breakfast.** Every day during phase 1, breakfast calls for a protein shake, which is a great traveling companion. If you are on the road, make sure to pack your protein powder and a shakable water bottle. Just put the powder in the bottle, fill it with bottled water, and shake. Voilà. Breakfast is served. If you'd prefer to eat your breakfast rather than drink it, you may do so as long as you eat lean protein. Your best option here is egg whites. This will give your body quality protein and all of the essential amino acids it needs. I ask you to make egg whites instead of whole eggs because most of the fat and calories of the egg are housed in the yolk. Start off your day with an egg white omelet full of your favorite vegetables. For great phase 1 egg dishes, try my Scrambled Egg Whites with Shiitake Mushrooms and Turkey Bacon and Scrambled Egg Whites with Ground Turkey and Chopped Tomatoes. (See Index.)

  Either way—protein shake or scrambled egg whites—you are putting protein into your system first thing in the morning. Although you may be used to starting the day with carbs, possibly in the form of a doughnut or, maybe slightly better, in the form of cold breakfast cereal, the sounder choice is nutritious protein. It will help you stay satisfied longer. Whereas you probably feel hungry an hour or so after eating a breakfast high in carbohydrate, this high-protein breakfast will keep you satisfied for most of the morning. It will also turn up your metabolic rate because your body burns more calories to digest protein than it does to digest carbohydrate.

  If you tend to skip breakfast, you must break yourself of that habit. To keep your metabolism humming along, your body needs regular doses of calories, about every three hours. After sleeping for eight hours, you need to get your metabolism moving, and the only way to do that is to eat.

- **Midmorning snack.** Your snacks during phase 1 will be low in fat and carbs and high in protein. Options include hard-boiled egg whites, raw almonds, chunk light tuna, a salmon burger, and much more.
- **Lunch.** Combine a source of lean protein (such as six ounces of salmon, tuna, or chicken or turkey breast) along with a hearty serving of your favorite steamed vegetable and/or mixed salad. I'd like you to eat your largest meal of the day around noon. It's more intelligent to eat as the Italians do, making lunch the biggest meal of the day and giving yourself the rest of the day to work off those calories. Lunch might consist of a lean source of protein, such as six ounces of chicken breast or fish, along with half a plate to a full plate of your favorite vegetable, such as steamed broccoli or spinach. Or, you might create a large salad. Fill a large plate with salad greens. Anything goes here as long as you stay away from carrots (because of their high carbohydrate content). Add a source of protein to your salad, such as a piece of salmon or tuna, sliced skinless grilled chicken breast, or sliced hard-boiled egg whites. Add some vinegar (any variety except balsamic, which contains sugar) along with a teaspoon of olive oil.
- **Midafternoon snack.** The logic here follows the same logic as the midmorning snack.
- **Dinner.** Again, your protein shake comes in handy. When you find yourself on the road, have a shake for dinner. Or, stick to the same formula you used for lunch. Make yourself a large salad with a lean source of protein. Pile on the vegetables (except for carrots) and place your favorite lean protein on top, ranging from grilled chicken breast to salmon to tuna.

I've devoted two weeks of your meal plan to phase 1, but, in reality, you might stay in phase 1 for a longer period of time depending on your weight-loss goal. If you have just 10 pounds to lose, two weeks should do it. If you have 50 pounds to lose, you might need to stick with it for 5 to 10 weeks to meet your goal. My mom has remained on phase 1—save the occasional cheat—for several months. She has been able to stay focused and motivated following the rigidity of this phase. Listen to your mind and your body, and if you feel that phase 1 is serving you well (as Mom does), then that is where you belong. Based on the results of the many people I've had on the plan, you can expect to lose up to seven pounds during each week of phase 1.

PHASE 2

During this phase, you'll learn how to maintain your weight loss. You'll add one daily serving of one of the A, B, C, D, E, and Fs back into your diet. In the meal plan, I've used this phase to teach you how to eat carbs healthfully. To this end, you'll find healthful, fiber-packed carbs such as quinoa, beans, lentils, and sweet potatoes served with lunch.

PHASE 3

I like to call this the "rest-of-your-life" phase. Although this part of the Eating Plan encompasses only four weeks, you'll spend the rest of your life in phase 3 in order to maintain all of the results you've worked so hard to get. During this phase you can eat a small serving (roughly 100 to 150 calories) of any carb of your choosing every day during your morning snack.

During phase 3, I want you to carefully monitor your weight, measurements, and clothing size and fit. Not everyone will safely be able to eat a daily serving from the A, B, C, D, E, and F list. If you start to gain weight, return to phase 2. Also, if you are extremely carb sensitive, adding certain carbs back in may set off a binge. Stay away from those foods that you've found addictive in the past. The longer you go without them, the less you'll want them.

For When You Fall . . .

As I began writing this section of the book, I had a telephone conversation with my mom, who has spent more than a few months living within the confines of phase 1. Although phase 1 generally spans two weeks, Mom had more than 150 pounds to lose. She couldn't lose all of that in two weeks, so, for her, phase 1 lasts as long as it needs to last. Until the week of our conversation, Mom had done very well, losing more than 60 pounds, but she still had a long way to go. In the previous week or so, however, she had lost her focus. As the "sabotage demons" started taking control over her decisions, the bagels and pizza found themselves on her breakfast and lunch plates. She was allowing outside influences to infiltrate her life and derail her.

I worried that she would soon fall into that vicious cycle of dwindling interest that leads to fewer results and in turn dwindles the interest even more. So I had a "make-or-break" conversation with her. Although she's heard it before, I exhorted her to remember the importance of not walking through life as a passive victim.

I also told her about the many things that I wanted to share with her—my future children and career successes. Quite selfishly, I also look to her for emotional and psychological support and want her to be around for many years. I told her that I wanted her to get healthy so she could be with me on this Earth for years to come.

I was as strong and as forceful with my mom as I have ever been; I left nothing to chance and explained that it was now or never for the program. She was failing or disappointing not me but rather herself. I had to make her realize that she was doing this for herself—not me, this book, or anyone else.

The day after that conversation, Mom completed her most challenging workout ever. I pushed her to her perceived limit and beyond. Two hours later, she was still feeling the effects of the extra cardiovascular exercise. She has had many more workouts like this since then. I am very proud of my mom and value the trust she has placed in me to help transform her. She is back on the program. I hope the story of her perseverance will help you to do the same if you ever find that your focus has strayed off course.

I tell you this story because it's probably sinking in just how challenging your journey ahead will be. Think positively as you embark on the Ultimate New York Diet, but also think realistically.

Each phase gets a little easier to adhere to. With each positive result and gain in confidence, you will find that this program represents a whole lot more than any diet you may have previously followed. More than just measuring your results in inches off your waist, you will see every aspect of your life with new eyes. The "new you" will have more self-respect and the strength and courage to lead a more productive, happy life.

3

The Ultimate New York Supplement Plan

My parents have always been strong advocates of taking supplements. A bodybuilder for the past 55 years, my dad has long looked to protein and vitamin supplementation to promote muscle growth. Back when he started, it meant taking concoctions made of eggs, brewer's yeast (I still gag at the smell and the taste), and wheat germ, among other ingredients.

Although my mom didn't always live the healthiest life in other respects, she always took vitamins, minerals, and antioxidants. Through supplementation, Mom was able to strengthen her body and fight off potential illnesses and physical problems that often beset people who are morbidly obese.

Because of my parents' influence, taking vitamins and supplements has always been second nature to me. When I was doing research for my own supplement line, I was determined to stick to those supplements that were tried and true—those that were safe, effective, and had little to no negative side effects. There have been countless studies concerning the efficacy of certain supplements and the warnings associated with some. I hope that after reading this chapter, you'll have a better sense of what supplements would be appropriate for you to take and which ones to avoid.

You may be wondering, "Can't I just lose weight simply by changing my eating and exercise habits? Do I really need supplements?" No, you don't *need* supplements. You could do it alone, but your journey would be much tougher. You'd feel hungrier, experience more cravings, and achieve results much more slowly. Even better, a new wave of supplements—backed by medical science—can aid you in your quest to sculpt a great body without making you feel jittery, giving you a headache, or ruining your health in the process. (Remember: I believe in wellness. I would never recommend something that might ruin your health.)

That said, you should know that old-school supplements marketed as an option for people who didn't want to exercise or change their eating habits *were* and *are* too good to be true. When I talk about weight-loss supplements, I'm not talking about eating all the cheeseburgers you want and then popping a pill. No, I'm talking about eating right, exercising, *and* supplementing.

The Ultimate New York Supplement Plan works synergistically with the Ultimate New York Eating and Fitness Plans. It will help support your efforts in the kitchen (or restaurant, as is the case with many of my clients) and the gym. I promote only foods, exercises, and supplements that are good for you. If something helps you lose weight but erodes your health in the process, it's not worth it.

In this chapter, you'll learn about the medical science behind a number of supplements that can help reduce hunger, improve energy levels, stop cravings for carbs, speed your metabolism, and more. Let's start with what I consider the most important supplement of all for people living the New York lifestyle—meal-replacement beverages.

Meal-Replacement Beverages

The Ultimate New York Eating Plan recommends you eat five meals a day, roughly every two to three hours. As I've mentioned before, I work with many very busy clients, many of whom never step foot in their kitchens. These on-the-go New Yorkers just don't have the time to cook five meals a day, making convenient liquid meals a must.

After the great success of *The Ultimate New York Body Plan*, I realized that this need for quick, convenient nutrition spans way beyond New York. I have heard from Body Plan participants literally all over the United States and around the world. These busy folks have told me that they could not have been successful on this plan had they not been able to drink some of their meals. Their meal-replacement shakes came in handy in many, many different situations.

Properly designed meal-replacement beverages arm you with great backup nutrition, eliminating the top excuses so many people use to backslide (and, believe me, at this point I'm pretty sure I've heard them all). For many people it's simply not realistic to try to cook three complete meals and two snacks a day. There just isn't time.

That's the beauty of making up to two of your meals shakes. It takes just a minute or two to mix up a protein shake. You can drink it wherever you find yourself—during your morning commute, during a board meeting, or during a sprint through the airport. I've found that protein shakes have helped my clients wean themselves off the fast-food lifestyle. Often, it means saying good-bye to vending machine foods and soft drinks—which is music to my ears.

Other clients use them when they visit friends and relatives. I must confess that my meal-replacement shakes have saved me from many a bad or inedible meal. In fact, I recommend that people have a meal-replacement drink before going out to a cocktail party or even on a blind date. Let's be honest, you're often too nervous to eat on those dates anyway. (Some of my clients turn to their protein shakes to help overcome alcohol-induced hangovers, but that's a topic of a different chapter in this book.)

Your shake ideally will provide you with the perfect mix of protein, carbs, healthful fats, fiber, and vitamins. When used properly, these meal-

Ellen Barkin

I've worked with actress Ellen Barkin in recent months, and she's become a very close friend. Unlike many people who come to me, Ellen didn't want to lose weight. She's been slender her entire life. She did, however, want to firm up and look as amazing as she could—and should—at age 51.

Q: **What were you hoping to get out of the program?**

A: As I got older and entered my 50s, I felt like I needed some serious training. I had exercised my entire life, but for a couple of years in my late 40s, I stopped. I guess I felt burnt out. Those two years, however, were crucial in terms of getting older.

I am very skinny by nature. I'm underweight. No matter what my history had been and no matter how oddly envious an outsider might be of my weight, to me it was always an issue. I also experienced all the usual things that happen to women as they age as a consequence of gravity, and I wanted to firm up.

Q: **Did the program deliver the results you were seeking?**

A: After just a few weeks with David, I was back to where I wanted to be.

He fixed all of the things that happen to women as they get older. I told him, "You are never going to make this go away. This is age. This is gravity. This is what happens to a body when it gets older." I have no butt. David works very hard to give me one. He has helped me to create a body that's proportioned and beautiful. Now, I'm the girl in the gym that everyone looks at and says, "She's how old?"

Q: **Unlike many people who try this program, you didn't want to lose weight. As a result, was it hard to motivate yourself to stick with the strict dietary regimen?**

A: At first I told David I couldn't follow it. I told him that I absolutely must have my potato chips. That drove him crazy, and he told me I had to give it all up. For a month I decided I would do everything by the letter. I am a very disciplined person. For 30 days I had no wine, no carbs, none of his A, B, C, D, E, and Fs. I also never missed an exercise appointment, and I saw extreme results.

Q: **How do you feel about the Supplement Plan?**

A: I take all of David's supplements, which are extraordinary. If I miss a day, I feel it. They give me more energy and more focus. I have two kids living at home, a full-time production company, a part-time acting career, and a teaching job. I have a stressful life, and these supplements help me to get through the day. When I don't take them, I crash around 5:00 P.M., which is the time I really need to go into action family wise.

Q: How has this plan changed the way you exercise?

A: I have spent 25 years exercising. I've worked with many trainers, but many of them wanted to bulk up my upper body and create noticeable muscles. David doesn't do that to me. He doesn't try to get me all pumped up. I am my age, and I am proud of it. I just want to look like a 50-year-old who is in good shape, and, thanks to David, I do.

Q: How do you stay on track when you travel?

A: I take along my DVDs, my medicine balls and light hand weights, and David's supplements. That does it for me.

Q: What have you learned during the past six months on this program that you wish you knew when you were 20 or 30?

A: I wish I knew to take better vitamins, to eat regularly, and not

to let anyone tell me what their dream body was for me.

ELLEN'S ADVICE FOR YOU: You don't need to train one-on-one with David to experience incredible results. Sometimes I'm out of town for three months at a time—months where David isn't there to motivate me to exercise or put me through a workout. During those months I use his books and videos. I make his recipes. Without fail, when I return to New York and start training with David again, I'm still in great shape.

POSTSCRIPT: *No smoke, no mirrors, no airbrushing. Ellen is the real deal! She is as New York as the Empire State Building and represents so many women in their early 50s who are trying to balance work and family with their own "inner peace." Through my program, Ellen can more effectively live her life, being present for herself as well as for those who are so important to her.*

replacement drinks offer a viable, time-saving meal choice. This will prevent hunger, give you the energy you need for your workouts, keep you satisfied, and provide the amino acids your muscles need to recuperate after your exercise sessions.

When studying the ingredients label of a protein drink, look for the following.

- **Type of protein.** Protein powders come from many sources ranging from whey to egg to bovine colostrums to casein to soy. Look for a shake that contains whey. Whey protein is essentially milk protein without the casein and sugar. I prefer it to other types because your body absorbs it most efficiently. Of all the protein sources, your body digests it most rapidly, shuttling amino acids to your muscles most quickly. In short, this type of protein will help speed your exercise recovery, allow you to sculpt muscle faster, and reduce soreness after your sessions.

    More important, whey also effectively reduces hunger. In a study completed at the University of Toronto, scientists sat 22 men in front of an all-you-can-eat pizza buffet. Men who had chugged a whey protein drink two hours earlier ate less pizza than men who had drunk soy- or egg-based protein drinks. Whey reduces hunger by triggering the gut to release several peptides (simple proteins that communicate messages throughout the body) that increase your sensation of fullness. Now, please take my word for it and don't try your own pizza study at home.

    When compared to other protein blends, whey proteins also contain the highest concentration of branched chain amino acids (BCAAs). These amino acids are an integral part of muscle metabolism and are the first aminos sacrificed during muscle catabolism (muscle wasting), a process all too common in most weight-loss regimens. Whey protein also enhances glutathione production. Glutathione is the body's most powerful naturally occurring antioxidant and also plays a role in immune system support.

    Now, you don't simply want whey protein per se. You want to see the following on the list of ingredients: *cross-flow microfiltered whey protein isolate*. With its average yield of 90 percent protein and its near absence of lactose and fat, this tops the list, with high-quality *cross-flow microfiltered whey protein concentrate*, with a yield of about 80 percent protein, running a close second. Cross-flow microfiltration is a process by which the proteins are physically separated by microscopic filters, thus avoiding the destruction of the proteins, which is typically the case with heat or acid separation methods. These high-quality whey proteins contain the highest concentration of intact protein microfractions, including immunoglobins, which help support the body's immune system, placing them at the top of the list for immune system support.

If whey protein is so good for you, why do so many meal-replacement beverages contain "proprietary protein blends"? Whey protein isolate is considerably more expensive than almost all other reliable protein sources except egg albumin, which is considerably lower in bioavailability. For this reason, whey protein isolates are either excluded from the mix or blended with the cheaper, more poorly absorbed garbage proteins such as caseinates and milk protein isolates and concentrates. These far lesser-quality proteins are also used for their taste appeal. If whey proteins appear in a blend of, let's say, two or three other protein sources, you are more than likely getting a mere spritz of the good stuff in addition to a whole lot of far less-valuable ingredients.

- **Carbohydrate.** The vast majority of companies marketing meal replacements do not seem to pay much attention to this component. Most use high amounts of maltodextrin, a cheap complex carbohydrate from corn that burns more like a sugar than a true complex carbohydrate. Some companies even add simple sugars on top of this, such as corn syrup. Needless to say, because of their higher carbohydrate content, such products are incompatible with an effective low-carb diet.

- **Flaxseed oil.** Flax contains essential fatty acids, important fats that our bodies can't make on their own and must be obtained through our diet. Flaxseeds are rich in alpha-linolenic acid (an omega-3 essential fatty acid) and linoleic acid (an omega-6 essential fatty acid). These important fats may increase metabolic rate and fat burning, improve insulin sensitivity, prevent body-fat storage, increase muscle tone, reduce muscle wasting by encouraging muscle receptors to increase insulin sensitivity, and help alleviate mood swings and mild depression during dieting.

Flax is a dynamite energy source that is high in soluble and insoluble fiber, which helps maintain regularity and healthy cholesterol levels. Flax also contains the highest concentration of lignans of any commercially available material. Lignans are powerful phytonutrients (plant compounds) that support a healthy immune system.

Few protein shakes contain this important ingredient, which is really too bad. A protein shake that contains flax provides a convenient way for you to get this all-important weight-loss power food into your system.

- **Medium chain triglycerides.** Other than the essential fatty acids, the only other fat source known for its usefulness in sports are MCTs or medium chain triglycerides. These medium length fatty acids are quickly converted to energy. MCTs are highly beneficial for endurance athletes as well as for people on low-carbohydrate diets (in other words, you!).
- **Fiber.** One of the downsides of a high-protein diet is that it tends to cause constipation. I've included many vegetables and legumes in your meal plan to help counteract that tendency. Getting a drink that contains a lot of fiber, from flaxseeds in particular, will help keep you regular.
- **Water based.** Ideally, your shake should come in the form of a protein powder that can be mixed with water. Stay away from shakes that recommend mixing with a juice, such as orange juice, or with yogurt. Both juice and yogurt are on your banned-food list. Even in phases 2 and 3 of this plan, I discourage you from mixing your protein powder with yogurt (frozen or otherwise) as it generally results in many more calories and grams of protein than you need at any one meal.

It's hard to find a commercially available meal-replacement powder that meets all of these requirements. I guess I just got tired of clients asking me to point them toward the right product, so after almost a year of in-depth consultations with some of the most prominent scientists and formulators in the field of sports nutrition and diet, I came up with a personally branded shake that contains the right blend of all of the mentioned ingredients. This relatively simple formula has a modified protein-to-carbohydrate ratio of 25:9 (with 5.5 grams from fiber). You can find information on this meal-replacement beverage in the Resources section at the back of the book, or read labels on other available shakes carefully to find the right blend.

Metabolism Boosters

As you know, the Ultimate New York Diet is all about rapid weight loss. Your meal plan combined with exercise will help you to take off serious pounds, but I've found that a few supplements will help to speed things along even more quickly. Look for supplements that contain the following ingredients.

- **Green tea extract.** By now you've probably heard that green tea promotes heart health and prevents cancer. You may not know that green tea also promotes weight loss. In a study completed at the University of Geneva, researchers put study participants on a typical Western diet of about 13 percent protein, 40 percent fat, and 47 percent carbohydrates. For six weeks, the men took two capsules consisting of green tea extract plus 50 milligrams of caffeine, 50 milligrams of caffeine alone, or a placebo with meals. After six weeks, the men who took the green tea extract had a significant increase in 24-hour energy expenditure (the number of calories the body burns in a 24-hour period) and a lower respiration quotient (a measurement of how well the body utilizes carbohydrates, proteins, and fats). A lower respiration quotient means that the body is burning more fats for energy. Men in the other groups did not show an increase in calorie or fat burning. The scientists determined that green tea contains substances called catechin polyphenols that alter the body's use of norepinephrine, a chemical transmitter in the nervous system, to increase the rate of calorie burning.

  In addition to speeding your metabolism, green tea can also help you exercise longer and harder. A study published in the *American*

Liv Tyler

I've been working with Liv for more than five years. Although she has always stayed in great shape, our time together often becomes more intense when she's getting ready for a role, a magazine cover, or an event. For a month (ideally) or two weeks (reality) before the Academy Awards or a screen role, her usual three workouts a week bloom into twice-daily sessions that span up to two hours in length. Her casual eating changes to a strict observance of the A, B, C, D, E, and Fs with one of my shakes for breakfast and dinner. About 10 months after giving birth to her son, Milo, Liv told me she again was ready to slim down and tone up. But this time, things were different.

Q: How has having a baby changed the way you see yourself and your body?

A: I have a whole new appreciation for my body. Before I got pregnant, I was so critical of it. The idea that I could create a human being inside of me changed that view. I feel so much better about my body and, at the same time, feel excited to keep pushing it. I want to get into the best shape I've ever been.

Q: In what ways were you overly critical of your body in the past, and how has that view changed?

A: I guess it comes from being in the business for such a long time, and from being human and being a young woman living in today's world. You see all of these media images and can't help but fall into the trap of comparing yourself to other people. David has helped me learn how to appreciate the things that are beautiful about me and not dwell so much on the things that are not. For example, no matter how skinny I am, I have a little tummy, but I don't gain weight in my thighs or hips. David always encourages me to "show more leg." Instead of obsessing about getting my stomach flat, I have learned to feel really good about myself because I know that I am doing the best I can. I am the way I am. This is what my body looks like, and I feel good about that.

Q: This program is pretty intense. How is it different from other diets you've tried?

A: I've tried everything from raw food to the Zone to fasting—everything. With those diets, I would always find that I could stick with it for a while and I would see quick results, but the results were always short lived. With David's plan, you also see fast results, but you don't suddenly lose those results two weeks later. You come out of the program feeling refreshed and liberated.

Q: How do David's protein shakes and Vitamin/Mineral Powder help you to stay on track?

A: The Vitamin/Mineral Powder helps me to drink more water. I add one pack to a huge bottle and drink it throughout the day. The Meal Replacement Powder helps me to avoid temptation. Say I'm staying at a fancy hotel, where everything they serve has cream and butter. I don't even tempt myself by looking at the room-service menu. I just make my shake and drink it. Or, if I know I'm going out to dinner, I'll have a shake for lunch and then eat what I want at dinner. It's all about balance and moderation.

Q: How do you balance staying in shape with your career and motherhood?

A: When I am doing an intense week or two with David, I make sure that's all I am doing that week. I tell my friends that I'm not going to be a good friend for a week or two, that I'm not going to be going out. I also tell my family that I love and adore them, but that I need to focus more on myself for a few days. Luckily my husband is an amazing hands-on father, and we have the luxury of having a wonderful nanny. They are both very patient with me and give me the time to focus on this transformation. For me, the time I spend exercising is an amazing release. It's an important part of my day. With my work and as a new mother, I'm so busy. Something is always going on, and someone always needs me. When I work out, I shut out all of those distractions and take time for myself. This is my selfish time, time for me to feel good.

LIV'S ADVICE FOR YOU: Don't trick yourself into thinking that you can lose weight through diet alone. I've tried every diet and every program out there. If you are not eating healthfully and exercising, then you will gain back everything that you lose. This program is about health. You will see lasting results, and you will see them quickly, but you must stick with it. With David's guidance and direction, I have the strength and confidence to be the best that I can be.

POSTSCRIPT: *The pressure of being a world-famous actress has never diminished the inner beauty that Liv possesses. She is like many women who have tried other plans with little success. She speaks to the strength of this program and reinforces one of its key elements—life transformation.*

Journal of Physiology found that mice given green tea extract paddled 24 percent longer in a swim and burned more fat than mice who did not get the extract.

Now you could simply drink multiple cups of green tea a day, and some of my clients do just that. They find that a cup of green tea after meals not only provides this nice metabolism boost but also instills a sense of closure to a meal. This makes it less likely that they'll find themselves foraging through the fridge and cupboards in search of something else to eat. That said, I've found that only the rare individual is willing to drink multiple cups of green tea a day, which makes green tea extract a convenient alternative. Interestingly, the extract in supplement form is actually better absorbed by the body than in tea form. Look for a supplement that contains at least 100 milligrams of extract.

- **Cinnamon.** A potent antioxidant, cinnamon bark extract has been shown to reduce blood sugar levels in people with diabetes, which in turn reduces insulin levels. High circulating insulin levels throw the body into a fat-storage mode and trigger sensations of hunger. As an added bonus, cinnamon also has been shown to boost HDL cholesterol levels and reduce total cholesterol and triglyceride levels. There are also studies to show that cinnamon can have a thermogenic effect on the body, speeding up your metabolism and causing you to burn fat at a higher rate. Look for a supplement that contains roughly 100 milligrams of cinnamon bark extract.
- **Banaba leaf.** This traditional antidiabetic herb helps reduce blood sugar and insulin levels, keeping the body out of fat-storage mode. In one study, obese mice who ate banaba reduced their fat levels compared to obese mice who did not eat banaba. Take roughly 10 milligrams daily.

These ingredients work so effectively that I've included them in many of my personally branded line of supplements. For example, my Flush and Cleanse supplement contains green tea extract, among many other herbs. My PM Appetite Suppressant contains banaba and cinnamon, and my protein shake contains essential fatty acids and fiber.

Energy Boosters

Various studies have now determined what most dieters already know at least on some level: dieting—at least temporarily—makes you dumber. In one classic study, researchers asked 33 dieting women and 33 non-dieting women to complete a series of memory tests. The women on restricted-calorie diets displayed a poorer ability to use central executive functioning, the ability of the brain to plan and think abstractly. Dieting can also make you tired.

The frequent meals in the Ultimate New York Eating Plan will help to regularly supply your body with the right foods at the right times to avoid these problems. That said, I'm all about eliminating excuses, and if you take a nap in the afternoon instead of exercise just because you are tired, well, a supplement could come in handy.

I encourage you to look for a supplement that contains the herb ginseng. In a study completed at the Human Cognitive Neuroscience Unit of Northumbria University in Tyne, United Kingdom, 15 volunteers took 400 milligrams of Panax ginseng before completing a battery of mental tests. Another 15 volunteers completed the same tests but did not take ginseng. Participants who took ginseng performed better on various tests of cognitive function, indicating they felt less mentally fatigued than those who did not take it. Ginseng may boost energy levels by helping to regulate blood sugar and increase blood flow. One of the best energy boosters around, ginseng can also help boost your immunity and overall wellness.

I include ginseng along with vitamin B_{12}, tyrosine, and vinpocetine in a supplement I call "Afternoon Energy." I tell my clients to take it to reduce what I call "afternoon burnout." If you tend to feel worn out toward the end of the day, these supplements can help. They also relieve stress, fatigue, and depression.

Appetite Suppressants

The increased protein and frequency of meals on the Ultimate New York Eating Plan will go a long way toward reducing between-meal hunger. I have found that some people, however, need a little extra help in this area. If you find yourself craving carbs or experiencing some stomach rumbling between meals, consider taking one of the following supplements.

- **Hoodia.** From the South Africa Kalahari Desert, this powerful supplement suppresses appetite and stops cravings for foods. San Bushmen who live in this desert have relied on this cactus fruit for thousands of years to reduce hunger during their long hunting trips. A molecule in the plant called P 57 affects the brain's ability to sense blood sugar levels. When you eat, blood sugar rises, causing certain brain cells to fire and signal the rest of the body to turn off the sensation of hunger. A study completed at the Hallett Center for Diabetes and Endocrinology at Brown Medical School in Providence, Rhode Island, determined that this supplement increases brain cell adenosine triphosphate (ATP) content in the hypothalamus, an area of the brain in charge of appetite. The study also determined that it decreases appetite by 40 to 60 percent. Providing more ATP to these brain cells triggers the right brain, hormonal, and appetite responses to turn down appetite and help you to eat less.

  In short, Hoodia triggers cells in the brain to send out the "no more food is needed" signal, even if blood sugar has not gone up—even if you have not eaten at all. As my mom, who takes it regularly, puts it, "When I take Hoodia, the refrigerator doesn't talk to me." As an added bonus, Hoodia is also a mild aphrodisiac and antidepressant that has no known side effects. Look for a supplement that contains at least 500 milligrams of Hoodia extract.

- **5-HTP (5-hydroxytryptophan).** If you're one of those people who craves carbs as soon as you stop eating them, go to the health food store right away and get some 5-HTP unless you are on an antidepressant. This works by boosting levels of brain chemicals that, in turn, turn down cravings. It's a precursor to the neurotransmitter serotonin, a feel-good brain chemical responsible for boosting mood, improving sleep, and reducing appetite. When you take 5-HTP supplements, they are absorbed into the bloodstream and make their way to your brain, increasing the synthesis of serotonin. Studies show that 5-HTP can reduce appetite and binge eating, as well as insomnia and migraines.

Research completed on rats shows it may even reduce alcohol consumption by boosting mood and soothing stress. Take 40 milligrams daily. Talk to your doctor first if you are taking an SSRI antidepressant such as Prozac, Zoloft, or Paxil, as too much serotonin can cause side effects such as confusion, agitation, and loss of coordination.

- **Fiber.** Most of my supplements—especially my meal-replacement shake—contain extra fiber to slow digestion and block fat absorption in the gut. Fiber slows the absorption of carbohydrate into the bloodstream, reducing postmeal insulin levels by up to 50 percent, making you feel more satisfied after eating, and reducing cholesterol levels. A study published in the *American Journal of Clinical Nutrition* compared satiety levels in participants after they ingested either grapes or grape juice or oranges or orange juice. When participants ate the whole fruit (which contained fiber) versus fruit juice (which did not contain fiber), they felt more satisfied for a longer period of time. Insulin levels did not rise as much when participants ate fruit versus fruit juice.

Look for a supplement that contains one of the following types of fiber (or both), in the highest amounts you can find.

- **Methylcellulose.** Studies show that this fiber type can reduce appetite by 10 percent. It works by adding bulk but not calories to your stomach and intestines, weighing them down to make you feel fuller on fewer calories.
- **Guar gum.** In one study, researchers compared the effects of two breakfasts—one high in guar gum and the other not—on postmeal satiety. Participants who ate the breakfast that contained guar gum rated their satiety levels higher during the 30 to 60 minutes after eating than participants who ate the meal without guar gum. Other studies show guar gum helps to even out blood sugar levels after meals, reducing appetite later in the day. It seems to prevent the increase in hunger, appetite, and desire to eat when calorie intake drops.
- **Chromium.** This mineral helps to regulate the action of the hormone insulin to turn down hunger. By making cells more sensitive to the effects of insulin, chromium allows the pancreas to secrete less of this fat-storage, hunger-promoting hormone. So, in addition to turning

down hunger, chromium also encourages your body to burn fat and preserve muscle. It also lifts mood, which can help reduce your cravings for carbs. In a small study completed at the Comprehensive NeuroScience Institute in White Plains, New York, depressed patients said they felt more positive, felt less hungry, and craved carbohydrates less often and less intensely compared to patients who did not take the supplement. As an added bonus, the supplement seems to lower blood fat levels, which can improve your health.

The human body does not easily absorb chromium from food, which is why you need a supplement. Also, chromium levels tend to decrease with age; the older you are, the more you need this supplement. Look for a supplement that contains 100 percent of the daily value for this mineral.

You can take the combination of supplements that works for you. I've also combined guar gum, cellulose, magnolia bark, cinnamon, banaba, chromium, and 5-HTP into an appetite suppressant that my clients swear by. When they take it in addition to Hoodia, their between-meal hunger vanishes, and they have no nighttime cravings for sweets or salty snacks.

Cleansing Supplements

Over the years, you've been exposed to numerous toxins in the form of air pollution, pesticide residue on your foods, heavy metal contamination in fish and poultry, and much more. To detoxify your system, your body has stored away these toxins in your fat cells. One of the unfortunate side effects of weight loss is this: as your fat cells release their fat, they also release these toxins into your bloodstream. To enable your body to deal with these toxins, I suggest the following supplements. They will help detoxify your body in a number of ways.

- **Senna leaf extract.** This small bark shrub grows in the upper Nile regions of Africa and the Arabian Peninsula. First used more than 3,500 years ago by ancient Egyptian physicians, senna has now been proven to be an effective remedy for constipation. The extra fiber that you'll be consuming on the Ultimate New York Eating Plan will help to encourage regular bowel movements, which in turn help to whisk impurities out of your system in a timely manner. That said, you may need a little extra help in this department, which is where senna comes in. Take 150 milligrams of senna before bed with a large glass of water to promote a morning bowel movement.

- **Milk thistle.** This herb has been used since Greco-Roman times to treat liver problems. Studies show that silymarin and other active substances in milk thistle protect the liver from damage caused by viruses, toxins, alcohol, and certain drugs. As an added bonus, one animal study found that silymarin worked as effectively as the cholesterol-lowering drug probucol, with the additional benefit of substantially increasing HDL (good) cholesterol. Take 200 milligrams a day.

- **Dandelion leaf extract.** Like milk thistle, this herb also helps to detoxify the liver. It's also a mild laxative that helps settle the stomach and prevent indigestion. Take at least one milligram a day.

Look for a supplement that contains these herbs in a convenient mixture. I suggest all of my clients take one of my personally branded supplements called Flush and Cleanse. It contains senna, dandelion leaf, milk thistle, and other cleansing herbs and minerals. As an added bonus, it also contains green tea extract for metabolism boosting.

Overall Good Nutrition

I recommend that all of my clients take a multivitamin. No matter how healthful your diet, you just never know if something is slipping through the cracks. A daily multivitamin mineral supplement helps seal those cracks.

In particular, make sure your supplement supplies 100 percent of the daily value for the following:

- **Zinc.** Deficiency in this mineral is actually very common, especially in highly active or highly stressed people. An important mineral for immunity, zinc helps prevent those colds that can derail your fitness efforts. Also, low zinc levels can lower your resting metabolic rate by interfering with thyroid hormone production. In one study, zinc supplements boosted resting metabolic rate in formerly zinc-deficient participants by 300 daily calories.

- **Magnesium.** You need 320 milligrams a day, but only 32 percent of Americans consume that much from food alone. This mineral helps regulate blood pressure, strengthen bones, and fight fatigue.

- **Vitamins C, E, beta-carotene, and coenzyme Q_{10}.** These powerful antioxidants lend their electrons to free radicals in your body, making them more stable and preventing them from destroying other cells. In turn, this can prevent a host of problems from general aging to heart disease to cancer to arthritis. Your best defense against free radicals is multilevel, and that's why I suggest taking all of these rather than just one. You can get all of these antioxidants, plus a dose of other helpful vitamins and minerals, from a few commercially available multivitamin and mineral supplements sold in health food stores.

- **Calcium.** For the first two weeks of this program you will be cutting dairy products out of your diet, which is one reason I suggest you supplement with calcium. A growing amount of research shows that this mineral may be integral to the process of fat burning. Take a supplement twice a day that contains about 500 milligrams of calcium, as your body can absorb only that much at once. This will give you the amount you need to maintain strong bones as well as boost your fat-burning furnace. Calcium supplements come in many forms and types, but I recommend coral calcium above the many others on the market. You can consume additional calcium in dark green vegetables such as broccoli and spinach.

- **Vitamin B_{12}.** You need this vitamin for energy production. Take a vitamin supplement that provides 100 percent of the recommended daily allowance in each pill.

In addition to that list of usual suspects, I've added spirulina and astragalus to my Vitamin/Mineral Super Juice. Spirulina is a micro algae that is rich in protein, beta-carotene, iron, vitamin B_{12}, and a rare essential fatty acid. It's considered one of the world's top superfoods. Astragalus is

What Not to Take

You'll find a number of weight-loss, fat-burning, and energy supplements out there from which to choose. Stay away from supplements with a high caffeine content and other stimulants such as theobromine. Note that many weight-loss supplements contain hidden caffeine in the form of bitter orange, guarana, and green coffee bean extract, totaling the amount of caffeine in five to six cups of coffee.

Please do be careful what you take, and read labels closely. My recommendations should help you make the right choices. I searched for such a long time for the perfect weight-loss supplements that I finally decided to design my own blends. I believe the three that my research team came up with—Vitamin/Mineral Super Juice, Afternoon Energy, and the PM Appetite Suppressant—are home runs in terms of health, vitality, and weight loss. But whatever you do, proceed with caution and be sure you're not getting hidden ingredients with the good stuff.

a Chinese herb that builds energy in the body. In doing so, it may bolster immunity and overall health.

Personally, I also take some Chinese herbs, including reishi, maitake, shiitake, and cordyceps mushrooms. They help build up and promote the immune system and provide general overall health and vitality. I take them in liquid form and will just drop them in my tea several times a day.

What You Need and Why

Used prudently and intelligently, supplements can improve and enhance your quality of life immeasurably. If you are on a budget and simply can't afford to buy the various supplements listed in this chapter, then I recommend you pare things down to the two most important essentials: a meal-replacement powder and a vitamin-mineral supplement.

If you hate protein shakes, the two supplements that people swear by are the Afternoon Energy and the Vitamin/Mineral Super Juice. Some have likened them to "David Kirsch crack."

For everyone else, I would definitely recommend trying the full line of supplements. That's not to say that they are all a prerequisite to success on the plan, but they will definitely enhance your experience and improve the chance of success and optimizing your results.

I have had many pregnant women use both my Meal Replacement Powder and Vitamin/Mineral Super Juice. That being said, please consult your physician as he or she should be the one advising you in this regard. Also, certain supplements can have an adverse effect on prescription medication that you may be on. Please consult your physician to determine if there are any contraindications for any supplements.

My dad—who has type 2 diabetes and has recently undergone quadruple bypass surgery—has been taking my Meal Replacement Powder and Vitamin/Mineral Super Juice to great effect. It actually feels really good to be able to guide and counsel both my mom and dad as they get older. I have put them both on a very strict nutrition regimen—Mom for weight loss and Dad for overall health and wellness. The supplements are helping both of them to thrive—and I know they will help you to do the same.

The Ultimate New York Fitness Plan

About a month before Sara Rotman began the Ultimate New York Diet, she wore a size 2 and weighed 118 pounds. She was her thinnest ever—but she was anything but healthy and fit. During the aftermath of a traumatic divorce, Sara had spent two years treating her body badly. She distracted herself from her anger and grief through work, using her demanding career as an excuse not to exercise. The stress from her job coupled with the grief of her failed marriage worked together to suppress her appetite. "I didn't eat; I had coffee for breakfast and a martini for dinner," she told me.

Although this caffeine-and-alcohol diet had shrunk Sara in size, she had lost weight from all the wrong places. Sara's muscle tone was gone. "I was skinny, but I had no tone. When I walked down the stairs, my body kept moving."

Sara's body-fat percentage was much higher than it should've been for someone who fits into size 2 jeans. Worse, the lack of muscle tissue meant that Sara's metabolism was now in serious need of a makeover. Each pound of muscle burns roughly 35 to 50 calories a day just to maintain itself. Sara's body was ready to put on fat as soon as she started eating again.

Sara visited her family doctor, complaining of debilitating chest pain. After a thorough workup, her doctor determined that there wasn't anything wrong with Sara's heart. Rather, he suspected her chest pain was caused by a combination of stress and a poor diet. He suggested she give up the coffee and start eating real food. She did, and she put on 15 pounds within 30 days.

A former athlete who rowed crew, Sara's body was now foreign to her. "I felt really bad about myself," she said. "Finally, one day, I told myself that I was simply not going to be divorced, fat, and unhealthy. I couldn't change the fact that I was divorced, but I could change everything else."

And she did. After two weeks on the Ultimate New York Diet, Sara dropped more than 10 pounds of fat, firmed up, and developed a glow to her skin that she hadn't seen in years. That chest pain? By the end of her first two weeks, she no longer noticed it.

As Sara learned, the hardest aspect of weight loss is the first step—taking control of your life. Sara did just that, and, as a result, she has a strong, positive, healthy attitude and a rocking body as well. The body is a bonus. Sara's true reward is her new, healthy attitude, one she'll need to maintain these results as time goes on.

Diet Plus Exercise Equals Success

Sara's story clearly illustrates the importance of exercise in a weight-loss program. Many dieters mistakenly think that they can lose weight through diet alone—without exercise. Well, as you can see from Sara's story, it's just not true. Yes, you can lose a lot of weight by not eating, and you can lose a lot of weight *quickly*, but you won't keep it off. When you diet without exercise, at least half of your weight loss comes from lean body mass (muscle, bone, and other nonfat tissue). This loss of lean body

David's Jiggle Test

The jiggle test is an efficient self-administered test that determines your level of muscle tone. Too often clients tell me that they've maintained their weight on vacations or work trips without ever stepping foot in the gym. Worse, they tell me they've done this while maintaining a less-than-stellar nutrition regimen. Because muscle weighs more than fat, all too often these clients have simply gained fat from overeating and simultaneously lost muscle from underexercising. Their weight on the scale may be the same, but they are "skinny fat." The best test of your fitness is a body-fat test administered by a professional, which gives you a true barometer of your lean tissue to fat mass percentage. In lieu of that, you can stand in front of a mirror and jiggle, shaking your arms, your rear, and your legs. If everything stays motionless, you're fit. If your skin is flapping, you've been skipping too many workouts.

mass profoundly slows your metabolism, setting you up for weight regain as soon as you increase your food intake.

When you train your muscles, your body responds by building more capillaries to those muscles. Simultaneously, the cells inside your muscles house more mitochondria, cell powerhouses that burn fat for energy. These adaptations nudge your body into fat-burning mode, coaxing fat out of those fat cells to be used as your body's primary energy source. Without exercise, the opposite takes place. The body holds onto fat and burns everything else it can, including muscle tissue.

Also, exercise enables your body to more efficiently burn blood sugar for energy. After your body converts the food you eat into blood sugar, your pancreas secretes the hormone insulin. This hormone acts as a key to unlock cells throughout your body to absorb sugar and burn it for energy. When you don't exercise, insulin does not work as effectively. So your pancreas secretes more and more insulin, allowing it to knock more loudly and forcefully to shuttle sugar past cell membranes. High insulin levels drive sugar to places where you don't want it—usually the fat cells in your abdomen. Interestingly, it also tends to make you feel hungry, triggering overeating.

Exercise becomes even more critical when you're losing weight quickly. Usually when you scale back your caloric intake, your body conserves calories. This survival mechanism is designed to keep you alive during a famine. Exercise helps trick the body so it's more likely to allow rapid weight loss without slowing the metabolism to compensate.

So, I hope you now agree that you must exercise to enable lasting weight loss. Now, I wouldn't be who I am if I didn't take things a step further. Weight loss isn't just about vanity. It's also about your health and your well-being, which gives you two more important reasons to include exercise in the weight-loss mix. When you exercise, you reap the following benefits:

- **Stronger heart, blood vessels, and lungs.** Too many of us "exercise" by walking roughly two and a half miles per hour from the couch to the refrigerator and from the front door to the car. This speed and distance does not stimulate the cardiovascular system. When you exercise, you exercise your cardiovascular system, which among other things allows your heart to pump more blood per beat. This means more oxygenated blood returns to your heart after making its way through your body, feeding your heart muscle with more oxygen. This also reduces blood pressure, which in turn cuts your risk of stroke and heart attack.
- **Fewer aches and pains.** Exercise strengthens the ligaments that link bones to bones and tendons that link muscles to bones. This helps stabilize your joints, reducing your risk of spraining an ankle or tweaking a knee. It also helps to soothe the symptoms of osteoarthritis.
- **Fewer sick days.** Regular exercise bolsters the function of natural killer cells, T cells, and other immune cells, making it less likely that an infection can take hold. This side benefit of exercise may also prevent certain types of cancer, including colon cancer.
- **More days on this planet.** Exercise reduces risk for a host of diseases, including heart disease, cancer, diabetes, and osteoporosis.
- **Better outlook on life.** People who exercise regularly report more positive moods, greater self-esteem, more confidence, and better brain function than people who are sedentary. Most notably, exercise may help you to more easily stick with the Diet by reducing depression.

- **Job promotion.** Studies show that regular exercise results in improvements in math, acuity, and reaction time.

David's Express Workout Plan (Better Known as Workouts in a New York Minute)

In my most recent book, *The Ultimate New York Body Plan*, I laid out an intense exercise program that required 45 to 90 daily minutes of vigorous exercise. Although I still feel this is the ideal exercise plan—as the thousands of people who bought that book will attest to—I have heard from many people who tell me it's more time than they are willing or able to commit to. I want you to succeed, so I designed an exercise plan that the busiest person on the planet could accomplish in any situation.

You'll find my excuse-proof plan in the following pages. Throughout, you will find a number of 10-minute workouts designed for different types of people with different lifestyles.

Ideally, I'd love for you to work out longer, combining 45 daily minutes of some form of cardio such as power walking, cycling, or running with at least a half hour of cardiosculpting or toning, workouts that I have outlined in great detail in *The Ultimate New York Body Plan* and on my videos. If you don't have those resources at your disposal, you can string together several of the 10-minute blasts into one longer, heart-pumping workout. (Consult David's 45-Minute Total-Body Blast and the Sample Schedule on pages 130–131 for guidance.)

On those really busy days when you just don't have time for that much exercise, turn to these 10-minute minisessions. In this way, you can let your life situation dictate *how* and *when* you work out, but not *whether* you work out. In the Ultimate New York Diet, it's not 45 minutes or nothing. These minisessions will get the heart pumping and, on some level, satisfy your body's urge to move.

At the *very least*, do one minisession on a given day. Ideally, however, I'd like you to do three or four of them, splitting up your sessions as time permits. For example, on a Monday, you might do a 10-minute session that focuses on your legs first thing in the morning. It's the perfect way

David's No Excuses Training

I don't believe in excuses, as any of my clients will tell you. Believe me, I've heard my share over the years. The classic New York reasons for not making it to exercise include late or broken-down subways, misguided and often disgruntled taxi drivers, rush-hour traffic, gym clothes forgotten at home, and those last-minute conference calls in the office, just to name a few. Those who know me and/or have trained with me know that I always have an answer to these often-used excuses. The response is: "And your point is?" No (or few) excuses are actually valid. You can always exercise. Consider:

- If the subway breaks down, I guess you're going to be doing some sumo lunges (if there's room) and plié squats while you wait for it to start up again. Not only will you burn some calories and tone your muscles, you'll also let off some steam and be more likely to get a seat on the train.
- If rush hour is your nemesis, then you'll do as my friend and client Stephanie often does—get out of the taxi and run over to the club. The running will definitely count as your cardio warm-up.
- If you're like some of my clients and you're stuck in the back of your chauffeur-driven car, then I guess you're going to be lying on the

to wake up and start your day. Then, do another one during your lunch break or in the middle of the afternoon. You'll feel as if you just had a shot of espresso. Finally, do another one when you arrive home from work. It will help blast away the stress of the day, allowing you to feel more alert and calm with your family. On a Tuesday, you could follow the same schedule, but pick an upper-body workout instead.

Time for a Mind Shift

I work with some of the busiest people on the planet. For example, Sara owns her own creative agency. To provide advertising, design, and marketing services to such clients as clothing designer Carolina Herrera, MTV, and heavy metal rock bands, she works 60 to 100 hours a week.

backseat, loosening up those jeans, and doing your crunches, bridges, and stretching.

- To prevent the "I don't have anything to wear to the gym" excuse, I try to always keep some extra appropriate gym wear around the club in addition to good training shoes. Many of my clients stash their gym wear and shoes at the gym, so they never have to worry about forgetting them.

- When stuck on a conference call in the office, use a speakerphone or headset, freeing up your hands and body for a quick set of push-ups. This will energize the brain while someone on the other end is droning on. If that's not possible, then do some alternate lunges, bench dips against the desk, and lateral squats. It will definitely get the heart pumping, and if there is no other benefit, you will at least be that much sharper for your conference call.

The idea is simple here. In my book, there are few acceptable reasons for not working out. Get up and move your body! You can and will feel better. Young, old, newcomer, and old-time fitness enthusiasts alike will all benefit from this healthy, take-charge attitude.

Yet, without fail, she's at the Madison Square Club every morning, five days a week. On the weekends, she stays active by horseback riding. On days when my friend and client Jack is not able to get his daily morning exercise, he tries to get in a three-mile run before heading home or out to dinner. These are the things that keep busy, successful New Yorkers like Sara and Jack at the top of their game. They respect the delicate balance of mind and body and are rewarded with solid minds, firm bellies, and perky butts.

If they can do it, so can you. It's not about time; it's about commitment. If you want to fit it in, you will. So, before embarking on this plan, I'd like you to think about your past attempts at exercise (if there have been any) or your past excuses to not exercise. Examine the reasons you fell off the exercise wagon or didn't get on it in the first place, and come up with the tools to surmount them. Often this soul-searching process will lead you

Marni Opatowsky

When Marni signed up for my program, she was out of work. Marni realized she could use this free time either constructively—by committing herself to a program to shed the extra 15 pounds she'd gained over the years—or destructively—by sitting on the couch and overeating. Her mother purchased a gym package for her as a Hanukkah gift, and thankfully Marni decided to use her time constructively.

Q: What caused you to gain the extra 15 to 20 pounds?

A: I gained it slowly over a period of two years. I worked a sedentary desk job and was often tempted by bagels and other foods that were always in the break room. My weight went up and down in a cycle. I would gain five pounds and then diet it off with Atkins or the Zone or Jenny Craig. Then I would gain 10 pounds and go on a diet. Then 15, then 20. I usually got to my goal weight, and I would maintain for a while, but eventually something would come up. I would go out with my friends and eat the wrong thing. I'd tell myself that I would get on track the next day, but I would end up eating the wrong thing so often that I'd just give up and regain the weight.

Q: How did the extra pounds affect your life?

A: I always felt self-conscious. I never felt I looked right. I didn't feel comfortable. I would see my thinner friends wearing all of these cute things, but if I tried to wear similar outfits I would feel self-conscious. I just didn't feel healthy.

Q: What changed for you that enabled you to maintain your results on this plan?

A: I finally realized that what I eat really affects how I feel. On New Year's last year, for example, I ate really badly and I felt like crap the next day. Rather than have five smaller meals as David prescribes, I just ate one big one. Also, I'm exercising a lot, and it really defeats the purpose if I go out and eat a burger

and fries every night. The exercise helps me find the motivation I need to eat right. For example, I used to eat when I was under stress, and now I've learned to break that cycle. I realized that the food doesn't make me feel better, but the exercise does. So, when I feel stressed, I go to the gym instead.

Finally, I've learned how to put myself first. I was not a priority before, at least not to the extent that I am now. I worried that I would miss out on my social life if I took time to go to the gym. Now, exercising is like brushing my teeth. I don't feel complete unless I do it, and I know I can meet my friends later.

Q: **What keeps you committed to the program?**

A: I've gotten great feedback from family and friends about how I look, and it makes me want to keep doing what I'm doing. I now wear more tank tops, halter tops, and lower-cut jeans, clothes that I didn't feel I could pull off before.

Also, my father was overweight for many years—often gaining and losing, gaining and losing. About five years ago, he had gastric bypass surgery. Thinking of that has helped me to stay committed because I know, if I don't, down the road I could end up like Dad.

Most important, I feel so much healthier. I have so much energy, and I *love* going to the gym. That's certainly something I never thought I would say! I go to the gym six or seven days a week. I feel so much better about myself, so much more confident. I'm happier. I feel as if I can accomplish anything.

MARNI'S ADVICE FOR YOU: If you ever feel discouraged and think that you can't make it, just promise yourself that you will give it a couple more days. Something happens on the third day where everything seems to come together. You start seeing things in yourself that you weren't able to see before.

POSTSCRIPT: *At the time of writing this book, it has been more than one year since Marni successfully completed the program. She has continued to improve upon and excel beyond her very impressive results (15 pounds in two weeks!), rarely missing a cardio day. Unlike many who say they are doing their cardio, Marni pushes it to the limit and beyond every time. She has learned her lessons well.*

to your personal "success key"—that unique formula that will drive and guide you down the wellness path toward your ultimate goal.

When it comes to sticking to an exercise plan, you need only three things: willpower, dedication, and your body. My mother, whose story I shared earlier, started working out for the first time in many years at age 69, when she was 150 pounds overweight. She admitted that it was tough for her at her age and weight to walk confidently into my club and work out next to much younger, much skinnier, and much more scantily dressed women. (As Mom likes to say, "The girls here wear dental floss for pants.") But Mom has gotten over all of this. Now, even though she still has 100 pounds to go, she walks into the club with confidence, wearing brightly colored outfits. She's been known to tell the younger, smaller, dental floss–wearing woman on the next treadmill, "Don't hate me because I'm beautiful." And on those days when she does feel self-conscious, she removes her glasses so she can't see the other women in the gym.

If Mom can do it, so can you. In a few short months, she's lost more than 60 pounds! Something that started out as an overwhelming chore has become a natural way of life for Mom. So, you are never too old, you are never too large, and you are never too out of shape. No matter your age, size, exercise background, career, or family commitments, you can exercise at any location and any time.

The Preworkout Test

If you are very out of shape, get a checkup and talk to your doctor about your fitness goals. In addition to helping you to better design the program for your health needs, this visit can also serve as a source of motivation. Many of my clients finally began exercising after years of inactivity only after this important checkup, when they learned that their cholesterol level, blood pressure, or some other health marker was in the danger zone. To further motivate yourself, ask your doctor to write a prescription for exercise, noting any restrictions you may have. In fact, if you are going to hire a trainer or join a gym, your health insurance may cover the fees if you have a doctor's prescription. Put it on your fridge or computer—wherever you'll see it most often.

Then take the following fitness test. Use it to gauge your starting point and pinpoint the best workout to use from day one. Although the various 10-minute workouts you'll find in this chapter are short on time, they are big on challenge. You'll need a certain level of fitness in order to do the moves correctly and gain the most benefit from them.

To assess your fitness level, do the following:

1. **KNEE BEND:** Stand with your feet slightly wider than shoulders' distance apart and your back against a wall. Firm your tummy and press your lower back into the wall. (Note: if you own a stability ball, put that between your back and the wall.) Walk your feet forward, about two feet away from the wall. Then bend your knees as far as you comfortably can, stopping once your thighs are parallel to the floor or sooner. Make sure your knees do not jut beyond your ankles. If they do, your ankles are too close to the wall. Hold as long as you can bear it, and watch the clock.

Write how long you held the knee bend here: _____ seconds/minutes

2. **AROUND THE WORLD:** Stand with your legs in a wide stance, hips' width apart. Bend your knees slightly. Grasp a medicine ball or a pair of three- or five-pound dumbbells in each hand and extend your arms overhead. Bend forward and slightly to the right, bringing your outstretched arms to the outside of your right foot. Then reverse the motion, lifting the dumbbells (or the medicine ball) in a half circle, up, overhead, and down the left side of your body. Continue to circle right and left as many times as you can, keeping count.

Write the number of half circles you completed here: _____

3. **PUSH-UPS:** You can do these either with your knees on the floor (the easier version) or with your legs extended (the more challenging version). Place your palms on the floor. Bend your elbows out the sides as you lower your chest toward the floor. Then press back up. Do as many as you can, keeping count.

Write the number of push-ups you completed here: _____

4. **KNEE LIFTS:** Stand with your feet under your hips about shoulder-width apart. Tuck your tailbone slightly so that you feel your lower tummy muscles firm and the curve in your lower back straighten. Shift your body weight onto your right foot. Bend your left knee and lift it toward your chest (as close to your chest as you can get it). Lower and repeat with the right leg. Lifting your right and then your left leg one time counts as one rep. Continue to alternate right and left legs as many times as you can without losing your balance.

Write the number of reps you completed here: _____

Don't read the following paragraph until you've completed this test.

SCORING YOUR TEST

OK, now you'll use the information you gathered in the test to pinpoint your fitness starting point. If you completed fewer than 15 push-ups, around the worlds, and knee lifts and held the knee bend for less than 20 seconds, I recommend you stick with the exercises in this pretest until you've mastered them. Do 15 repetitions of each exercise (holding the knee bend for 30 seconds) three times a day for two weeks. After that amount of time, you will have built the strength and balance needed for

Willpower Helpers

To improve your success at starting and sticking with the Ultimate New York Fitness Plan, do the following:

- Stick to a regular exercise time every day. It will help make exercise a habit, like brushing your teeth.
- Sign a contract committing yourself to exercise. The worst promise you can break is the one you make to yourself.
- Put exercise appointments on your calendar. Make them nonnegotiable.
- Remember that exercise is not an all-or-nothing proposition. When your time does not permit a 45-minute workout, one of my "express" workouts is sure to do the trick.
- Keep a daily log or diary of your activities. It will help to keep you honest, make you feel accountable, and help you see how much you're improving.
- Check your progress. Find out your blood pressure, cholesterol, resting heart rate, body-fat percentage, and other health factors before you start. Also keep tabs on your fitness milestones. Can you do more push-ups than when you began? Or is your heart rate slower now? These results—as well as your weight loss—will fuel your motivation.
- Use your favorite pair of jeans or bathing suit to help you measure your success. There's nothing like the feeling of slipping into those jeans, zipping them up, and feeling sexy and wonderful!

all of the 10-minute routines in this chapter. If in the pretest you completed more than 15 push-ups, around the worlds, and knee lifts and held the knee bend for longer than 20 seconds, you already have the strength and balance to complete any of the routines in this chapter.

Your Equipment

For some of the express workouts, you will need the following fitness essentials:

- **Stability ball.** Look for a burst-resistant ball, and buy the right-sized ball for your height. When you sit on the ball with your feet on the floor, your knees should bend at a 90-degree angle. Generally, that means the following ball sizes work for the following heights.

Ball Diameter	Height
55 cm (21″)	4′11″ to 5′4″
65 cm (25″)	5′5″ to 5′11″
75 cm (29″)	6′+

- **Dumbbells.** Start with two- or three-pound dumbbells and move up to five-pound dumbbells once (if ever) the workout feels too easy. Look for dumbbells with a soft coating, and buy a color you like. You're more likely to use them if you like them.
- **Medicine ball.** Today's medicine balls are covered in soft plastic coating and come in many colors and weights, starting at just over 2 pounds and ending at 24 pounds. You'll want a ball that weighs between 2 and 10 pounds. Some of these balls are often weighted in kilograms. If so, choose a ball that weighs between 1 and 4 kilograms.

Express Workouts (aka Workouts in a New York Minute)

In the following pages, you will find a number of short but challenging workouts designed for just about any situation you may find yourself in. Each workout is designed to last roughly 10 minutes. In the beginning, as you get used to the movements, the routines may take longer. Warm up before all routines with a couple of minutes of marching or jogging in place.

WORKOUTS FOR THE OFFICE

One of my clients, Greg Namin, a systems engineer, does miniworkouts in his cubicle in addition to his morning workout. "I've shifted from just getting through the day to not facing the day until I've done what I need to do to be healthy," he says. On his upper-body workout days, he supplements his morning workout session with push-ups in his cube. On lower-body days, he adds lunges throughout the day. "I give myself a break from whatever I'm working on. I don't wait for it to happen. I just do it. These minisessions help me to stay more productive because my mind is sharper."

I hear this sentiment a lot from my career-focused clients. Rather than take time away from work, exercise actually helps them achieve more because they feel more focused, creative, and alert. Richard Jones, a corporate CEO, began exercising for the first time ever about a year ago. (He, by the way, overhauled his diet and quit smoking at the same time.) He told me, "People who work for me, peers at work, and people who I report to all said to me that they felt inspired by what I've done. I get more respect from them and feel motivation from them to continue."

Even in a small office or cube, you can stash a stability ball and medicine ball to enable more effective office workouts. If you have no other place to put it, use your stability ball as your office chair. As you sit on it, you'll work your core muscles all day long. I think you'll find that you'll come to like it much more than your old alternative. Stash the medicine ball under your desk.

Greg Namin

Greg was one of six participants in a Fox News Challenge who wanted to lose weight and shape up—with my advice. Greg, a former army recruit, did some of my work for me by sending a daily e-mail to the other participants, motivating them to stick with the plan. His determination and ability to follow the plan to a tee paid off. He lost 10 pounds and trimmed six inches from his waist within just two weeks. More important, his cholesterol and triglycerides dropped from "dangerous" levels to healthy levels without the aid of medicine. After the challenge, he continued to lose weight, dropping 35 pounds overall.

Q: **When did you gain the excess weight?**

A: When I was in the army, it was not difficult for me to keep my weight down. If you got fat in the army, they put you in a special physical training program or you got kicked out. So, between the regimented exercise and regimented meals, I stayed fit and trim. After I left the army, however, I stopped exercising. I was eating pretty much the same foods, but the lack of exercise caused me to gain weight.

Q: **What diets had you tried in the past?**

A: At one point, I tried the Atkins diet and was able to lose 30 pounds. It didn't require much effort and, because of that, was as easy to fall off as it was to get on. Once off, I gained most of that weight back.

Q: **How did the excess weight affect your life?**

A: I was five feet eight inches tall, and I weighed 230 pounds. My knees hurt when I walked. My back hurt when I got out of bed. My baby daughter liked to lie on my stomach because it was so soft and offered so much padding. My cholesterol was 243. I still have photos of myself when I was bigger, and I look at them sometimes and

wonder how I got like that. Some people may be happy or content with being heavy. Not me. It's not in my blood. The aches and the pains were getting old.

Q: What drew you to the Ultimate New York Diet?

A: It required a big commitment, which resonated with my army background. I liked the idea that I would have to challenge myself. It required a big change of attitude, but that was important for me. It's that initial challenge that has helped me to succeed. Because it requires work, it helps to create a sense of accomplishment and fulfillment. I've worked hard to get this far. I'm not going to turn back now! When you switch your mind-set to this plan and realize how much you've invested in it, you're not going to go back.

Q: How have your results changed your life?

A: My stomach is now hard and firm, and, as a result, my daughter no longer treats me like a pillow. I also had to go out and buy a new wardrobe because I went from a size 42 to a size 36 pants. When I wake up in the morning and look in the mirror, I say, "Wow."

Q: How have your priorities changed as a result of this program?

A: I've changed from someone who just tries to get through the day to someone who doesn't start his day unless he's done what he needs to do to be healthy. I work out five days a week without fail. The last time I did that was when I was in the army.

Q: How do you motivate yourself to maintain your results?

A: This is a lifelong thing for me. I have a history of diabetes in my family. I want to live long enough to see my kids grow up and go to college. I want to see my grand-children. To reach those goals, I have to keep this up.

GREG'S ADVICE FOR YOU: Ask yourself whether you really want this. If you are not committed, you won't make it. Once you are committed, everything falls into place. Your commitment is the essential ingredient.

POSTSCRIPT: *For all of you guys out there who think this is a program just for women, think again. Greg is living proof that the Ultimate New York Diet is nondiscrimina-tory. It works for everyone—men and women, old and young, fitness beginner or former athlete.*

Abs/Core

Low Plank and High Plank on Stability Ball

1. Walk out into a push-up position with the balls of your feet on the stability ball and your palms on the floor under your chest. Keep your abs tight. Don't allow your hips to sag downward. *Hold for 15 seconds.*

2. Switch your body position so that your palms are on the stability ball and the balls of your feet are on the floor. Your legs should be extended, and a diagonal line should form from your heels to your head. *Hold for 15 seconds.*

3. *Return to the low plank and repeat the low plank and then high plank one to two times.* Finish with the low plank and remain in that position for the pike.

Pike with Stability Ball

1. From the low-plank position with the balls of your feet on the stability ball, raise your hips toward the ceiling as you bring the ball in toward your hands, keeping your abs tight and legs extended. Your torso should form an upside-down V shape.

2. *Hold 10 to 15 seconds.*

Hyperextensions with Stability Ball

1. Lie with your tummy against the stability ball. Place the bottoms of your feet against a wall for support. (As you grow stronger, you can do this exercise without the wall for a greater challenge.)

2. Extend your back as you reach your head, shoulders, and elbows toward the ceiling.

3. Lower and *repeat 15 to 20 times.*

Side Crunch with Stability Ball

1. Lie with your left side against the stability ball. Scissor your legs so your right leg crosses over your left, giving yourself a wide base of support. Place your left palm against your abdomen or waist. Grasp a small medicine ball in your right hand. Hold the ball at eye level with your elbow bent.

2. Crunch sideways as your eyes follow the movement of the medicine ball.

3. *Lower and repeat 15 to 20 times, and then switch sides.*

Oblique and Lower Abs with Stability Ball

1. Kneel, placing your forearms on the stability ball and knees on the floor, with your legs crossed at the ankles. Roll the ball forward with your arms as you bring your torso forward, feeling your abs kick in as they stabilize your body. *Hold 15 seconds, return to the starting position and repeat three times.* For added intensity, roll the ball on a 45-degree angle with your arms as you bring your torso forward, feeling your obliques kick in as well.

2. *Repeat the entire sequence one or more times for a total of 10 minutes.*

OFFICE WORKOUT #2

Total Body, High Energy

Jog in Place with Medicine Ball

1. Stand with your feet under your hips about shoulder-width apart. Grasp a medicine ball with both hands. Extend your arms in front at chest level.

2. *Jog in place for 30 seconds* with the medicine ball extended at chest level. Do not put all of your weight in your toes, as this will stress your knee joints.

3. Continue to jog in place as you rotate your torso to the left with your arms extended. *Jog for an additional 30 seconds.* Then rotate your torso to the right and *jog for 30 seconds.*

Squat Thrusts with Medicine Ball

1. Stand with your feet slightly wider than hips' distance apart. Grasp a medicine ball with both hands at chest level with your elbows bent.

2. Bend your knees, stick your butt back, and come into a squat.

3. Continue to bend your knees as you bend forward from the hips, placing the medicine ball on the floor under your breastbone.

4. Press your hands into the medicine ball as you jump and extend your legs behind your body, coming into a push-up position. Keep your abs tight the entire time. Recoil your legs, and rise to the starting position.

5. *Repeat 10 to 15 times.* During your last repetition, remain in the modified push-up position and proceed directly into mountain climbers.

Mountain Climbers with Medicine Ball

1. From the push-up position in the squat thrust, bend your right knee and jump it in, bringing your right thigh under the right side of your torso.

2. Jump your right leg back as you simultaneously bend your left knee and jump it in.

3. *Continue alternating right and left for 15 to 30 seconds.*

Jumping Lunges Holding Medicine Ball

1. Stand with your feet under your hips shoulder-width apart. Hold a medicine ball to your chest. Take a large step forward with your right foot. Sink down into a lunge, forming right angles with both legs.

2. Spring upward, with your energy emanating through your heels, launching both feet off the floor, and switch positions with your legs so your left foot is in front and right leg behind. Land and sink down into another lunge.

3. *Alternate your legs 10 to 15 times on each side.*

Squat Jumps with Medicine Ball

1. Stand with your feet slightly wider than shoulders' distance apart and your toes turned out. Hold a medicine ball in front of your chest. Squat down while sticking your butt out. Keep your knees just above—not in front of—your toes.

2. Spring up while thrusting your arms overhead. Tap your heels together and then bring your feet apart before you land on your heels, rolling forward onto your toes. *Complete 15 repetitions.*

3. *Repeat the entire sequence one or more times for a total of 10 minutes.*

Legs/Butt

Side Step Squat with Medicine Ball

1. Stand with your feet slightly wider than hips' distance apart. Grasp a medicine ball in both hands at chest height, with your elbows bent.

2. Bend your left knee, and lower yourself into a half squat, keeping the right leg extended. As you squat, press the ball away from your chest as you extend your arms, keeping your arms parallel to the ground. *Hold for a count of five.*

3. *Rise and repeat 15 times, and then switch sides.*

Single-Leg Squat with Stability Ball

1. Stand with a stability ball about 12 inches behind your right leg. Bend your right knee, and place the ball of your right foot on top of the stability ball.

2. Bend your left knee as you simultaneously straighten your right leg, pressing the stability ball back behind you.

3. Rise to the starting position and *repeat 10 to 15 times.*

Medicine Ball Sissy Squats

1. Warning: don't try this exercise if you have bad knees. Stand with your feet under your hips. Place a medicine ball between your knees, squeezing your knees into the ball to hold it in place. Place one hand against a wall, doorknob, chair, or table for balance.

2. Bend your knees as you thrust your hips forward and squat downward, shifting the weight into the balls of your feet as you squat down.

3. Once your shins are just about parallel to the floor, extend your legs up by pressing up through the balls of your feet.

4. Lift back to the starting position. Lower your heels and *repeat 10 to 15 times.*

Bridge with Stability Ball

1. Lie with your back on the floor. Place your heels on top of the stability ball. Rest your hands about 90 degrees away from your sides with your palms facing down.

2. Lift your hips toward the ceiling until only your head, shoulders, and arms are in contact with the floor. Pulse upward through your hips over and over *for 20 to 30 seconds.* Remain in this position and proceed to the hamstring curls.

Hamstring Curls with Stability Ball

For this exercise, choose from option A (the easier version) or option B (the more challenging version).

- **OPTION A:** From the bridge position, bend your knees and pull the ball in toward your buttocks. Push the ball back out into the bridge position. *Repeat 10 times.*

- **OPTION B:** From the bridge position, raise your left leg toward the ceiling, balancing on your right heel, shoulders, arms, and head. Bend your right knee, and pull the ball toward your buttocks. Extend your leg as you press the ball away. *Repeat 5 to 10 times.* Then switch legs and repeat.

Reverse Prone Scissors

1. Lie facedown on the floor. Spread your legs as wide as you can.

2. Press your hips into the floor as you exhale and lift your flexed feet up as you squeeze them together in one fluid motion. Squeeze your heels together at the top of the movement. Inhale as you lower. *Repeat 15 to 20 times.*

3. *Repeat the sequence one or more times for a total of 10 minutes.*

Upper Body

Around the World with a Medicine Ball

1. Stand with your legs slightly wider than hips' distance apart. Place a medicine ball just in front of and to the outside of your right foot. Bend forward from the hips, and grasp the ball with both hands near your foot.

2. Lift the ball in a half circle, up the right side of your body, overhead, and down the left side of your body, until it rests on the floor near the outside of your left foot. Repeat a half circle to your right. Continue circling right and left, left and right.

3. *Circle for 30 seconds.*

Push-Ups on Stability Ball

1. Place your tummy on the stability ball and palms on the floor in front of the ball. Walk your hands forward as you slide your torso forward on the ball, until you come into a push-up position with your thighs, shins, or balls of your feet on the ball. (Note: placing your thighs on the ball is the least challenging option, your shins slightly more challenging, and the balls of your feet or your toes the most challenging.) Place your palms on the floor under your chest. Make sure your abs are tight and back is flat. Do not allow your hips to sink downward.

2. Bend your elbows out to the sides as you bring your face and chest toward the floor. Exhale as you extend your elbows and push up to the starting position.

3. *Repeat 10 to 15 times.*

Ultimate Shoulder Shaper on the Stability Ball

1. Lie with your chest or tummy (whichever is more comfortable for you) against the stability ball. Place the bottoms of your feet against a wall for support. (As you grow stronger, you can do this exercise without the wall for a greater challenge.) Grasp a dumbbell in each hand, placing your hands just above the floor with your arms extended.

2. Raise the dumbbells until your arms are parallel with the floor and in a straight line with your shoulders.

3. Bring your arms around in a semicircle until they are extended from your shoulders at right angles to your torso.

4. Lower the dumbbells to the floor. Then reverse the process, lifting the dumbbells to the right-angle position at shoulder height and bringing them around in front.

5. *Complete 20 to 30 repetitions.*

Bench Dips on Stability Ball

1. Sit on the floor. Place your heels or calves against the top of the stability ball. Place your palms on the floor behind your hips with your fingers facing forward.

2. Press your body weight into your palms as you extend your elbows and lift your buttocks off the floor. Bend your elbows as you lower your buttocks toward the floor without touching. Then extend your elbows.

3. *Repeat 20 to 30 times.*

Hyperextensions with Stability Ball

1. Lie with your tummy against the stability ball. Place the bottoms of your feet against a wall for support. (As you grow stronger, you can do this exercise without the wall for a greater challenge.)

2. Extend your back as you reach your head, shoulders, and elbows toward the ceiling. Lower and *repeat 15 to 20 times.*

3. *Repeat this sequence one or more times for a total of 10 minutes.*

HOTEL ROOM WORKOUTS

Many people who travel for work find themselves eating bad foods and taking a break from their exercise routine. Yet, traveling often provides you with ripe opportunities for exercise. For one, if you are traveling for business, you don't have a family to keep you busy in the morning or evening, opening up time for your workout. So, when you find you're saying, "I can't work out because I'm on the road," say to yourself, "And your point is?" and start moving to one of the following routines. They can all be done within the confines of a hotel room without equipment.

————————— HOTEL WORKOUT #1 —————————
Abs/Core

Basic Crunch

1. Lie on your back on the floor, knees bent and feet on the floor. For added abdominal emphasis and reduced lower-back strain, place your legs on top of the bed or sofa (if you have one in the hotel room). Place both hands as far down your upper back as possible, so that your head is resting on your forearms. Visualize gravity pulling your belly button to the floor, flattening your lower back.

2. Focus on your abs as you relax your back, neck, shoulders, and arms. Gaze at the ceiling. Exhale as you crunch up, starting the contraction at your lower tummy and curling one vertebra at a time until you reach your shoulders. Lift from your shoulders, making sure not to use your hands or arms to yank your head off the ground. Once you can curl up no higher, slowly lower your body. Go directly into your next repetition before your shoulders reach the floor to keep a constant contraction in your abs.

3. *Repeat 10 to 15 times.*

Double Oblique Crunch

1. Lie with your back on the floor. Bend your elbows out to the sides, and place your fingertips behind the back of your head. Bend your knees, and lift your feet until your shins are parallel with the floor.

2. Exhale as you crunch your knees in toward your right nipple as you simultaneously lift your shoulders. Lower and repeat by bringing your knees in toward your left nipple.

3. *Continue alternating left and right for 20 to 30 complete repetitions.*

Leg Circles

1. Sit on the floor with your hands behind your butt and your fingers pointing forward. Your legs should be bent and raised in front of you.

2. Making sure to keep your ankles together, slowly draw circles with your feet, going both clockwise and counterclockwise.

3. *Make 15 to 20 circles in each direction.*

Pillow Handoff

1. Lie on your back. Place a pillow between your knees and shins. Extend your legs toward the ceiling, forming a 90-degree angle (or as much as you are able to) with your torso. Extend your arms overhead.

2. Curl your tailbone toward your navel as you lift the pillow up and over, bringing your arms and shoulders up to meet the pillow.

3. Grasp the pillow between your hands. Lower your hands and pillow to the floor overhead and your legs to the floor. Repeat by using your arms to lift the pillow and hand it back off to your legs. Continue to switch handing it off from your legs to your hands and hands to your legs.

4. *Switch off a total of 10 to 15 times.*

Superman

1. Lie on your tummy with your legs extended. Place your hands behind your head. Squeeze your glutes and tighten your abs.

2. Bring your shoulders and feet off the floor as you exhale, making sure to keep your abs and glutes tight. Lengthen and press out from the crown of your head and toes to lengthen your body as you lift. *Hold 10 to 15 seconds.* Inhale as you lower. *Repeat three to four times.*

3. *Repeat the entire sequence at least once, for a total of 10 minutes.*

Legs/Butt

Step-Ups onto Desk Chair into Reverse Lunge

1. Stand facing a desk chair (one that is sturdy and does not have wheels). Place your right foot onto the chair. Press into your right heel as you extend your right leg and lift your body up onto the chair.

2. Bring your left knee into your chest.

3. Lower your left foot to the floor. Step back with your left leg. Bend both knees at right angles, lowering yourself into a lunge.

4. *Repeat 10 to 15 times on that side and then switch legs.*

Sumo Lunge with Side Kick and Frog Jump

1. Stand in a "sumo" position with your feet slightly wider than shoulders' distance apart, your knees bent, and your body weight over your heels.

2. Take a large step sideways with your right leg, bringing your right knee in toward your chest and then over to the right in one continuous motion.

3. As soon as your right foot touches the ground, bring your knee back into your chest and complete a side kick, kicking your right heel out to the side into the stomach of an imaginary opponent (or jaw if that imaginary person is height compromised).

4. Lower your right leg to the floor into the "sumo" position. Squat down while sticking your butt out. Keep your knees just above—not in front of—your toes.

5. Spring up while thrusting your arms overhead. Land on your heels, rolling forward onto your toes. Repeat with a sumo lunge and side kick with your left leg and another frog jump.

6. *Continue alternating right to left until you have completed 10 lunges on each side and 20 frog jumps.*

Wall Squats

1. Stand with your back to the wall and your feet hips' distance apart. Bend your knees as you squat down, sliding your back down the wall. Squat until your thighs are parallel with the floor. Tuck your tailbone, flattening your lower back against the wall. (Note: your knees should be over your ankles. If they come farther forward, move your feet out away from the wall.) *Hold 20 to 30 seconds.*

2. Rise, widen your stance about a foot on each side, and repeat.

3. Rise, widen your feet about a leg's distance apart with your feet turned out 45 degrees, and repeat.

4. If you are able to, turn the wall squat into a plié toe squat by squatting and rising on your toes at the same time. To really advance the move, stay up on your toes throughout the entire set of squats.

5. *Repeat the entire set 15 to 20 times.*

Donkey Kicks Deluxe into
Prone Glute Crossover

1. Get on the ground on all fours with your hands under your chest and your knees under your hips. Suck in your abs and keep them tight throughout the movement.

2. Bring your right knee in toward your chest.

3. Exhale as you press your right foot toward the ceiling, keeping your foot flexed and your leg bent at 90 degrees.

4. Bring your leg back into your chest, and then extend it behind again, this time keeping it straight as you lift through your glutes.

5. Cross your right leg over your left, keeping your right foot flexed and tapping your right toes to the floor about a foot to the left of your left shin. Lift back to center.

6. *Alternate legs, and repeat 15 to 20 times for each leg.*

Hydrants Deluxe

1. Get on the floor on all fours with your hands under your chest and your knees under your hips.

2. Bend your right leg out to the side until your thigh and calf are parallel with the floor. Lift through your hips.

3. Extend your right leg and see if you can lift a tiny bit higher. Return to the starting position and *repeat 10 to 15 times.* Switch sides.

4. *Repeat the entire sequence at least once, for a total of 10 minutes.*

Total Body

Standing Asymmetrical Lunges with Rear Foot on Desk Chair or Bed

1. Stand with your feet hips' distance apart. Facing away from the bed or desk chair, place the ball of your left foot on top of the bed or desk chair. Place your hands on your hips for support.

2. Bend your right knee as you sink into a lunge, anchoring your weight in your right heel.

3. *Repeat 15 to 20 times, and then switch legs.*

Push-Ups with Feet on Bed

1. With your feet on the bed and hands on the floor directly under your chest, come into a push-up position with your hands slightly wider than shoulders' distance apart. Tighten your abs, and tuck your tailbone to flatten your back.

2. Bend your elbows out to the sides as you lower your chest toward the floor. Exhale as you press up. *Repeat 10 times.*

3. Then, move your hands closer together so they are just under your chest. *Push up 10 times.*

4. Move your hands even closer, at an angle with your fingers touching. *Push up 10 times.*

Half Handstand

1. With your feet on the bed or desk chair and hands on the floor, come into a half handstand with your hips directly above your head. To get into position, start with your belly on the bed. Place your hands on the floor and then shimmy your body off the bed as you walk your hands forward about one foot and bring the balls of your feet toward the bed's edge.

2. Bend your elbows as far as you can and then straighten them.

3. *Repeat 10 to 15 times.*

Reverse Scissor Crunches

1. Lie on your back on the floor with your arms out to your sides, palms facing down. Lift your legs up so they are perpendicular to your body. Open your feet to form a V with your legs.

2. Lift your hips straight up and bring your heels together simultaneously. Lower your hips, and open your feet into a V. (For added resistance, use ankle weights as shown.)

3. *Repeat 15 to 20 times.*

Reverse Prone Scissors

1. Lie facedown on the floor. Spread your legs as wide as you can.

2. Press your hips into the floor as you exhale and lift your flexed feet up as you squeeze them together in one fluid motion. Squeeze your heels together at the top of the movement. Inhale as you lower. *Repeat 15 to 20 times.*

3. *Repeat the entire sequence at least once, for a total of 10 minutes.*

WORKOUTS FOR HOME

You need not join a gym to get in a great workout. You also need not spend a fortune on exercise equipment for your home. And even if you are short on space, you can still get in a great home workout. You need only a set of dumbbells and a stability ball. If you are short on space, use your stability ball as a chair or footrest when you are not exercising (some clients also find it makes a great active plaything for their children).

HOME WORKOUT #1
Total Body

Plié Squat with Hammer Curl into a Shoulder Press

1. Stand with your feet slightly wider than hips' distance apart. Turn your toes out and your heels in. Grasp a dumbbell in each hand, holding your hands at your sides, palms facing your hips.

2. Bring your body weight back into your heels as you bend your knees and squat down while pushing your butt out.

3. As you squat down, curl your arms up toward your shoulders, keeping your elbows close to your sides.

4. Hold the plié squat as you press your arms overhead without fully locking out the elbows. Lower your arms in the reverse order that you raised them. Extend your legs and return to the start.

5. *Complete 20 to 30 biceps curls and presses as you squat.*

David's Ultimate Shadow Boxing

1. Grasp a dumbbell in each hand. Stand with your abs tight and your back flat. Punch your right fist out diagonally, ending at torso level in front of your left ribs, completing a crossover punch.

2. Pull back as you bend your knees into a squat, as if you were ducking an incoming punch. Repeat on the other side as you extend your legs, driving up through your heels and butt. *Repeat 20 to 30 times on each side.*

3. With your right elbow against your ribs and your knuckles turned up, punch in an upward motion, as if you were punching someone in the jaw under their chin with an uppercut punch, trying to lift him off the ground. (When done correctly, the uppercut really engages the abs and obliques.) Pull back as you bend your knees, sitting back onto your heels. Repeat with the other arm as you extend your legs. *Repeat 20 to 30 times on each side.*

4. Bring your bent right arm up so it is parallel with the floor. Throw a hook punch, as if you were trying to cock someone on the side of the jaw. Pull back as you bend your knees, sitting back onto your heels. Repeat on the other side as you extend your legs.

5. *Repeat the entire sequence for one minute.*

Squat Jumps with Medicine Ball

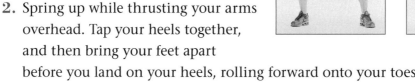

1. Stand with your feet slightly wider than shoulders' distance apart. Hold a medicine ball in front of your chest. Squat down while sticking your butt out. Keep your knees just above—not in front of—your toes.

2. Spring up while thrusting your arms overhead. Tap your heels together, and then bring your feet apart before you land on your heels, rolling forward onto your toes.

3. *Complete 15 repetitions.*

Sumo Lunge with Side Kick and Frog Jump

1. Stand in a "sumo" position with your feet slightly wider than shoulders' distance apart, your knees bent, and your body weight over your heels.

2. Take a large step sideways with your right leg, bringing your right knee in toward your chest and then over to the right in one continuous motion.

3. As soon as your right foot touches the ground, bring your knee back into your chest and complete a side kick, kicking your right heel out to the side into the stomach of an imaginary opponent (or jaw if that imaginary person is height compromised).

4. Lower your right leg to the floor into the "sumo" position. Squat down while sticking your butt out. Keep your knees just above—not in front of—your toes.

5. Spring up while thrusting your arms overhead. Land on your heels, rolling forward onto your toes. Repeat with a sumo lunge and side kick with your left leg and another frog jump.

6. *Continue alternating right to left until you have completed 10 lunges on each side and 20 frog jumps.*

Platypus Walk with Medicine Ball

1. Stand with your feet in a wide plié squat. Grasp a medicine ball with both hands, and extend your arms overhead. Sit into a squatting position with your knees aligned with your toes and your butt sticking back as far as you can.

2. Keep your core tight as you walk forward, pushing off through each heel. If you perform the move correctly, your butt and inner thighs will be on fire. Walk across the room in one direction, and then reverse and walk backward. If your room is small, repeat crossing the room one time.

3. *Repeat the entire sequence at least once, for a total of 10 minutes.*

WORKOUTS WITH CHILDREN

Several years ago, a client of mine had a baby. It was summertime, and she was eager to participate in my boot camp class that I was conducting on the beach in the Hamptons. I offered to take over baby duty, which she gladly accepted. The Baby Bjorn carrier was strapped on, and Olivia and I bonded while Lisa planked, platypused, and sprinted along the beach. There's always a way.

The following workouts will help to excuse-proof your fitness efforts because they allow you to work out *with* your children. That said, I encourage you to carve out some personal time just for you to do some form of exercise without your kids. Do what works best and fits best into your schedule. Ask a neighbor to watch your kids while you do a half hour run or power walk, and offer to do the same in return. A couple times a week, work out at a gym that offers child-care services. Or alternate child care with your partner. Your partner watches the kids during your workout. You come home, shower, and take over the child care so your partner can exercise.

In the following pages, you'll find routines for babies and toddlers. With older children, try doing any of the other dumbbell-free exercises in this chapter. Children love to jump, skip, and race, so think jump squats, sumo lunges, jumping jacks, walking lunges (call them "giant steps") and you'll be well on your way to designing a great fitness routine for the entire family.

With Infants Age Zero to One Year

Plié Squats with Baby in a Front Pack

The great part about exercising with your baby is that you'll get stronger as your baby gets heavier. Yet, the change will take place so gradually, you won't even notice it's happening. Place your baby in a front-style baby carrier. (If you prefer, hold your baby in your arms—you'll get the added bonus of strengthening and toning your arms.)

1. Stand with your feet slightly wider than hips' distance apart. Turn your toes out and your heels in.

2. Bring your body weight back into your heels as you bend your knees and squat down while pushing your butt out.

3. *Rise and repeat 15 times.*

Platypus Walks with Baby in a Front Pack

1. Place your baby in a front-style baby carrier. (If you prefer, hold your baby in your arms—you'll get the added bonus of strengthening and toning your arms.) Sit into a squatting position with your knees aligned with your toes and your butt sticking back as far as you can.

2. Keep your core tight as you walk forward, pushing off through each heel. If you perform the move correctly, your butt and inner thighs will be on fire. Walk across the room in one direction, and then reverse and walk backward. If your room is small, repeat crossing the room one time. As your strength and endurance builds, *repeat the walk 2 or 3 times.*

Ultimate Multitasker

Burn calories while you soothe a crying baby. Sit on your stability ball and bounce while holding your baby. Or, hold your baby while standing, and do the grapevine and other bouncy movements. Snuggle your baby up in a sling or front pack and walk up and down your steps. Put your baby in a stroller and walk. Babies—especially colicky ones—respond to bouncy movements and vibration. It helps them to fall asleep, giving you some much-needed quiet time.

My friend Erin and her adorable son agreed to be in the photos shown here. She is happily expecting her second child and, God willing, will have added a beautiful girl to her family by the publication of this book. You can exercise when you are pregnant, but you do have to be careful, so if you are expecting, please consult your doctor before doing any of the moves shown here.

Push-Ups over Baby

For women who have recently given birth, push-ups will at first feel challenging. Stay the course. As you get stronger and your postpartum body responds, they'll become easier and easier.

1. Start with your knees on the floor. As you get stronger you can progress to extended legs. Place your baby under your chest and between your arms throughout the push-up. Try to maintain eye contact with your baby at all times to facilitate bonding.

2. Get in a push-up position with your hands under your chest. Firm your abs, and tuck your tailbone.

3. Bend your arms, and lower yourself toward your baby, keeping eye contact.

4. Straighten your arms to raise yourself.

5. *Repeat 15 times.*

Bridge with Baby on Tummy

1. Lie on your back with your knees bent and thighs touching each other. Depending on your baby's size and motor development, place your baby along your thighs or on your tummy with his or her feet toward your face. Hold your baby in place with your hands.

2. Tuck your tailbone and press into your heels as you lift your hips. Continue to keep your tailbone tucked; this will help to activate your lower tummy. Keep your knees close together as well. Your natural tendency will be to allow them to splay outward. *Hold for 30 seconds.*

3. *Lower and repeat one time.* As you get stronger, hold for 30 seconds, rest, and repeat one or two more times.

Crunches with Baby Resting on Bent Legs

1. Lie on your back with your knees bent and thighs touching each other. Place your baby on your shins with his or her head facing you. Hold your baby in place with your hands.

2. Drop your belly button toward the floor, flattening your lower back. Exhale as you crunch up, starting with your lower belly muscles and curling one vertebra at a time until your abdominals are fully contracted. Then slowly lower to the floor and *repeat 15 times.*

3. *Repeat the entire sequence at least once, for a total of 10 minutes.*

With Babies and Toddlers
Six Months to Two Years

Ticktock

You can do this movement as soon as your baby has firm head control. It helps to start it while your baby is young because it will get progressively more challenging as your baby gains weight.

1. Stand with your knees soft and slightly bent, your feet shoulder-width apart. Hold your baby under his or her arms with your arms outstretched. Say, "Ticktock, ticktock, the mouse ran up the clock." As your clock "ticks," shift your arms so your baby ticks like the pendulum of a grandfather clock.

2. Then say, "The clock strikes *one*!" As the clock strikes, bring your arms up overhead in a sweeping motion. Your baby will laugh hysterically.

3. Say, "Ticktock, ticktock, the mouse ran up the clock," repeating the pendulum motion. Then, bring your arms overhead as you say, "The clock strikes *two*!" At first, you may be able to complete only two strikes before your shoulders are singing. Over time, work up to 5:00.

Ring Around the Rosy

You can play this "game" with one or more children. They will love it, and their enthusiasm will keep you going long after your legs have tried to call it quits.

1. Have everyone hold hands as you walk, skip, or run in a circle and sing, "Ring around the rosy, pocket full of posies, ashes, ashes, we all fall down."

2. When you say, "We all fall down," do a knee bend or squat. Get up and repeat until your children's interests are satiated. If you literally can't do another squat, try falling down and rolling around. It will make your children laugh and is a fun, active way to burn extra calories.

London Bridge

1. Lie on your belly. Clasp your hands together, and raise your body so that you are balancing on your forearms and the balls of your feet. Your body should be parallel to the floor and your abs tight. Suck your abs in, and don't drop your butt or curve your back.

2. Raise your hips into a pike position. Push your body weight back toward your feet, and lift through your tailbone. Sing the song "London bridge is falling down, falling down, falling down. London Bridge is falling down, my fair lady." As you sing, encourage your toddler to crawl or walk under the bridge formed by your body.

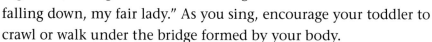

3. When you finish the verse, let the bridge "fall" by coming into the first position. Make it a game to see if you can fall and catch your toddler under the bridge (carefully, of course). Also, don't worry if your toddler or baby doesn't at first crawl under your bridge. He or she might try to crawl up your back or just sit and watch. Anything is fine as long as your baby is safe and within eyesight and you are getting in your workout. Don't push yourself past any safe limit on this one. Remember, you have precious cargo under that bridge!

Airplane

1. Lie on your back with your knees bent. Hold your toddler over your chest with your palms cupping his or her chest. (Note, if your toddler is tall or finds this uncomfortable, rest your forearms against your toddler's torso.)

2. Make airplane noises and deliver fun commentary as your toddler "flies." Simulate nosedives by bringing your arms overhead and down. The more creative you are with your arm movements, noises, and commentary, the more your toddler will laugh.

3. *Repeat the entire sequence at least once, for a total of 10 minutes.*

WORKOUTS FOR ACTIVE VACATIONS

I can personally attest to the fact that you can stay active anywhere you find yourself. During the summer of 2005 I spent three weeks vacationing in Turkey, where I power walked four to six hours daily through Istanbul. There were many beautiful sites to see, so I never got bored.

After Turkey, I headed down south to the Aegean Sea for seven days on a 100-foot sailboat. There, I filled my days with very challenging rock climbs, energetic swims, stretching, and yoga (and lots of backgammon with my friend Sam on the boat). I started every day with push-ups, pull-ups (on the boom, that thing that holds the main sail), and crunches. I followed this with very healthy breakfasts of plain no-fat yogurt, egg whites (omelet or frittatas), and a little Turkish coffee (I was on vacation and felt the need to indulge a bit).

So, you can see, you can turn anywhere into a "wellness zone." To help you along, I've included the following workout for the beach, the backyard (if you're having a low-key vacation at home), or the local park.

Platypus Walk

1. Place your hands behind your head with your elbows out to the sides. Sit into a squatting position with your knees aligned with your toes and your butt sticking back as far as you can.

2. Keep your core tight as you walk forward, pushing off through each heel. If you perform the move correctly, your butt and inner thighs will be on fire. Walk to the water (imaginary or otherwise), and then sprint back to your beach blanket three times. (Don't cheat by placing your beach blanket at the water's edge.) You can also do this exercise on a boat, provided there is enough room to walk at least 10 to 15 feet back and forth. Please be mindful of the edge, as I don't want anyone platypusing overboard!

Side Plank to Forward Plank

1. Lie on your belly. Clasp your hands together and raise your body so that you are balancing on your forearms and the balls of your feet. Your body should be parallel to the floor and your abs tight. Suck your abs in, and don't drop your butt or curve your back.

2. Lift into a side plank on your right side by bringing your right hand forward so your forearm is perpendicular with your body and your left hand is on your hip. *Hold two seconds.*

3. Return to the plank and then lift into a side plank on your left side. *Continue to alternate sides 10 times.*

Squat Thrusts

1. Stand with your feet slightly wider than hips' distance apart.

2. Bend your knees, stick your butt back, and come into a squat.

3. Continue to bend your knees as you bend forward from the hips, placing your hands on the floor under your breastbone.

4. Press your hands into the floor as you jump and extend your legs behind your body, coming into a push-up position. Keep your abs tight the entire time. Recoil your legs, and rise to the starting position. *Repeat 10 to 15 times.* During your last repetition, remain in the modified push-up position and proceed directly into mountain climbers. (Incorporating a medicine ball as on page 93 adds a higher degree of difficulty to this exercise.)

Mountain Climbers

1. From the push-up position in the squat thrust, bend your right knee and jump it in, bringing your right thigh under the right side of your torso.

2. Jump your right leg back as you simultaneously bend your left knee and jump it in.

3. *Continue alternating right and left for 15 to 30 seconds.*

Reverse Walking Crabs

1. Sit with your hands behind your butt, your fingers pointing toward your butt and your knees bent.

2. Press through your triceps to lift your butt off the ground.

3. Walk backward on your hands and feet. You should feel your triceps screaming. Keep your shoulders back and your elbows soft. Don't arch your lower back. Walk to the water's edge, and then return to your towel.

Football Drills

1. Do football/basketball crossover sprints to the water and back. On the first sprint, stand with your left side facing the water. Cross your right leg in front of your left and then behind your left leg over and over as fast as you can. Return and do 15 push-ups. Then do a crossover sprint with your right side facing the water.

2. *Repeat the entire sequence at least once, for a total of 10 minutes.*

Putting It All Together

As I've mentioned, you can do the 10-minute workouts listed in this chapter separately, during the spare snippets of time that you manage to carve out of a day, but I encourage you as much as possible to assemble them into a longer 45-minute total-body blast. Ideally, commit yourself to this weekly exercise goal:

- 45 minutes of continuous cardiosculping (such as my 45-Minute Total-Body Blast) three to four days a week
- 30 minutes of cardiosculpting (either split into multiple 10-minute segments or all at once) the remaining days of the week
- 30 to 45 minutes of your choice of cardio—running, power walking, cycling—*every day*, in addition to your cardiosculpting workout (For ideas on fitting this type of cardio into your day, see Chapter 5.)

All told, you should have your body in motion for an hour to an hour and a half every day. Following you'll find a longer 45-minute blast that allows you to do just that; it takes various exercises from the miniworkouts from this chapter and assembles them into a complete cardiosculpting workout. You'll also find two shorter upper- and lower-body-focused workouts that you can alternate between to keep your mind—and your body—engaged.

David's 45-Minute Total-Body Blast

Jog in Place with Medicine Ball

Squat Thrusts with Medicine Ball

Mountain Climbers with Medicine Ball

David's Ultimate Shadow Boxing

Reverse Lunge with Torso Twist

Good Mornings with Rotation

Jumping Lunges Holding Medicine Ball

Squat Jumps with Medicine Ball

Plié Squat with Hammer Curl into a Shoulder Press

Forward and Reverse Crossover Lunges with Biceps Curls

Sumo Lunge with Side Kick and Frog Jump

Platypus Walk with Medicine Ball

Low Plank and High Plank on Stability Ball

Pike with Stability Ball

Side Crunch with Stability Ball

Oblique and Lower Abs with Stability Ball

Incline Dumbbell Press/Fly/ Pullover on Stability Ball

Push-Ups on Stability Ball

Bench Dips on Stability Ball

Wide Dumbbell Rows on Stability Ball

Handoff

Double Crunch with Ball

Trunk Crunches

Football Drills (Do jumping jacks if space does not permit.)

Reverse Walking Crabs

SAMPLE SCHEDULE

Use this schedule as a guide for mixing and matching your 10-minute workouts. Regardless of where you find yourself, try to fit in the 45-Minute Total-Body Blast at least three days a week (as the schedule suggests). On alternate days you'll find ways to mix and match various 10-minute workouts depending on your lifestyle: office worker, stay-at-home parent, vacationer, or business traveler. With this schedule, you'll firm every area of your body every day.

Alternatively, you might decide to focus on a specific body area on a specific day. For example, if your legs are your number one pet peeve, you might assign Tuesday and Friday as official leg days, picking from the various 10-minute lower-body workouts in this chapter. Or, for variety, you might declare Tuesday abs day, Thursday upper-body day, Friday lower-body day, and Sunday the day you really zero in on your trouble spot. The options are endless!

	Monday	Tuesday (office work example)	Wednesday	Thursday (vacation example)	Friday (home-based example)	Saturday (total-body day)	Sunday (business travel example)
Morning	David's 45-Minute Total-Body Blast	Home Workout #1 (before work)	David's 45-Minute Total-Body Blast	Vacation Workout	Home Workout #3 (before kids wake up)	David's 45-Minute Total-Body Blast	Hotel Workout #1 and #2
Midmorning							
Lunch break		Office Workout #3			Home Workout #1		
Midafternoon		Office Workout #1		Home Workout #1 (while kids nap)			
Early evening				Vacation Workout	Home Workout #2 (on bathroom floor while kids bathe)		Hotel Workout #3

Exhilarating and Efficient

You have now seen all of my exercises for the Ultimate New York Fitness Plan. Feel free to adjust and adapt any of these workouts and, if need be, personally customize them to suit your particular needs or time constraints. Consistent with and supportive of my principle of "no-excuse" training, the intensity and energy expended in these "express" sessions far exceeds the traditional "two-hour" workouts that I have witnessed at other fitness clubs. Workouts in a New York Minute (all right, 10 New York minutes) is an exhilarating, efficient, and results-oriented program that will bring about lifelong rewards.

The Ultimate New York Walking Plan

To get ready for my dad's quadruple bypass surgery, Mom and Dad moved into the city to be closer to the hospital and dad's many doctors. As a consequence, at 71 and 69, respectively, and after 40 years of suburban living, they got rid of their car and Mom decided to walk to the grocery store, walk the dog, and, for longer trips, walk to the bus stop to take the bus. The image of Mom walking to the bus stop and walking to her office really pleased me. The thought that she was getting up first thing in the morning and getting her heart pumping was a big plus.

Now there was no more suburban lethargy. No more driving to the office, eating at the desk, getting back in the car, returning home, eating, vegging out in front of the television, and falling into bed. "Wherever I had to go, this fat ass had to walk," Mom likes to joke. "In our old home, you get in the car to drive to the end of the driveway to get your mail. In New York, I had to walk everywhere."

These walks caused my mom to lose 10 pounds during the first couple of weeks she was in the city. Since that time, she has embraced my entire program—using daily exercise, a strict diet, and my supplements to peel the pounds off even faster. It's the walking, however, that got her started—a form of movement that Mom didn't even think of as exercise.

The World's Walking Capital

I have lived in New York City for almost 25 years and have always been captivated by the inherent energy that permeates every aspect of daily living. But even with all of the reasons to move, it's just as easy to find a way to stay put. New York City is the "delivery capital" of the world. Everything from your laundry to your groceries and hot meals can be delivered at a moment's notice.

Before working out at my gym, some of my clients had never before exercised in their lives. For example, Richard Jones, a corporate CEO, never exercised a day in his life before he met me a year ago. Despite his successful career, he admitted to finding the gym quite intimidating. Well, you know what? Now, not only does he exercise four days a week at the Madison Square Club, but he also plays tennis or basketball with his teenage children on the weekends. Every day, he hikes up 10 flights of stairs to his loft in downtown Manhattan. The simple act of climbing those stairs every day burns approximately 200 to 300 calories. All told, Richard has lost more than 60 pounds in the past nine months and has totally embraced the concept and philosophy of the Ultimate New York Diet.

Whenever I encounter such a fitness newbie, I get excited because I know the metamorphosis from fitness novice to fitness-minded happens rapidly and dramatically. This transition follows Newton's first law of motion, which states that an object at rest tends to stay at rest, and an object in motion tends to stay in motion. Once these former couch potatoes begin moving, they usually can't stop.

This metamorphosis takes place because the urge to move is encoded in our genes. Infants, babies, and toddlers are drawn to the notion of movement. They can't wait to move, stand, walk, run, and discover. Unfortunately, for many of us, as we get older, we stop doing those simple things and adopt a more sedentary lifestyle.

Walking Works

Numerous and repeated bouts of "unofficial" exercise pay off in big dividends. First, they provide a nice caloric buffer in the rare event that you do miss your "official workout." Second, these short snippets of exercise help to boost your mood and energy levels throughout the day. I find that there's no better solution to a midafternoon slump than climbing a few flights of stairs, taking a quick power walk around the office, or doing a set of push-ups near your desk. Third, your unofficial exercise will help to further condition your heart and lungs, making you a stronger, more energetic, and healthier person. Fourth, unofficial exercise encourages you to remain on the "motion" end of Newton's first law of motion. The more often you put yourself in motion, the more likely your chances of staying in motion. Last but not least, I have found that one tends to eat healthier when constantly on the move. It's a lot easier to slurp down one of my meal-replacement drinks while you are in motion than it is to chow down on a street vendor hot dog.

You need not live in New York or any other city to experience this metamorphosis. It doesn't matter whether you live in rural America, suburbia, an urban center, or somewhere else entirely. You have many opportunities every day to sneak in extra calorie burning. You need only pay attention to and take advantage of them. The advice in this chapter will help you to do just that.

In this chapter, you will find a number of ideas that will help you log more time on your feet. Based on the advice you will find in the following pages, I want you to set the following goal for yourself. Within eight weeks, you will log 10,000 to 12,000 incidental steps a day, roughly three to five miles depending on your stride. That's the number of daily steps

Richard Jones

I met Richard Jones soon after his 50th birthday. He stood six feet two inches tall and weighed 247 pounds. A CEO and the father of teenage twin boys, his plate was quite full, literally and figuratively. But he was determined to change, and he did just that. Within four months, he lost 40 pounds and has changed his whole outlook on life. He dresses, acts, and carries himself around with a newfound confidence.

Q: **What made you decide to turn your life around?**

A: I spent the first 35 years of my life thin, but not healthy and not muscular. When I was 35, my eating habits caught up with me and I slowly began putting on weight. By age 50, I was heavy and smoking one and a half to two packs a day. I had not been to the doctor in many years. When I turned 50, I went in for a checkup. My blood pressure was quite high. My doctor was concerned that I could have a stroke. It was a wake-up call for me.

I made a decision that I wanted to be alive for a while more. I wanted to be around for my family, so I quit smoking, changed my eating habits, and started exercising for the first time in my life.

Q: **That's quite a lot to tackle all at once. Did you ever think you might have bitten off more than you could chew?**

A: Everyone said to me that I should tackle just one lifestyle change at a time. To me, it is just one change. It's about being healthy. Quitting smoking, exercising, and changing my eating habits all fostered each other and were interconnected. I'm not sure I could have made one change without making the others.

Q: **What habit was the hardest for you to break?**

A: I was really addicted to sugar. Dealing with that was hard at first. It took time, but looking back on it, not that much time. You can't expect to change something like that in a week or two, but I did overcome it over a period of months. It's

experts recommend you take to improve your heart health, and it's also the number of steps studies show help to enable weight loss.

To achieve this goal, you'll need a pedometer, a simple device sold at most sporting goods stores. You wear it on your waistband. It will not gone, but it has gotten easier. And when I do backslide a little and give in to a sugar craving, I don't punish myself afterward. I don't use it as an excuse to do it all the time. I have learned that moderation is key.

Q: How has your view of exercise changed?

A: At first, I felt incredibly intimidated to walk into the gym. I have a lot of confidence and am very successful in my professional life, but I didn't feel that way about exercise. Now I enjoy more physical things, like going for bike rides. I take great pleasure from physical activity that I did not take before.

Q: What results amaze you the most?

A: It amazes me that I was able to do it. I don't consider myself an enormously disciplined person. I had been so undisciplined in terms of eating and smoking for so long that it really surprises me that I could turn all of it around.

Now I weigh 185, I have more muscle than ever, and I feel great. I don't smoke. I feel very healthy and active. I feel really good and confident about myself in a way that I haven't felt for a long time. When I was heavy, I used clothing to mask my body. Now I'm able to wear real clothes again. Instead of double-extra-large sweaters and shirts draped around me, I wear vintage jackets and fitted clothing.

RICHARD'S ADVICE FOR YOU: This needs to be a serious priority in your life. Don't be scared of the changes that lie ahead. If I can do this, anyone can, really.

POSTSCRIPT: *Richard represents every guy out there who may be reading this book (or perhaps the husbands of some of the women reading it). I am particularly proud of Richard's accomplishments, as he has had to maintain a very active social and business life at the same time. When he has the "occasional dietary indiscretion," he answers with an intense cardio session. He has learned to take the lessons of my program and translate and transform them to suit his life.*

sense your movement, counting your steps for you. Wear your pedometer for a day or two just to get a baseline reading of how many steps you typically take. You'll probably find that you take somewhere between 900 and 3,000 steps a day during your usual activities. Once you know your baseline, start adding steps. Make it your goal to add 20 percent more steps each week. In other words, if you recorded 3,000 steps as your baseline, you'll want to walk 3,600 daily steps during week one of the program. (Note: this doesn't include your Ultimate New York Fitness Plan workouts, which you will complete in addition to your daily 10,000 to 12,000 steps.)

Walk These Ways

Once you strap on your pedometer, you'll find you take additional steps somewhat automatically. Concentrate on adding more steps both formally and informally.

ONE FORMAL WALK AND MANY INFORMAL WALKS

Devote time to one major walking (or running or some other type of cardio) session at least a few times a week. Start with whatever amount of time you can physically maintain, increasing the duration each week by about five minutes. Do intervals for most of your walk. That means doing bursts of faster walking (or running, depending on your fitness) that will seriously increase your heart rate and work your muscles to the max. You can do your intervals outside or on a treadmill. Start by walking (or jogging) five minutes at your usual pace to warm up. Then alternate two minutes of faster walking or running with two minutes of recovery walking or running. Your faster pace should feel like an 8 on a scale of 1 to 10 in intensity, and your easy pace should be a 4 or 5. If you prefer to cycle, row, or do some other form of cardio, go right ahead, alternating two minutes of faster-paced work with two minutes of recovery exercise.

In addition to a formal daily walk, take numerous miniwalks throughout the course of the day.

ADDING STEPS FOR . . .

Here are some ways to add a few daily miniwalks, depending on your lifestyle.

Busy Parents with Young Babies. Nearly all infants love riding in a stroller. More often than not, the stroller will soothe your baby to sleep. As an added bonus, if you have a colicky baby, your stroller time may be your only quiet time during your day. I knew one mother whose colicky baby cried from 3:00 P.M. to midnight on most days. She often put the baby in a stroller and walked a half-mile loop around her neighborhood—over and over again. Without fail, the screaming always stopped by the time she reached the end of the driveway, giving her the entire walk to collect her thoughts and wits before returning home. If you have more than one child, bring the older one along on your walks or walk with the baby around the playground while keeping an eye on the older one playing on the equipment.

In addition to giving yourself some needed quiet time, daily walks with your infant will help you to reduce stress and lift your mood, which can help fight off the postpartum blues that stem from shifting hormone levels. You'll also bathe yourself and your baby in sunlight, which, research shows, will help you both to sleep better at night, particularly if you take a morning walk.

In addition to burning calories by walking, you'll also tone your chest and arms as you push the stroller, especially if you take things uphill.

Start with an infant stroller that allows you to place your baby in a car seat facing you. This provides your baby more comfort, as many newborns don't particularly like being flat on their backs. It also provides a better vantage point for you to see what your baby is doing. By around six months, when your baby can sit upright, you can progress to a jog stroller, which is lighter and easier to maneuver than the typical baby stroller.

For a little more variety, consider taking things off road by placing your infant in a front-style or backpack baby carrier, depending on his or her age. This adds weight to your body, forcing your legs to work harder. As with the stroller, your infant will probably fall asleep in the pack, giving you needed quiet time.

If you are stuck indoors on a rainy day, you can still sneak in more steps. Put your infant in a sling or baby carrier and walk up and down the steps in your home or apartment. Or, drive to an indoor mall and power walk as you window-shop.

Busy Parents with Children Age One and Older. Some parents tell me that their children at around age one just say "no" to the stroller, backpack, and bike trailer. These on-the-go children simply don't want to be contained. If that's the case, I strongly encourage you to carve out some "you" time where you can get in a longer, uninterrupted walk at a brisk pace. Perhaps you can share babysitting with another parent. One day you watch the kids so your friend can have some child-free time. On another day he or she watches them so you can walk or run.

Consider forming a walking club for other parents with young children. Meet at a nearby track or park. Everyone should bring blankets, toys, and, of course, children. During each meeting, one or two parents sit it out to supervise the kids while the other parents walk or run. Use these additional ideas to sneak in more steps:

- **Play chase and other active games.** Encourage your son or daughter to chase you around the yard or house and vice versa. As your children age, take part in the active games they devise. Join in on tag, baseball, soccer, and other games rather than sitting and watching.
- **Take a nature walk.** Young children love the outdoors. Head to a nearby park and meander. In addition to allowing your toddler or older child to expend some energy, you'll be able to teach him or her about trees, leaves, plants, flowers, and other aspects of nature. You'll also build your patience as your child stops every few steps to inspect leaves, sticks, and other treasures.
- **Go up and down the steps.** Most toddlers are fascinated by stairs. Rather than always gating them off, every once in a while open the child-safety gate and encourage your toddler to climb up and down while you follow close behind. This allows your toddler time to practice an important skill as you also get in some active time.
- **Use a wagon.** If your toddler hates the stroller, you might have some luck pulling him or her in a wagon, especially if you pack it full of stuffed animals and set off on a fun adventure. Head downtown and pull your child around Main Street or the mall. Let him or her out as needed.

People Who Work Lots of Hours at a Desk Job. Many of my clients spend more time at work, thinking about work, and getting ready for work than they do any other activity. Even when they're not in the office, they generally are still working either by cell phone or notebook computer—or both. I often ask them what they do to stay active during the day, and here I've compiled some of their tricks.

- **Take a break.** No matter how stressed you feel to get a project completed, take at least two breaks a day, one in the morning and one in the midafternoon. During this 5 to 10 minutes of nonwork time, go for a brisk walk around the office or—if possible—outside. This 5- to 10-minute session will not only help you burn a few extra calories but will also recharge your mental and physical batteries. On top of these two official breaks, take a walk break whenever you find yourself spinning your wheels. All of us have segments during the day when our brains partially shut down, whether we like it or not. A brisk walk helps lift the brownout, sharpening your brain for the rest of the day.

- **Hold a conference walk.** Walk with colleagues to brainstorm or solve problems. Movement has a way of simultaneously opening up the creative mind while shutting down the critical mind. Those folks who annoy you during meetings because they seem to talk just to hear the sound of their own voices? They'll be less likely to do so while in motion. The walk-and-work session will help keep everyone on track—no pun intended.

- **Use the least important parking space.** Who cares that you clawed your way to the top in order to get the chosen space with your name on it right next to the office door? Park your car in the spot farthest away from the door and hoof it in. The short, brisk walk will help wake you up in the morning, readying you to face the day. Follow this mind-set no matter where you need to park your car. As one of my clients, Christine Capulong, puts it, "Rather than wasting my time circling a parking lot in search for a space closest to the store, I instead look for the space closest to the entrance of the lot." She also never takes elevators, mounting stairs two at a time.

- **Discuss matters in person.** I'm not sure when it became commonplace for workers to call or e-mail each other rather than speak face-to-face. When you need something from someone in your office, make it a point to get out of your chair and physically place yourself in the same space as the person you are talking to. Not only will this help you to log more steps, but you'll also be more likely to effectively get your point across when you can use body language and tone of voice in addition to your actual words.

- **If you dine out for lunch, walk to your destination.** Pick some dining spots 10 to 15 minutes away, and walk to and from lunch.

People Who Travel for Business. Although you can't help but remain motionless during a certain part of the travel experience, you probably have more opportunities to sneak in steps than you think. Consider the following tactics.

- **Never use the moving walkways.** Store your luggage in an airport locker, or invest in a backpack carry-on. This allows you to more comfortably walk the concourses. Also, invest in comfortable travel shoes. Timberland and other companies now make fashionable dress shoes with comfortable rubber soles designed for airport navigation. Once you have the right shoes and luggage, you can more easily take the stairs instead of the elevator or escalator (you'll probably have them to yourself and can avoid the crowds).
- **Move in the morning.** As soon as you arrive at your destination, take a walk. This will help to prevent jet lag. Then, especially if you've skipped multiple time zones, follow up with a brisk walk or hike early during your first morning at your destination. Your morning walk will help to reset your body clock to your new time zone.
- **Go prepared.** Pack one of your favorite exercise books or DVDs (mine will always work in a pinch), and if your room does not have a DVD player (check ahead of time), you can always watch the program on your laptop.

People Who Are on Vacation. Although many people backslide during their vacations, I personally think your time off from work and away from home is the easiest time to sneak in fitness. Each vacation destination will offer up its unique set of touristy ways that can keep you fit on the road. If you are staying near a lake or pond, look into paddleboat, canoe, or rowboat rentals. If you are staying in snow-capped mountains, look into skiing, snowshoeing, and snow hiking. If you're at the shore, try some bodysurfing, bodyboarding, paddleball, beach football (my favorite), and beach volleyball. If you're staying at a vacation home, see if there's a horseshoe pit and start up a game. Walk on the beach. Wade through the hotel swimming pool. Consider the following options.

- **Take walking breaks during road trips.** If you are driving to your destination, stop every few hours at a town park, playground, or restaurant with a play area. Allow your children to romp around as you walk. Or, join in with them by playing tag or kicking a ball.
- **Take an active cruise.** Some large ships house pools, golf simulators, rock walls, basketball hoops, fitness centers, jogging and walking areas, and instructor-led fitness classes. During your sea and land excursions you can burn calories as you snorkel, swim, hike, scuba dive, and horseback ride. While on a cruise in Turkey, I started every morning doing push-ups and sit-ups and taking a morning swim followed by an invigorating hike. One hour under the Turkish sun made breakfast taste that much more delicious and worthwhile.
- **Walk everywhere.** You can get in plenty of unstructured exercise by walking as you sightsee. One of my clients, Sabina, arrived in France about a week before her wedding. She spent each morning walking the French countryside. "It helped me to connect with my environment," she said. Stroll through your destination's downtown, the local zoo, and other destinations. If you're staying in a city, walk the streets to pick your nightly restaurants rather than relying on the hotel staff, phone book, or travel guide. Check out menus and make your reservation. You can easily get in three hours of walking a day just by seeing the sights on foot.
- **Schedule an educational vacation.** Wrap your entire vacation around an activity, such as learning to sail, ski, swim, hike, or play a sport. Travel agents can hook you up with any number of vacation packages that will keep you active and satisfy your yen for knowledge. If you have children, look for packages that include excavating dinosaur bones and other anthropological expeditions.
- **Sign up for an adventure vacation.** Numerous companies will not only help you stay in shape while you are on vacation, they'll help you

get in the best shape of your life. For example, one adventure travel company, Backroads, organizes cycling, kayaking, and hiking trips all over the world. Another company, Trek Travel, organizes cycling trips through Tuscany, Provence, and Denmark, among many other destinations. Many of these companies offer gentle, intermediate, and hard-core excursions, matching their adventure vacations to your fitness level and skills.

Living the Ultimate New York Diet

During the past 20 years, I've worked with countless personalities—men, women, young, and old. I've trained corporate CEOs, supermodels, actresses, stay-at-home moms, rock stars, chefs, interior designers, public relations professionals, and every career and lifestyle in between. Some of my clients split their time between New York, L.A., London, and other cities. They live out of suitcases. Others never step foot out of the city. Some love to cook. Some eat out or order in every single meal. Some have wanted only to firm up, others wanted to lose 5 or 10 pounds, and still others wanted to lose more than 100 pounds.

Yes, they come from every walk of life and every lifestyle, but, in all of them, I see a common thread emerge. In order to transform their bodies from flabby to firm, chubby to slender, and toxic to healthy, they must simultaneously transform their minds. They must reach deep down into their souls to uncover the drive needed to maintain healthful eating and exercise habits. They must confront the negative thoughts that drive them to self-destructive behavior. In short, to effect a lasting physical change, you must first examine and strengthen your mind.

I've been there when my clients have sheepishly dragged themselves into my club after a night of martinis and pretzels. I've called them when they've skipped exercise sessions and gotten them back on track. I've listened as they've told me about their stress, emotions, and other eating triggers. Most important, I've worked with them to find a way to overcome their hurdles to wellness.

Based on those experiences, I've over the years developed a training program for the mind. In the following pages, you'll find that plan. You may not need to work on every aspect of it, but I'm pretty sure you'll find at least one part of your mental, emotional, and spiritual self that could use a little attention. As you read, be honest with yourself about your abilities, feelings, and knee-jerk reactions. This inner candidness will help you to uncover the parts of yourself that need work—the parts of yourself that will either trip you up on the road to wellness or pave your way to success.

Believe in Yourself

To be successful on this—or any other—plan, you must learn to give up your desire to control what you cannot and assume control over what you can—your personal choices. You *can* be the best that you can be. You can't control your weight on the scale or even your clothing size, but you can control the foods you put in your mouth and the movements you do with your body. You can also control whether you allow outside influences—situations, people, and places—to filter into your everyday life. In other words, you do have control over the bag of chips (crisps in some parts of the world) that wind up in your hands (and ultimately, your mouth) after a particularly stressful day at the office.

As I write this chapter, I am munching on a handful of organic raw almonds—my favorite snack food. It has been a particularly stressful time in my life, but in spite of this (or maybe because of this), I find myself staying focused and trying "to keep it all together." Keeping control over the little things—things I eat or what I do with my downtime—really helps me keep my eye on the "bigger picture."

I've worked with many clients who, before the Ultimate New York Diet, had tried many other diets. Each time they lost some weight. Each time they eventually hit a plateau and then gained the weight back. They succeeded on the Ultimate New York Diet not because of the Meal Plan, the Exercise Plan, or the Supplement Plan (although, of course, that all certainly helped). They succeeded because they finally took control. They finally made a mental shift to *choose* a new way of eating, exercising, supplementing, and thinking.

"I've had a weight problem since I was 10 years old," Christine Capulong, one such client, told me after she had lost 10 pounds and two dress sizes on the plan. "I've spent so much money trying to lose weight. I've tried Weight Watchers and Jenny Craig. I've gone to diet centers. I've enrolled in hospital-based programs. I even spent five months at a fat camp. Each time I lost weight but then hit a plateau. Then I would be off whatever program I was on and the weight went back up. This time was different. This time I took ownership and control of the process. It's not a diet; it's a lifestyle. I don't have to depend on someone else to control my weight for me now. I took control." Within two days of starting the program, I got the distinct impression that Christine was going to not only succeed but excel. Her enthusiasm and positive energy were infectious and helped guarantee her success.

How do you get in control? How do you get to the same place that Christine finally got to after so many years of floundering? To put yourself in control you must develop a sense of inner confidence. Studies show that people with more self-confidence are more likely to succeed at adopting new habits.

The rapid results you will experience on this program will help to bolster your confidence. If you continue to nurture it, you'll reap benefits that extend far beyond the size of your swimsuit. You'll improve your career, your relationships with others, your relationship with yourself, and your overall outlook on life. You won't build this inner sense of confidence overnight, but you must constantly work on nurturing it. Here are some ways to do just that:

- **Keep an accomplishment list.** At the end of each day, write down your successes—the hard-boiled egg white you ate instead of the morning bagel, the steps you climbed instead of taking the elevator, the glass of water you had instead of the Coke.
- **See slipups as opportunities to learn about yourself.** So you had a latte, chocolate chip cookie, or bag of potato chips. Rather than get mad at yourself (or at the food) or the person who "caused you to eat it," learn from what you did—and move on. Why did you eat what you did? Pinpoint the reason, and then think up constructive ways to overcome that problem in the future.
- **Consciously change the way you think about yourself.** We all have a broken record somewhere inside our heads that fuels us with self-destructive chatter. These undermining comments are a little different from person to person, but common themes go something like this:

"Who do you think you are going to the gym?
You are not a gym person."

"You're a fat person. Just get used to it. You'll never be skinny."

"You hate to exercise. Why are you doing this to yourself?"

"You'll never be able to do this."

I encourage you to carry a journal with you and jot down such thoughts whenever they pop into your head. At first, you might not even notice them. Eventually, however, with practice, you'll notice them as soon as they surface, and you'll be able to counter them with something that's more empowering and, more important, accurate. In this way, you'll no longer be the "out-of-shape guy who hates to exercise" or the "fat lady who loves ice cream." You'll become the "disciplined person who makes healthful eating choices" and the "fit person who exercises for her health."

Find Your Success Key

At one point in Mom's journey to wellness, she had already lost more than 60 pounds, but she was clearly at a critical point, the point at which many of you (who have a significant amount of weight to lose) may be at some point in this program. She had missed a couple of workouts, and my dad was having some physical problems. Those were the beginning tell-tale signs that she was veering off course a bit. The occasional bagel was followed by Caesar salad dressing on her otherwise-plain grilled chicken salad. Then, at my niece's pizza party in Pennsylvania, she feasted on the only thing being offered that day—fatty, greasy pizza. What was I going to do? How was I going to address the situation in a positive way and not scare her away? I was hard on her, forcing her to restate her desire to lose weight in a healthy way. At first I heard the excuses. I heard that she was pushing 70, that she still had 100 pounds to lose. I heard about her fear, her sadness, her sense of loss and frustration. I heard that she had other things going on in her life—such as my father's heart problems—that were more urgent than her own health.

"What about you, Mom?" I asked her. "Don't you want to do this for you?"

After thinking about that question, my mom looked at me and said, "I do need to do this for me. Before I leave this Earth, I want to do something for me, something that's selfish. I want to be able to say that I could do it, that I started something and I finished it, and that I finished it myself without anyone helping me." Well, maybe she got a little help (or prodding) every now and again.

Since that "tough love" conversation, Mom has not missed many days at the gym. Additionally, she has been cooking her own meals at home—following my recipes and avoiding the Chinese takeout and the morning bagel. Now, as the pounds fall off, Mom is being totally transformed—mind, body, and spirit. She now isn't doing this for me or for my dad or for anyone else. She has found the reason—what I call the "success key"—to make the right choices that lead to weight loss.

For my mom, what started out being something she was doing for me and my dad and the rest of the family has now become predominantly about her. Where she initially approached this as if she were helping

Shannon Lyons

I've never met Shannon face-to-face, but I feel as if I've known her for many years. She e-mailed me not long after completing the two-week program outlined in The Ultimate New York Body Plan. *She had experienced amazing success and asked for advice on maintaining it. So, over e-mail, she and I conversed, and I helped her transition to the Ultimate New York Diet.*

Q: **To what do you attribute your past battles with weight?**

A: All through my high school and college years, I worked out. I maintained a size 2 or 4 in high school and college, but even then I wasn't happy with my body. After I got married, I put on 10 pounds and went up to a size 6, and then an 8. I continued to go to the gym. I even trained for and ran a marathon. I thought all the running would help me get that runner's body I had always wanted. It didn't.

When I got pregnant, I gained 70 pounds. It was not a pretty sight! After I had the baby, I lost all but 15 of it. I got pregnant again and gained 50 pounds. By the time my youngest turned one, I still had 25 pounds to lose. I had no idea what to eat, and my trips to the gym were doing nothing.

I just didn't know how to start, where to start, what to eat, and how to work out. When you have a lot of weight to lose, it's daunting, and it's hard to "attack" it.

Q: **How did the excess weight affect your life?**

A: I felt "yuk" all the time. I felt like my body looked like a mess. I just felt so bad about myself, especially after the births of my two children. I didn't want to be seen in public. I was consumed with wanting my body to be something it wasn't. It became mentally exhausting. I would always try and look nice, but when you're overweight, just trying to get dressed or to go to the gym is a nightmare. I would think about wanting to be thin every day, even dream about it. I felt embarrassed. I also felt defeated, knowing I had so much to lose.

Q: **Why did this plan help, whereas others did not?**

A: With other diets, I wasn't working out like I was with David's plan, so yeah, I lost weight, but my body wasn't really changing. This was different because I was seeing my body change. I had never seen

these types of results with those other plans, so that's why I gave up on them. With David's plan, I saw results in that first week, and that fueled my motivation to keep going. When I started, I weighed 140, and now, two months later, I'm 123. I haven't seen those numbers on the scale in years. I'm wearing clothes that I haven't been able to wear in years, and some of them are a little too big on me.

Q: **What kept you going when the little voice in the back of your head told you to give up?**

A: I was desperate to change my life. I told myself, every second of every day, "I can do this." I have realized that my mind is a very powerful thing. I have to talk to myself and God every day to keep me on track and, at times, get me back on track.

Yes, I have bad days every once in a while, and I splurge. On those days, I remind myself of the hard work, and that gets me recommitted. If I do have a bad day, I just work out really hard the next day.

Q: **How have you adapted the plan to your personal lifestyle, culinary tastes, career, and family situation?**

A: I have a pretty good routine now, so some of that has just become a habit. I take each day one at a time. I force myself to make choices. If I know I have an event one evening, or on the weekend, I try to make that day extra good, work out harder, and really watch what I eat. I have more control now, and it really is because I know how hard it was to get to this point. I don't want to lose it.

Q: **How has this plan changed your life?**

A: I feel so good about myself. I feel thinner, healthier, sexier, free of bad toxins. Being able to get into jeans that I haven't worn in three years (and they are a little big) feels great. I feel like myself again. Feeling good about yourself is priceless. You really can do anything if you have the self-esteem. Doing the program, conquering it, and seeing the results gave me more confidence and more self-esteem, and that's changed how I feel inside.

SHANNON'S ADVICE FOR YOU: You *really* can do *anything* you set your mind to. Once those first few days go by, you see the results, and those results will take you to the end. Believe in yourself; you owe it to yourself. For once in your life, give it your all, and make this last attempt to change. You will be amazed.

POSTSCRIPT: *Shannon stresses the idea that anything is possible. I am a true believer in this concept and am very proud of Shannon's successes and transformation.*

me finish one of my homework assignments, she now views it as a self-mission. Succeeding on this program has become about her. That is the ultimate reward.

I've seen this time and time again. This is so important that I hope you will bear with me as I tell you another story that I think will really help to illustrate my point. I met Greg Namin when I was promoting *The Ultimate New York Body Plan*. He and five other participants agreed to try my plan for two weeks as Fox News Channel chronicled their results (you've previously read about Greg and another participant, Christine). Greg had tried to lose weight in the past, but he came into the Fox News Challenge with a kind of commitment I had not before seen. He told me that his daughter had started calling him the retired version of "Mr. Incredible" because of his gut. He said his excess weight now made his knees and back hurt on a constant basis. He had recently gone to the doctor for a checkup. His cholesterol was 243 and his triglycerides 900. He tried cholesterol-lowering medication, but it hadn't helped.

He wanted to be a true Mr. Incredible for his daughter. He not only wanted to look good and lose his gut, but, more important, he wanted to feel good. "I felt so bummed out all of the time. My knees hurt when I walked and when I got out of bed in the morning." He wanted to be around to see his daughter grow up. That's heavy stuff. That's the stuff that fuels motivation.

Within two weeks, Greg's cholesterol dropped to 168 and his triglycerides to 89. He's still working toward his goal weight, but the last time I spoke to him he had lost 35 pounds and was still going strong.

Now it's time to focus on you. What are your reasons for losing weight? Are you doing this for yourself? If your knee-jerk reaction is similar to my mother's, then I want you to spend more time thinking about that question. You might think you want to do this to make your husband happy or to get your doctor off your back. Those reasons are good ones, but they won't carry you through. You need to do this for you. To light that inner fire and keep it lit, find your personal reason for weight loss, the one that resonates most powerfully for you. Is it about your health, your energy levels, your self-esteem, your self-worth, or your sense of enjoyment in life? Think about it. Then write it down in the space provided. Whenever you start to backslide on the program, revisit this question and your answer.

In this way, you'll be able to give yourself the same pep talk that I gave my mother on this all-important day—and you'll get yourself back on track.

I want to lose weight and get in shape because _____
_____.

Give Yourself Permission to Be Your Top Priority

I met Sue Blake when she was hired to promote my second book. At age 43, Sue had spent years putting others, including her family, friends, and clients, first. "In years past, I thought I had enough to do that I couldn't possibly bring something else—like a wellness program—on board, even if it was something that would improve my health," she told me. "In trying to be magnificent on their behalf, I fed my own needs through comfort eating and excessive sleeping.

"When I started the Ultimate New York Diet, I finally gave myself permission to rank myself higher than *everybody* else," she said. This wasn't easy. Sue had to make tough choices. Choosing to get out of bed at 6:00 A.M. to go to the gym meant that she wasn't home in the morning to shepherd her teenage daughters out of the house for school. It meant giving up her morning routine of a full-fat large cappuccino and a bacon sandwich. It meant putting a voice to her emotions rather than soothing them with food.

So many people—women in particular—put everything else and everyone else first. In an attempt to be all they can be for their kids, clients, and spouses, they skimp on sleep and ignore their body's needs. In the words of one of my clients, successful weight loss is about "honoring yourself." That requires a shift in mind-set. To enable this shift, take a moment and really think about these questions.

- Who are you doing this for and why?
- If after eight weeks on the plan you lost no weight but would still be healthier, feel more energetic, and have an incredible sense of accomplishment, would the plan still seem worth it to you?

- Do *you* matter to you?
- In what positive ways will losing weight and getting fit affect you? How can you benefit from this program?
- Will you have the strength and confidence to translate these changes into your everyday life by doing such things as cooking healthier meals for your family and leading fun-filled family fitness weekends?

Once you answer those questions, I want you to make a promise to yourself. I want you to promise that for the next eight weeks and beyond, you will honor yourself. Yes, you can fulfill your many other roles in life as mother, father, husband, wife, grandmother, and so on, but your first priority for the next eight weeks will be you. No more will you put others' needs in front of your health and your wellness. You are many things to many people, but first and foremost you are you.

Stop the Panic-Eat-Panic-Eat Cycle

I've seen it happen many times. People start on a diet and it seems to be working. Then *something* happens. Perhaps it's a rough day at work. A vacation. Traveling. A wild night out with friends. A relationship breakup. The death of a loved one. A prolonged period of stress. It doesn't matter what the *something* is. The effect generally is the same. That diet? Gone. Not to be tried again.

Does any of this sound familiar to you? I call this response the panic-eat-panic-eat cycle. It's triggered not only by negative thinking but also by inaccurate thinking. Thoughts such as, "Now I've blown it. I might as well . . ." fuel dieting sabotage. The panic over eating one cookie leads to eating the whole box.

It doesn't have to be like this. You *can* break this cycle. I know because I've watched many of my clients do just that. I've even seen my mother do it.

Not long ago, at a regular checkup with my dad and his cardiologist, Mom and Dad learned that Dad needed four stents in one of his coronary arteries. This news sent Mom into a tailspin, worrying about what she would do if something happened to him. Later that day, she found herself in front of the refrigerator, staring inside and searching for comfort.

"I stood there looking and looking. I found a frozen bagel in the freezer, took it out, toasted it, and ate it. Then I ate another one. It wasn't about the bagel. If I could have run home to my mother, now, that would have been nice. I realized that eating wasn't going to solve anything, so I had a cup of coffee and then removed myself from the kitchen to go put things in perspective."

Yes, Mom fell off the wagon. She ate two bagels and had a cup of coffee. The important thing is that the next day she was back on the program. I considered this a turning point in Mom's struggles with emotional eating. She was getting in control of it—on her own. She was making a concerted effort to battle the "unconscious" stress-induced eating that has plagued her for years.

My relationship with food is definitely a response to the environment I grew up in. Raised in a house where food represented so many things—comfort, sustenance, celebration, and escape—I had to find my way with it all. I needed to discover that healthy balance. I chose the road of restraint and discipline. Not that I don't cheat every once in a while. I still love Mexican food and the occasional pecan pie. On Thanksgiving my cousin asked me how I could feel satisfied on just two bites of pecan pie. Having discipline requires a break in the cycle. Rather than panic-eat-panic-eat, I stop and think about what I am eating and/or drinking. By doing this, I end up enjoying the food, and I also give my brain a chance to kick in and remind me about what I am doing and what consequences it may have on my waist and overall wellness program. It's having the thought, "Do I really need to eat the whole thing?" before I eat rather than thinking, "I can't believe I ate the whole thing!" afterward. On Thanksgiving it meant putting the fork down after thoroughly enjoying two bites of pecan pie and saving myself the agony of a major stomachache.

Nearly all of my clients who have ridden the dieting roller coaster much of their lives told me that, in order to succeed on the Ultimate New York Diet, they had to break this panic-eat-panic-eat cycle. "I don't have to panic. I just go to the gym. I stop the negative tailspin and get back on track. I get on the treadmill or the rowing machine if I was really bad, and I'm done with it," says Sara Rotman, one of my clients.

This mind-set is so critical to your success, because there will be times when—for whatever reason, legitimate or not—you go off the plan. When

Sue Blake

I met Sue Blake more than a year ago. Reading and promoting my book gave her the motivation she needed to finally make healthful eating and exercise her top priority. In just over a year, she lost four dress sizes and 35 pounds. What started as a business relationship, I am proud to say, has turned into a lifelong friendship.

Q: **Why did you turn to the Ultimate New York Diet?**

A: After I read David's book, I realized I had had *enough* of being over-weight and unfit. At the time I was size 20 (and had some 22s for if I was going out to eat). I had recently returned from holiday, one that I went into fat and came back fatter.

Squeezing into a swimsuit (*not* a bikini) and feeling bloated and disappointed was enough to wake me up. David's program made total sense. He wasn't telling me to diet for diet's sake. I resonated with the mind, body, and spirit approach. To me, it said "self-empowerment." I began at the beginning in a quiet, low-key way, not telling a soul in case I failed. Footnote: a year on, I wore a bikini on holiday for the first time in more than 15 years.

Q: **How did your outlook on exercise change?**

A: I was the child who was allowed to forgo sports at school if I said I did not feel like it. I had never known how great exercise could feel. I also had used my asthma as an excuse not to exercise. I'd had enough of panting at the top of a flight of stairs, so I made myself think "can do" rather than "can't, so won't." For me the program represented an attitudinal change on every level. I used to think turning up at the gym was an achievement (it was!), and over time, with focused thoughts, I even accomplished the rowing machine from a basic level at two minutes to the top level at

you eat one of the A, B, C, D, E, or Fs or skip your workout, you need to be able to talk yourself through the self-blame, guilt, and fear—and get back on track. This goes for small indiscretions—such as a glass of wine—as well as large ones—such as a two-day binge.

an hour and a quarter within nine months. Needless to say, my asthma has improved enormously. As for the cardiosculpting, well, if you think you can't, then you likely won't. Once I learned how to do most of the exercises and got over the shaky wobbly stage, I was rocking. My body had never been in places like David's exercises took it.

Q: **Of what results are you most proud?**

A: Totally the fact that I have done it! This is life changing. The more I've worked out, the more energy I've gained. The better I eat, the more vibrant I feel. My eyes are brighter. My skin glows. I've lost all the cellulite off my bum, not to mention inches everywhere else, and, for the first time in a long time, I can see my toes. Just a few months into the program, I knew, just knew, that I would continue to treat myself better in every way, every day, and I have. I've been maintaining my results for more than nine months and lost more weight. My body shape has really changed.

I am who I am at last, and I'm proud of it. I am having the time of my life, and I am on the cusp of 45. If I knew a program like this existed, I'd have done it years ago. Don't get me wrong, this program was the hardest thing I have ever done, yet in some ways it was the easiest to achieve and stick with as the results were quick. Job done? Almost. I'll be at target weight by my next birthday.

SUE'S ADVICE FOR YOU: Don't wait a second longer to transform your life. Get real with yourself sooner rather than later if you really want to *live in* (not just have) a healthier body. Today is not a rehearsal for tomorrow, and life's challenges are *all* different when you feel better about yourself.

POSTSCRIPT: *Sue represents the majority of you out there who never found the time to devote to yourself. She has seen that by honoring herself and successfully completing this program, she is actually more present now for herself, her family, and her friends than she has ever been before.*

For example, while in phase 2 of the plan, Richard Jones went on a business trip. One night, alone in his hotel room, he opened his minibar and started eating. He sat up *all night* eating peanut butter cups, M&M's, and other sugar- and fat-packed candy bars. He ate everything in the bar.

For some people, such a binge would have been the end. They would have called it quits. The next morning, Richard was mad at himself and probably a little nauseated and "sugar stupid"—who wouldn't be?—but he recommitted himself to the program. "It was a bump in the road. I went on, and that's all it was. I didn't use it as an excuse to eat like that all the time."

To break the panic-eat-panic-eat cycle, follow these pointers:

- If you need to shed the guilt of eating, do so in a constructive way. Rather than feed your guilt with even more food, go to the gym and punish yourself with an hour on the treadmill, or do the longest cardiosculpting session of your life.
- See the forest through the trees. Too often, people equate a slipup with weight gain, which isn't necessarily the case. One night of martinis or pizza isn't going to undo all of your hard work. To prove this to yourself, get on the scale and see for yourself. Take your measurements. Try on that pair of unforgiving jeans. Assess the damage and move on.
- Own your choices. During every meal and snack, you have a choice. You can choose between a piece of grilled chicken and a piece of fried chicken. No one is holding a gun to your head telling you to eat the fried chicken. If you eat it, do it because you *choose* to eat it. Stop blaming your hectic schedule, mood, or spouse. This is about you. Do you choose health, or do you choose to be a victim?

Solve Problems Rather than Give In

Think back to your past attempts at weight loss. What triggers caused you to slip up? Think forward to what this plan requires. What in your life may make the plan difficult to achieve?

None of us has a perfect life. All of us are busy. We all struggle in our own way to create time to exercise and eat healthfully. To be successful on this plan, you must identify your personal unique challenges and take effective actions to overcome them. Following you'll find ways to do just that for some of the most common challenges to weight loss and wellness.

Sugar Stupidity

Food comas or rendering oneself "sugar stupid" often come after overindulging in sweets, carbs, or alcohol. The physical result is often a feeling of extreme lethargy and self-loathing. Your body is craving the carbs, as this is what you think will give you energy while you're mentally beating yourself up for failing yourself on the program. In reality, you need the exact opposite: lean protein. When you are feeling sugar stupid, try a protein shake and a good dose of exercise. Chances are, you'll snap out of it.

- **Find an outlet for eating.** My mom loves fresh bread and pastries. The smell brings her back to childhood, creating a sense of warmth and comfort. She can't eat these foods on the plan, so, for her, she does the next best thing. She window-shops. She'll take a power walk by some of the best French pastry shops in New York, look in the windows, and take a deep breath. This satisfies her enough that she doesn't feel tempted to go inside. Sue satisfied her yearning for coffee in those early months by simply smelling it sometimes. This isn't always going to work, but I have also used the "sniff" method when it comes to one of my favorite hot beverages—skim lattes with an extra shot of espresso.

- **Be prepared.** You never know when you'll be too busy to prepare a meal, so keep a stash of quick-and-easy healthful foods available to you at all times. Carry almonds, bottled water, and one of my Vitamin/Mineral Super Juice packets in your purse, or stash them in your desk. Stash other easy foods in your desk such as a can of tuna or salmon, protein powder, and broth-based soup. Virginia Gordon, who lost 10 pounds during her first two weeks on the plan, used to skip meals routinely. Now she carries almonds, water, and protein powder with her at all times. Because she likes her shakes well blended, she'll pop into a restaurant and ask them to blend the water and powder for her for a fee. She keeps three pounds of almonds in her kitchen at all times and puts them next to her purse along with bottled water at night so she can grab them in the morning on her way out the door.

- **Cut back on your TV and Internet time.** The television and Internet contribute to weight gain in three ways. First, they eat up time that could be spent preparing healthful foods or exercising. Second, they generally suck you into the couch or recliner, where you'll burn very few calories. Finally, they tend to encourage eating. It's no wonder a Harvard study linked watching 86 or more minutes of TV a day with an increased risk of obesity.
- **Find something to do with your hands during typical munching hours.** If you tend to eat after 7:00 P.M., knit, clean, or give yourself a manicure during that time.
- **Speak your truth.** If you are mad at someone, either tell them or get over it. Don't use it as an excuse to punish yourself further by eating. The same goes for feeling overwhelmed. Learn how to ask others for help rather than wallowing in stress and turning to food as a life vest. Put a voice to your anger, sadness, and other emotions rather than stuffing them down with food.

Think Long Term

I've said this so many times, but it bears repeating. The Ultimate New York Diet may include an eight-week Meal Plan, but it lasts the rest of your life. If you tend to think of diets as a short-term fix, I want you to change your thinking.

Everyone's personal makeup is slightly different. Your reasons for wanting to lose weight are different from someone else's. You are coming to the Ultimate New York Diet with different needs, challenges, emotions, and life circumstances. Not only will you change what you eat and how you exercise, you are going to change the rest of your life, too. Be ready for that. This isn't a diet. It's a life transformation.

You will be pleasantly surprised at the transformation that can and usually does take place. Your attitude about diet, exercise, and your overall wellness will be forever changed. Your relationship with food and your body will never be the same. I know these are very large claims, but after years of tweaking my program and seeing the most encouraging results with thousands of men and women all over the world, I say them with complete confidence.

By the time you finish this plan, you not only will look great, but you will also feel great. You'll be fit and healthy and have more energy. You'll also think more clearly and effectively. You'll have learned how to nurture yourself, stick up for yourself, and be yourself.

You'll also learn that exercise is not a chore or a punishment; rather, it's a way of honoring yourself. It's a reward. You'll learn that healthful eating isn't a prison sentence. Rather, it's a freeing experience.

After eight weeks, you'll look back and realize that, damn it, you worked hard. You'll have created an awesome sense of accomplishment. It's my sincere wish for you that you will—at eight weeks—look back at the person who started this plan and not recognize who that person was.

In navigating this plan for the rest of your life, you will backslide. You will experience setbacks, but you probably will never again slide all the way back into the shoes of the person who started this plan. If you keep picking yourself up, dusting yourself off, and recommitting yourself to success, each day, week, month, and year will lead you to a more effective, self-empowered you.

So, please, promise yourself that, once and for all, you are not going on a diet. Rather, you're going on a lifelong project. Call it Project You.

The Ultimate New York Meal Plan

Welcome to the Meal Plan, the part of the book that tells you what to eat day in and day out for the next eight weeks. The menus that you will find in the following pages put into practice everything you learned about eating when you read Chapter 2.

I've broken the following eight-week Meal Plan into three phases. You're about to embark on phase 1, the strictest phase of the plan. During phase 1, you will eat no foods from the A, B, C, D, E, and F list. In other words, no alcohol, no bread, no starchy carbs, no dairy, no extra sweet foods, and no fruit or excessive fat (the phase does allow a reasonable amount of healthful fat from almonds and olive oil).

Phase 1

In addition to serving as the strictest phase of the plan, phase 1 also serves as the rapid-weight-loss part of the plan. If you have a lot of weight to lose, you'll remain in phase 1 for longer than two weeks, until you reach your goal. If this is the case, you may pick and choose various days of this phase to follow. For example, if you loved the Turkey Chili, you might serve that up for dinner more often than another dish. The phase allows for that type of leeway. Just don't add any foods that you don't see listed, especially if they come from the A, B, C, D, E, and F list.

If you have more than 15 to 20 pounds to lose, you may find that you simply cannot stick to the confines of phase 1 for the length of time it will take to reach your goal. Don't beat yourself up over this. Guilt only leads to overeating. Instead, move on to phase 2 for a while, allowing yourself some more carbs for a few weeks, and then move back to phase 1 when you are ready. Some of my clients who had a lot of weight to lose split their weight-loss goal into miniphases, alternating between phases 1 and 2 of the plan until they reached their overall goal.

YOUR HOMEWORK

Before you embark on the Meal Plan, I'd like you to complete a few tasks that will help guarantee your success.

- **Look over the first week of the Meal Plan and the accompanying pantry list on page 167.** Go through your kitchen cabinets and refrigerator to see what items you already have on hand and which ones you'll need. Then head to the grocery store and stock up.
- **As you go through your cabinets and fridge during step one, do so while holding a large garbage bag.** Toss everything into the bag that doesn't fit into the confines of the plan—that means all the breakfast cereal, crackers, snack chips, ice cream, cheese, yogurt, bread, rice, pasta, fatty meats, fruit, and desserts. If you feel guilty about tossing out that much food, donate it all to a food bank or soup kitchen. You'll be much less tempted to eat chips and other A, B, C, D, E, and F foods if they aren't in your house.
- **Hard-boil a dozen eggs.** You'll find my recipe for the perfect hard-boiled egg on the following page.

Once you've completed those tasks, you're ready to start the plan. Good luck. I'll be waiting for a leaner, more focused you at phase 2.

PHASE 1 COOKING STRATEGIES

During phase 1, you will find yourself eating the following staples often: hard-boiled egg whites, steamed or sautéed vegetables, and mixed-greens salads. I recommend you hard-boil a dozen eggs at the beginning of every week, so you have them handy for snacks. Remember, this is a no-excuses meal plan. If you don't have time to prepare one of the suggested afternoon snacks, opt for a few hard-boiled egg whites or 10 raw almonds. If you don't have time to prepare a meal, opt for a protein shake. You always have healthy, quick, and easy choices.

Here you will find the advice you need for making New York Diet staples.

- **David's perfect hard-boiled egg.** Place the eggs in a saucepan and fill with enough cold water to cover the eggs. Place the uncovered saucepan on high heat (electric stove) or medium-high (gas). When the water starts to boil, turn off the heat, cover the pot, and leave the pan on the burner for eight minutes. Remove the pot from the stove, drain the water, and run the pot and eggs under cold water to cool the eggs and halt the cooking process. To peel, gently crack the eggs and then roll each one on a paper towel. The shell should peel right off, and you'll be left with a perfectly cooked egg. If you're like me and my friend Desiree, you'll prefer to eat the eggs while they are warm. (I hate them refrigerated.) Just sprinkle them with a little freshly ground black pepper, a pinch of salt, and, if you're living on the wild side, a touch of Dijon mustard. Eat only the whites. Toss the yolks, or, if you have a fit dog, then you can treat him with a yolk.
- **David's perfect mixed-greens salad.** You can use your creativity when making your salads. Try to mix at least two cups of leafy greens (they can be the prepacked, prewashed variety) with one cup of chopped veggies (such as cucumber, bell pepper, radishes, cauliflower, or broccoli). Items that cannot go into your salad include bacon bits, croutons, cheese, lunch meat, carrots, corn, and raisins. Top your salad with up to two tablespoons of my Red Wine Vinaigrette (see Index),

or create your own oil and vinegar mixture. Use only one teaspoon of oil on your salad.

- **David's perfect steamed or sautéed veggies.** You'll eat vegetable side dishes every night with dinner and sometimes for lunch as well. Usually you will steam your veggies. This is one of the best ways to cook veggies, as it helps to seal in the vegetables' natural taste and nutritional content and requires no added fat. To steam them, bring an inch or two of water to boil in a large pot over high heat. While you wait for the water to boil, wash, trim, and chop your veggies. Cut the veggies uniformly; this will ensure they cook evenly. Place a bamboo steamer rack over the pot and your veggies on the steamer rack. Steam for one to three minutes, checking them for doneness frequently. To sauté veggies, spray a nonstick skillet with olive oil cooking spray. Add a teaspoon of olive oil, and place the skillet over medium-high heat. Add one tablespoon of finely chopped garlic and sauté, stirring frequently until golden. Add the veggies to the pan. Sprinkle the veggies with freshly ground black pepper and half a teaspoon of crushed red pepper flakes (optional), and stir for approximately two minutes.

PHASE 1 APPROVED SNACK LIST

You'll find recipes for some of these snacks in Chapter 8. Because of the midmorning snack choices, the nutritional analysis that accompanies each day of the Meal Plan does not account for your morning snack. For the numbers people out there who want to figure out the overall nutritional stats for a given day, you need only add together the nutritional analysis of the snack you choose from this list to the day's nutritional analysis. For the rest of you, rest assured that whatever snack you choose from the approved list will fit nicely into the rest of the day's meals, enabling fast, lasting weight loss. Choose from the following options for your morning snack:

- One small can (about three ounces) chunk light tuna: 90 calories, 20 g protein, 0 g carbohydrate, 1 g fat, 0 g saturated fat, 0 g fiber, 0 g sugar
- One small can (about three ounces) wild salmon: 120 calories, 21 g protein, 0 g carbohydrate, 2 g fat, 0 g saturated fat, 0 g fiber, 0 g sugar

David's Phase 1 Pantry Items

Keep the following items on hand at all times. Purchase chicken, turkey, fish, and fresh herbs and vegetables as needed. If possible, buy organic meats, poultry, and produce.

Large container of raw almonds

Three dozen eggs

Box of protein powder

Salad greens

One bag of baby spinach

One head of broccoli

Container of cherry tomatoes

Low-sodium soy sauce

Two to three heads of garlic

Gingerroot

Thai chili paste

Extra-virgin olive oil

Red bell pepper

Dried oregano

Dried marjoram

Two containers each of all-natural
   chopped and stewed tomatoes

Nonfat, low-sodium chicken broth

Tabasco sauce

Nonfat vegetable cooking spray

Rice wine vinegar

Red wine vinegar

Sesame oil

Dijon mustard

Crushed red pepper flakes

Freshly ground black pepper

Five to seven scallions

Three to four cans chunk light tuna,
   packed in water

Three to four cans or bags of wild
   sockeye or red salmon

One can sun-dried tomatoes
   (not in oil)

- Two to three hard-boiled eggs (just the whites): 50 calories, 11 g protein, 1 g carbohydrate, 0 g fat, 0 g saturated fat, 0 g fiber, 0 g sugar
- 10 raw almonds: 70 calories, 3 g protein, 2 g carbohydrate, 6 g fat, 0 g saturated fat, 1 g fiber, 1 g sugar
- One Spicy Wasabi Salmon Burger (see Index): 205 calories, 28 g protein, 3 g carbohydrate, 9 g fat, 1 g saturated fat, 1 g fiber, 0 g sugar
- One Wild Salmon Burger (see Index): 179 calories, 26 g protein, 2 g carbohydrate, 7 g fat, 1 g saturated fat, 0 g fiber, 0 g sugar
- One Mexican Turkey Burger with Jalapeño Peppers and Mexican Salsa (see Index): 129 calories, 22 g protein, 7 g carbohydrate, 2 g fat, 0 g saturated fat, 2 g fiber, 3 g sugar

- One Salmon Cake (see Index): 183 calories, 26 g protein, 1 g carbohydrate, 7 g fat, 1 g saturated fat, 0 g fiber, 1 g sugar
- One serving Sesame Chicken Fingers (see Index): 195 calories, 26 g protein, 2 g carbohydrate, 8 g fat, 1 g saturated fat, 2 g fiber, 0 g sugar
- One serving David's Low-Fat Egg Salad (see Index): 91 calories, 14 g protein, 3 g carbohydrate, 2 g fat, 1 g saturated fat, 1 g fiber, 0 g sugar
- One serving Scrambled Egg Whites with Shiitake Mushrooms and Turkey Bacon (see Index): 130 calories, 16 g protein, 2 g carbohydrate, 6 g fat, 1 g saturated fat, 0 g fiber, 1 g sugar
- One serving Scrambled Egg Whites with Ground Turkey and Chopped Tomato (see Index): 92 calories, 18 g protein, 3 g carbohydrate, 1 g fat, 0 g saturated fat, .5 g fiber, 2 g sugar

PHASE 1 MENUS

Day 1

Breakfast: David's Protein (Meal-Replacement) Shake (either see Index for David's recipe, or see Chapter 3 for guidelines on choosing an appropriate shake)

Snack: selection from approved snack list

Lunch: Turkey Chili (see Index) with mixed-greens salad

Snack: 10 raw almonds

Dinner: protein shake *or* Herb-Crusted Turkey Breast (see Index) with steamed broccoli

Total: 805 calories, 104 g protein, 48 g carbohydrate, 23 g fat, 5 g saturated fat, 18 g fiber, 16 g sugar

Day 2

Breakfast: David's Protein (Meal-Replacement) Shake (either see Index for David's recipe, or see Chapter 3 for guidelines on choosing an appropriate shake)

Snack: selection from approved snack list

Lunch: Roasted Turkey Basil Salad (see Index)

Snack: Sesame Chicken Fingers (see Index)

Dinner: protein shake *or* Shrimp Marinara (see Index), one cup steamed spinach, and mixed-greens salad

Total: 925 calories, 141 g protein, 46 g carbohydrate, 19 g fat, 4 g saturated fat, 21 g fiber, 13 g sugar

Day 3

Breakfast: David's Protein (Meal-Replacement) Shake (either see Index for David's recipe, or see Chapter 3 for guidelines on choosing an appropriate shake)

Snack: selection from approved snack list

Lunch: Chopped Salad with Roasted Chicken, Tomatoes (see Index)

Snack: Wild Salmon Burger (see Index)

Dinner: protein shake *or* Southwestern Pepper Chicken (see Index), one cup steamed asparagus, and mixed-greens salad

Total: 866 calories, 117 g protein, 62 g carbohydrate, 17 g fat, 4 g saturated fat, 19 g fiber, 22 g sugar

Day 4

Breakfast: David's Protein (Meal-Replacement) Shake (either see Index for David's recipe, or see Chapter 3 for guidelines on choosing an appropriate shake)

Snack: selection from approved snack list

Lunch: Poached Chicken Breast (see Index), one cup steamed broccoli, and mixed-greens salad

Snack: David's Low-Fat Egg Salad (see Index)

Dinner: protein shake *or* Sun-Dried Tomato–Crusted Baked Halibut (see Index), Roasted Brussels Sprouts (see Index), and mixed-greens salad

Total: 947 calories, 140 g protein, 57 g carbohydrate, 17 g fat, 4 g saturated fat, 22 g fiber, 11 g sugar

Day 5

Breakfast: David's Protein (Meal-Replacement) Shake (either see Index for David's recipe, or see Chapter 3 for guidelines on choosing an appropriate shake)

Snack: selection from approved snack list

Lunch: Turkey Meat Loaf (see Index) with mixed-greens salad

Snack: 10 raw almonds

Dinner: protein shake *or* Horseradish-Encrusted Salmon (see Index), one cup sautéed bok choy, and mixed-greens salad

Total: 891 calories, 92 g protein, 49 g carbohydrate, 36 g fat, 7 g saturated fat, 17 g fiber, 20 g sugar

Day 6

Breakfast: David's Protein (Meal-Replacement) Shake (either see Index for David's recipe, or see Chapter 3 for guidelines on choosing an appropriate shake)

Snack: selection from approved snack list

Lunch: Chopped Salad with Roasted Chicken, Tomatoes (see Index)

Snack: Mexican Turkey Burger with Jalapeño Peppers and Mexican Salsa (see Index)

Dinner: protein shake *or* Spicy Wasabi Salmon Burger (see Index), one cup steamed spinach, and mixed-greens salad

Total: 813 calories, 112 g protein, 51 g carbohydrate, 20 g fat, 4 g saturated fat, 21 g fiber, 14 g sugar

Day 7

Breakfast: David's Protein (Meal-Replacement) Shake (either see Index for David's recipe, or see Chapter 3 for guidelines on choosing an appropriate shake)

Snack: selection from approved snack list

Lunch: Turkey Chili (see Index) with mixed-greens salad

Snack: two to three hard-boiled egg whites

Dinner: protein shake *or* Sesame Chicken Fingers (see Index), Asian Broccoli Stir-Fry (see Index), and mixed-greens salad

Total: 829 calories, 96 g protein, 57 g carbohydrate, 23 g fat, 6 g saturated fat, 22 g fiber, 19 g sugar

Day 8

Breakfast: David's Protein (Meal-Replacement) Shake (either see Index for David's recipe, or see Chapter 3 for guidelines on choosing an appropriate shake)

Snack: selection from approved snack list

Lunch: Turkey Meat Loaf (see Index) with mixed-greens salad

Snack: 10 raw almonds

Dinner: protein shake *or* Branzino (Sea Bass) Puttanesca (see Index) with Roasted Vegetable Caponata (see Index)

Total: 894 calories, 90 g protein, 63 g carbohydrate, 28 g fat, 6 g saturated fat, 18 g fiber, 29 g sugar

Day 9

Breakfast: David's Protein (Meal-Replacement) Shake (either see Index for David's recipe, or see Chapter 3 for guidelines on choosing an appropriate shake)

Snack: selection from approved snack list

Lunch: Poached Chicken Breast (see Index), one cup steamed broccoli, and mixed-greens salad

Snack: David's Low-Fat Egg Salad (see Index)

Dinner: protein shake *or* Herb-Crusted Turkey Breast (see Index), Cauliflower Hash (see Index), and mixed-greens salad

Total: 966 calories, 149 g protein, 57 g carbohydrate, 15 g fat, 5 g saturated fat, 21 g fiber, 13 g sugar

Day 10

Breakfast: David's Protein (Meal-Replacement) Shake (either see Index for David's recipe, or see Chapter 3 for guidelines on choosing an appropriate shake)

Snack: selection from approved snack list

Lunch: Roasted Turkey Basil Salad (see Index)

Snack: 10 raw almonds

Dinner: protein shake *or* Southwestern Pepper Chicken (see Index), one cup steamed asparagus, and mixed-greens salad

Total: 819 calories, 118 g protein, 56 g carbohydrate, 14 g fat, 2 g saturated fat, 19 g fiber, 20 g sugar

Day 11

Breakfast: David's Protein (Meal-Replacement) Shake (either see Index for David's recipe, or see Chapter 3 for guidelines on choosing an appropriate shake)

Snack: selection from approved snack list

Lunch: Chopped Salad with Salmon (see Index)

Snack: Mexican Turkey Burger with Jalapeño Peppers and Mexican Salsa (see Index)

Dinner: protein shake *or* Asian Pepper Chicken (see Index), Cauliflower Mushroom Mash (see Index), and mixed-greens salad

Total: 852 calories, 115 g protein, 57 g carbohydrate, 20 g fat, 3 g saturated fat, 22 g fiber, 19 g sugar

Day 12

Breakfast: David's Protein (Meal-Replacement) Shake (either see Index for David's recipe, or see Chapter 3 for guidelines on choosing an appropriate shake)

Snack: selection from approved snack list

Lunch: Turkey Meat Loaf (see Index) with mixed-greens salad

Snack: David's Low-Fat Egg Salad (see Index)

Dinner: protein shake *or* Sesame-Encrusted Tuna (see Index), one cup steamed asparagus, and mixed-greens salad

Total: 955 calories, 115 g protein, 61 g carbohydrate, 27 g fat, 7 g saturated fat, 19 g fiber, 22 g sugar

Day 13

Breakfast: David's Protein (Meal-Replacement) Shake (either see Index for David's recipe, or see Chapter 3 for guidelines on choosing an appropriate shake)

Snack: selection from approved snack list

Lunch: Turkey Chili (see Index) with mixed-greens salad

Snack: 10 raw almonds

Dinner: protein shake *or* Asian Pepper Chicken (see Index) with Asian Broccoli Stir-Fry (see Index)

Total: 814 calories, 95 g protein, 53 g carbohydrate, 25 g fat, 6 g saturated fat, 19 g fiber, 19 g sugar

Day 14

Breakfast: David's Protein (Meal-Replacement) Shake (either see Index for David's recipe, or see Chapter 3 for guidelines on choosing an appropriate shake)

Snack: selection from approved snack list

Lunch: Shiitake Chicken Paillard (see Index) with mixed-greens salad

Snack: Wild Salmon Burger

Dinner: protein shake *or* Turkey Meat Loaf (see Index), one cup steamed broccoli, and mixed-greens salad

Total: 973 calories, 122 g protein, 63 g carbohydrate, 26 g fat, 7 g saturated fat, 20 g fiber, 18 g sugar

Phase 2

Congratulations on finishing phase 1 of the plan. Whether your phase 1 spanned two weeks, two months, or much longer, you've pushed yourself to your limits and beyond. You've endured, overcoming inertia, laziness, fatigue, cravings, and addictions. By putting yourself first, prioritizing your life, and staying on track, you've taught yourself skills that will carry over into many other aspects of your life. I'm proud of you, and I hope you are, too. There's no better feeling than the feeling of accomplishment.

During phase 2, you will add back one daily carbohydrate serving. That's it. So, don't expect to make any trips to Krispy Kreme, Cold Stone Creamery, or Pasta Bella during the next two weeks. You'll eat your carbohydrate during either your midmorning snack or lunch, when your body is most receptive to using and burning carbs for energy. As with phase 1, you may choose your midmorning snack from the approved snack list. Although I still recommend a shake for breakfast during phase 2, I provide a little more leeway during this phase. The basic protein shake is optimal, but if you prefer, you can try one of two additional shake recipes that I've suggested. You can also use an expanded variety of salad dressings. Just consult the Sauces, Dips, and Dressings section under Phases 2 and 3 Recipes in Chapter 8 for options.

During the next two weeks, you can expect to lose even more weight—albeit more slowly. This middle phase of the plan will help you to cement everything you learned during phase 1 into your life in a permanent way. By now, your cravings for certain foods probably have already diminished (well, mostly anyway). Whereas, during week one you may have told yourself, "As soon as this program is over, I'm going to stuff myself silly with X, Y, and Z," you may now think to yourself, "I don't want to reverse everything I've worked so hard to achieve. Plus, X, Y, and Z don't seem too interesting to me anymore." In fact, one of my clients, Nina, recently was moaning while sweating out a glass of cabernet from the previous evening that before she did this program, she was able to have several glasses of red wine in the evening to no great effect. Now, after the program's completion, she can barely finish one glass without feeling its effects immediately after and the following morning. She actually dumped most of the second glass of this very good wine down the drain.

If you haven't gotten to that point just yet, don't worry. Soon you will, and you'll find yourself wonderfully liberated from the cravings that have held you prisoner to overeating and excess fat during your life. At this point also, you will have a greater understanding of how your body works and responds to "cheating." A bag of chips, a glass of wine, or a burger shouldn't throw you into a tailspin; rather, you will have the knowledge and the confidence to pick yourself up, dust off, and get back on your personal wellness track. This shift doesn't happen all at once, and it takes place on a slightly different time line for each individual, but I can tell you that, if you stick with me and give this plan everything you have, it will happen. So, promise me and promise yourself that you will tackle phase 2 with the same zeal, willpower, and confidence that you did phase 1. You'll be amazed by how well you're able to maintain your results and, as is often the case, improve upon them.

Good luck on the plan, and I'll see you in phase 3!

PHASE 2 APPROVED SNACK LIST
Choose from these morning snacks during phase 2.

- One small can (about 3 ounces) chunk light tuna: 90 calories, 20 g protein, 0 g carbohydrate, 1 g fat, 0 g saturated fat, 0 g fiber, 0 g sugar
- One small can (about 3 ounces) wild salmon: 120 calories, 21 g protein, 0 g carbohydrate, 2 g fat, 0 g saturated fat, 0 g fiber, 0 g sugar
- Two to three hard-boiled eggs (just the whites): 50 calories, 11 g protein, 1 g carbohydrate, 0 g fat, 0 g saturated fat, 0 g fiber, 0 g sugar
- 10 raw almonds: 70 calories, 3 g protein, 2 g carbohydrate, 6 g fat, 0 g saturated fat, 1 g fiber, 1 g sugar
- One Spicy Wasabi Salmon Burger (see Index): 205 calories, 28 g protein, 3 g carbohydrate, 9 g fat, 1 g saturated fat, 1 g fiber, 0 g sugar
- One Wild Salmon Burger (see Index): 179 calories, 26 g protein, 2 g carbohydrate, 7 g fat, 1 g saturated fat, 0 g fiber, 0 g sugar
- One Mexican Turkey Burger with Jalapeño Peppers and Mexican Salsa (see Index): 129 calories, 22 g protein, 7 g carbohydrate, 2 g fat, 0 g saturated fat, 2 g fiber, 3 g sugar
- One Salmon Cake (see Index): 183 calories, 26 g protein, 1 g carbohydrate, 7 g fat, 1 g saturated fat, 0 g fiber, 1 g sugar

David's Phase 2 Pantry Items

Large container of raw almonds

Three dozen eggs

Box of protein powder

Salad greens

One bag of baby spinach

One head of broccoli

Container of cherry tomatoes

One to two limes

Low-sodium soy sauce

Head of garlic

Gingerroot

Thai chili paste

Extra-virgin olive oil

Red bell pepper

Dried oregano

Dried marjoram

Two containers each of all-natural
    chopped and stewed tomatoes

One can chickpeas

One can kidney beans

Nonfat, low-sodium chicken broth

Tabasco sauce

Olive oil nonfat cooking spray

Rice wine vinegar

Sesame oil

Dijon mustard

Crushed red pepper flakes

Freshly ground black pepper

Five to seven scallions

Three to four cans chunk light tuna,
    packed in water

Three to four cans or bags of wild
    sockeye or red salmon

One can sun-dried tomatoes
    (not in oil)

Quinoa

Lentils

Steel-cut, slow-cooking oatmeal

Cinnamon

Two to three sweet potatoes

Salsa

- One serving Sesame Chicken Fingers (see Index): 195 calories, 26 g protein, 2 g carbohydrate, 8 g fat, 1 g saturated fat, 2 g fiber, 0 g sugar
- One serving David's Low-Fat Egg Salad (see Index): 91 calories, 14 g protein, 3 g carbohydrate, 2 g fat, 1 g saturated fat, 1 g fiber, 0 g sugar
- One serving Scrambled Egg Whites with Shiitake Mushrooms and Turkey Bacon (see Index): 130 calories, 16 g protein, 2 g carbohydrate, 6 g fat, 1 g saturated fat, 0 g fiber, 1 g sugar
- One serving Scrambled Egg Whites with Ground Turkey and Chopped Tomato (see Index): 92 calories, 18 g protein, 3 g carbohydrate, 1 g fat, 0 g saturated fat, .5 g fiber, 2 g sugar

- Frittata with Broccoli Rabe, Sun-Dried Tomatoes, and Parmesan (see Index): 151 calories, 16 g protein, 7 g carbohydrate, 7 g fat, 3 g saturated fat, 1 g fiber, 2 g sugar
- Turkey Bacon, Spinach, and Egg White Frittata (see Index): 72 calories, 10 g protein, 2 g carbohydrate, 3 g fat, 1 g saturated fat, 0 g fiber, 1 g sugar
- Turkey Bacon, Sweet Potato, and Green Onion Frittata (see Index): 96 calories, 9 g protein, 9 g carbohydrate, 2 g fat, 1 g saturated fat, 2 g fiber, 4 g sugar
- One serving Tuna Salad with Whole-Grain Mustard and Water Chestnuts (see Index): 113 calories, 22 g protein, 3 g carbohydrate, 1 g fat, 0 g saturated fat, 1 g fiber, 1 g sugar

PHASE 2 MENUS

Day 15

Breakfast: David's Energy Boost, David's Protein (Meal-Replacement) Shake, *or* Breakfast Shake (either see Index for David's recipes, or see Chapter 3 for guidelines on choosing an appropriate shake)

Snack: selection from approved snack list

Lunch: Grilled Chicken and Bean Salad (see Index) with mixed-greens salad

Snack: 10 raw almonds

Dinner: Sun-Dried Tomato–Crusted Baked Halibut (see Index), one cup steamed broccoli, and mixed-greens salad

Total: 907 calories, 105 g protein, 79 g carbohydrate, 18 g fat, 4 g saturated fat, 27 g fiber, 21 g sugar

Day 16

Breakfast: David's Energy Boost, David's Protein (Meal-Replacement) Shake, *or* Breakfast Shake (either see Index for David's recipes, or see Chapter 3 for guidelines on choosing an appropriate shake)

Snack: selection from approved snack list

Lunch: Tuna and Quinoa Salad (see Index)

Snack: Mexican Turkey Burger with Jalapeño Peppers and Mexican Salsa (see Index)

Dinner: Turkey Meat Loaf (see Index), mixed-greens salad, and one cup sautéed spinach

Total: 962 calories, 104 g protein, 64 g carbohydrate, 34 g fat, 6 g saturated fat, 20 g fiber, 18 g sugar

Day 17

Breakfast: David's Energy Boost, David's Protein (Meal-Replacement) Shake, *or* Breakfast Shake (either see Index for David's recipes, or see Chapter 3 for guidelines on choosing an appropriate shake)

Snack: selection from approved snack list

Lunch: Almond Lentil Loaf (see Index) with mixed-greens salad

Snack: Tuna Salad with Whole-Grain Mustard and Water Chestnuts (see Index)

Dinner: Herb-Crusted Turkey Breast (see Index), Cauliflower Hash (see Index), and mixed-greens salad

Total: 914 calories, 116 g protein, 74 g carbohydrate, 17 g fat, 3 g saturated fat, 23 g fiber, 17 g sugar

Day 18

Breakfast: David's Energy Boost, David's Protein (Meal-Replacement) Shake, *or* Breakfast Shake (either see Index for David's recipes, or see Chapter 3 for guidelines on choosing an appropriate shake)

Snack: selection from approved snack list

Lunch: Leftover Almond Lentil Loaf (see Index) with mixed-greens salad

Snack: Wild Salmon Burger (see Index)

Dinner: Guiltless Barbecue Burger (see Index) with Cauliflower Mushroom Mash (see Index)

Total: 913 calories, 106 g protein, 70 g carbohydrate, 25 g fat, 5 g saturated fat, 22 g fiber, 18 g sugar

Day 19

Breakfast: David's Energy Boost, David's Protein (Meal-Replacement) Shake, *or* Breakfast Shake (either see Index for David's recipes, or see Chapter 3 for guidelines on choosing an appropriate shake)

Snack: selection from approved snack list

Lunch: Red Peppers Stuffed with Quinoa (see Index) and mixed-greens salad

Snack: Sesame Chicken Fingers (see Index)

Dinner: Ginger-Glazed Halibut (see Index) with Asian Broccoli Stir-Fry (see Index) and mixed-greens salad

Total: 870 calories, 92 g protein, 84 g carbohydrate, 19 g fat, 3 g saturated fat, 25 g fiber, 29 g sugar

Day 20

Breakfast: David Kirsch's Power Pancakes (see Index)

Snack: selection from approved snack list

Lunch: Turkey Chili (see Index) with mixed-greens salad

Snack: David's Low-Fat Egg Salad (see Index)

Dinner: Thai Shrimp Sauté (see Index) with one cup steamed broccoli and mixed-greens salad

Total: 916 calories, 102 g protein, 77 g carbohydrate, 25 g fat, 10 g saturated fat, 23 g fiber, 23 g sugar

Day 21

Breakfast: Frittata with Broccoli Rabe, Sun-Dried Tomatoes, and Parmesan (see Index)

Snack: selection from approved snack list

Lunch: Baked Falafel with Yogurt-Mint Dressing (see Index) with mixed-greens salad

Snack: 10 raw almonds

Dinner: Chicken Satay (see Index) with one cup sautéed spinach and mixed-greens salad

Total: 976 calories, 93 g protein, 77 g carbohydrate, 33 g fat, 6 g saturated fat, 28 g fiber, 23 g sugar

Day 22

Breakfast: David's Energy Boost, David's Protein (Meal-Replacement) Shake, *or* Breakfast Shake (either see Index for David's recipes, or see Chapter 3 for guidelines on choosing an appropriate shake)

Snack: selection from approved snack list

Lunch: Leftover Baked Falafel with Yogurt-Mint Dressing (see Index) over mixed greens

Snack: Tuna Salad with Whole-Grain Mustard and Water Chestnuts (see Index)

Dinner: Shiitake Chicken Paillard (see Index) with one cup steamed broccoli and mixed-greens salad

Total: 914 calories, 112 g protein, 92 g carbohydrate, 14 g fat, 3 g saturated fat, 31 g fiber, 22 g sugar

Day 23
——

Breakfast: David's Energy Boost, David's Protein (Meal-Replacement) Shake, *or* Breakfast Shake (either see Index for David's recipes, or see Chapter 3 for guidelines on choosing an appropriate shake)

Snack: selection from approved snack list

Lunch: Shrimp and Whole Wheat Pasta with Arugula Dressing (see Index) with mixed-greens salad

Snack: Sesame Chicken Fingers (see Index)

Dinner: Herb-Crusted Turkey Breast (see Index) with one cup sautéed spinach and mixed-greens salad

Total: 1,006 calories, 129 g protein, 73 g carbohydrate, 22 g fat, 3 g saturated fat, 26 g fiber, 14 g sugar

Day 24
——

Breakfast: David's Energy Boost, David's Protein (Meal-Replacement) Shake, *or* Breakfast Shake (either see Index for David's recipes, or see Chapter 3 for guidelines on choosing an appropriate shake)

Snack: selection from approved snack list

Lunch: Turkey Chili (see Index) with mixed-greens salad

Snack: Spicy Wasabi Salmon Burger (see Index)

Dinner: Asian Pepper Chicken (see Index) with Asian Broccoli Stir-Fry (see Index)

Total: 958 calories, 120 g protein, 56 g carbohydrate, 28 g fat, 7 g saturated fat, 20 g fiber, 19 g sugar

Day 25
——

Breakfast: David's Energy Boost, David's Protein (Meal-Replacement) Shake, *or* Breakfast Shake (either see Index for David's recipes, or see Chapter 3 for guidelines on choosing an appropriate shake)

Snack: selection from approved snack list

Lunch: Tuna and Quinoa Salad (see Index) and one cup steamed broccoli

Snack: 10 raw almonds

Dinner: Guiltless Barbecue Burger (see Index), Cauliflower Hash (see Index), and mixed-greens salad

Total: 869 calories, 96 g protein, 69 g carbohydrate, 26 g fat, 4 g saturated fat, 20 g fiber, 16 g sugar

Day 26

Breakfast: David's Energy Boost, David's Protein (Meal-Replacement) Shake, *or* Breakfast Shake (either see Index for David's recipes, or see Chapter 3 for guidelines on choosing an appropriate shake)

Snack: selection from approved snack list

Lunch: Grilled Chicken and Bean Salad (see Index)

Snack: Mexican Turkey Burger with Jalapeño Peppers and Mexican Salsa (see Index)

Dinner: Branzino (Sea Bass) Puttanesca (see Index), mixed-greens salad, and Roasted Vegetable Caponata (see Index)

Total: 1,021 calories, 117 g protein, 90 g carbohydrate, 17 g fat, 6 g saturated fat, 26 g fiber, 32 g sugar

Day 27

Breakfast: David Kirsch's Power Pancakes (see Index)

Snack: selection from approved snack list

Lunch: Poached Chicken Breast (see Index), one cup steamed broccoli, and mixed-greens salad

Snack: David's Low-Fat Egg Salad (see Index)

Dinner: Turkey Meat Loaf (see Index) with mixed-greens salad and Cauliflower Hash (see Index)

Total: 1,006 calories, 129 g protein, 74 g carbohydrate, 22 g fat, 10 g saturated fat, 20 g fiber, 22 g sugar

Day 28

Breakfast: Turkey Bacon, Spinach, and Egg White Frittata (see Index)

Snack: selection from approved snack list

Lunch: Almond Lentil Loaf (see Index), mixed-greens salad, and Cauliflower Mushroom Mash (see Index)

Snack: 10 raw almonds

Dinner: Herb-Crusted Turkey Breast (see Index), Roasted Brussels Sprouts (see Index), and mixed-greens salad

Total: 819 calories, 87 g protein, 74 g carbohydrate, 22 g fat, 2 g saturated fat, 24 g fiber, 23 g sugar

Phase 3

Welcome to phase 3 of the Meal Plan, to what I like to call the "rest-of-your-life" phase. Throughout the following pages, you'll find four weeks' worth of meal plans to guide you in your wellness journey. Think of these meal plans as a blueprint, an optimal plan that you can either follow verbatim or tweak as needed to make it work for your lifestyle, food preferences, and tastes.

Just as you must continue to exercise to maintain your results, you also must continue to eat well. Although phase 3 of the Ultimate New York Diet is not as strict as phases 1 and 2, you will still abide by your A, B, C, D, E, and F dietary rules most of the time. The meal plans that span the next four weeks will show you how to work one or two of the A, B, C, D, E, and Fs back into your diet without gaining weight. The process may take a bit of experimentation to see exactly what you can add back in—and what you can't.

Unfortunately, not all bodies are created equally, and some people can cheat more than others without seeing the results line their thighs, butt, or abdomen. Some unlucky few can barely cheat at all. So be careful and monitor your clothing fit as you embark on phase 3. Eventually, eating according to the Ultimate New York Diet will become a way of life and you'll maintain your weight loss without thinking about it.

HOW PHASE 3 WORKS

During phase 3, you'll eat the same number of meals and snacks as you did during phases 1 and 2, except you'll be adding a second serving from your A, B, C, D, E, and F list as well as a once-a-week cheat meal. You may follow the Meal Plan verbatim or create your own meals by using this formula.

- **Breakfast.** On most days, I recommend a protein shake, either the standard shake or one of the variations that includes berries or dairy. On weekends, when you have more time to prepare breakfast, consider having a wholesome, high-fiber carbohydrate choice such as slow-cooking oats or my pancake recipe. Just remember that this will count as one of your A, B, C, D, E, and F options. If you'd like to splurge later in the day with a cheat meal or night out on the town, then choose a protein-packed breakfast of scrambled egg whites or one of my egg white frittata recipes.

- **Morning snack.** Optimally, you want to eat your carbs before 2:00 P.M., so morning snack is a great time to indulge if you are feeling a craving for something crunchy. Again, if you plan on eating carbs (or having another A, B, C, D, E, or F later in the day), then opt for one of the "Optimal" snack choices on the list on pages 185–186. If you want to use one of your two A, B, C, D, E, or F options, however, then choose a carbohydrate snack off that list.

- **Lunch.** Most of the time, I recommend you continue to combine a source of lean protein (such as six ounces of salmon, tuna, or chicken or turkey breast) along with a hearty serving of your favorite steamed vegetable and/or mixed-greens salad. Again, this is the optimal time to work in a healthful carbohydrate such as quinoa, sweet potato, lentils, or something else. I'd much prefer you had your carbs for lunch than for dinner.

- **Midafternoon snack.** Keep it simple and healthy. Choose from the "Optimal" section of your snack list.

- **Dinner.** Stick to the same lean protein and veggie formula you used for lunch. Once a week, you may substitute a cheat meal for dinner. You'll find some of my favorite cheat meal options on page 190. If you have a glass of wine or beer with dinner, count that as one of your A, B, C, D, E, or Fs for the day, meaning you should have eaten only one other item from that list earlier in the day. If dinner is your cheat meal, try to eat as cleanly as possible throughout the day, having nothing from the A, B, C, D, E, and F list.

IT'S ALL ABOUT CHOICES

As you add foods back in, start with the healthiest A, B, C, D, E, and Fs first, the ones that are least likely to spike your blood sugar and send you on a binge. The more your food resembles something that grows in nature (comes from a natural source), the better. Whenever you sit down to a meal or snack, ask yourself whether you are making the best choice. Often, just a simple switch can make all the difference in your health, energy level, and waistline. Following you will find simple switches that yield an incredible amount of nutrition for minimal sacrifice.

- Switching from instant oatmeal to old-fashioned, slow-cooking oats (such as McCann's Steel Cut Irish Oatmeal) yields a higher percentage of hard, compact starch granules and fiber. The compact starch granules are harder for the body to break down, which slows the digestive process and keeps you feeling satisfied for a longer period of time. In contrast, the starch in instant oats has been presoftened, speeding digestion.
- Switching from white bread to 100 percent whole wheat bread yields more fiber to slow digestion and even blood sugar. Taken a step further, switching from whole wheat bread to stone-ground whole wheat again yields bread that contains coarser starch granules that are difficult for the body to break down and digest.
- Switching from a plain mixed-greens salad to a salad with tomatoes creates a slightly acidic environment to slow digestion and lengthen your staying power.
- Switching from a crunchy snack of plain pretzels to a sliced apple with almond butter provides your body with vitamins and minerals it needs for optimal health as well as monounsaturated fat to slow digestion and promote satiety.
- Switching from instant rice to basmati rice yields more compact starch granules that are difficult for your body to digest. Switching to brown rice provides fiber to slow digestion and steady blood sugar levels. Brown rice contains 3.5 grams of fiber for every .6 fiber grams in white rice.

I could go on and on, but I think those examples help to paint a picture of optimal food choices. The coarser, less processed, and more wholesome the food, the better. For even more direction in making the right choices, consult the following A, B, C, D, E, and F pointers.

- **Alcohol.** Alcohol is one of the trickiest foods to reintroduce to your diet (just ask my friends Nina and Sam). If you stuck to phases 1 and 2 religiously, then your body is now like a clean, dry sponge. When you drink alcohol—any alcohol—your body will soak it up like a sponge. You'll find that you feel bloated and your skin is puffy soon after drinking. That's why I suggest you stick with red wine. Red wine contains a number of nutrients that are good for your heart. It also has a rich flavor, which encourages you to drink it slowly. Finally, it contains many fewer calories and carbs than other types of alcohol. (For more tips on alcohol choices, see Chapter 9.)

- **Bread.** I have nothing good to say about bread. Even whole-grain bread often contains quite a bit of white flour. Reserve bread for your cheat meal, and, even then, minimize it as much as possible. For example, if ordering pizza, order a thin crust. When having a sandwich, order it open-faced with just one slice of bread. When eating out, choose just one piece of bread from the basket and then send the basket away. Sourdough bread and whole-grain bread will break down somewhat more slowly than other varieties, making them slightly better choices.

- **Starchy carbs.** Stick to whole-grain varieties such as quinoa, lentils, beans, brown rice, and slow-cooking oatmeal.

- **Dairy.** Choose organic low- and nonfat versions of milk and yogurt. Use these mostly in recipes rather than as true meal servings. For example, use plain nonfat yogurt in place of mayo. Stay away from cups of flavored yogurt, which are two banned foods in one because they contain so much sugar. The same goes for chocolate milk. Although chocolate milk is a big no-no, there are certain brands of cocoa mix that are unsweetened and taste rather delicious. Two of my favorite brands of cocoa are Ghirardelli and Droste.

- **Extra sweets.** There's no such thing as a good sweet. Reserve these for your cheat day.

- **Fruit and fat.** Choose the lower-carb and -calorie varieties of fruit such as blueberries, strawberries, cantaloupe, kiwi, apples, and pears. Stay away from sweet, tropical fruits such as papaya, mango, and pineapple. As for fats, stick to the type in oily fish such as wild salmon, nuts, avocados, and olive oil. Raw almonds, walnuts, and organic raw peanuts are all healthy choices. The fat in flaxseeds and flax oil is also very good for you.

DAVID'S APPROVED SNACK LIST

Choose from these options for your morning snack. Whenever possible, try to choose from the "Optimal" section of the list. Count any choices from the "Still Healthy" section as one of your A, B, C, D, E, and Fs for the day. Limit yourself to the "To Satisfy Your Craving" category just once or twice a week.

Optimal

- One small can chunk light tuna: 90 calories, 20 g protein, 0 g carbohydrate, 1 g fat, 0 g saturated fat, 0 g fiber, 0 g sugar
- One small can wild salmon: 120 calories, 21 g protein, 0 g carbohydrate, 2 g fat, 0 g saturated fat, 0 g fiber, 0 g sugar
- Two to three hard-boiled eggs (just the whites): 50 calories, 11 g protein, 1 g carbohydrate, 0 g fat, 0 g saturated fat, 0 g fiber, 0 g sugar for 3 egg whites
- 10 raw almonds: 70 calories, 3 g protein, 2 g carbohydrate, 6 g fat, 0 g saturated fat, 1 g fiber, 1 g sugar
- One Spicy Wasabi Salmon Burger (see Index): 205 calories, 28 g protein, 3 g carbohydrate, 9 g fat, 1 g saturated fat, 1 g fiber, 0 g sugar
- One Mexican Turkey Burger with Jalapeño Peppers and Mexican Salsa (see Index): 129 calories, 22 g protein, 7 g carbohydrate, 2 g fat, 0 g saturated fat, 2 g fiber, 3 g sugar
- One serving Salmon Cakes (see Index): 183 calories, 26 g protein, 1 g carbohydrate, 7 g fat, 1 g saturated fat, 0 g fiber, 1 g sugar
- One Wild Salmon Burger (see Index): 179 calories, 26 g protein, 2 g carbohydrate, 7 g fat, 1 g saturated fat, 0 g fiber, 0 g sugar
- One serving Sesame Chicken Fingers (see Index): 195 calories, 26 g protein, 2 g carbohydrate, 8 g fat, 1 g saturated fat, 2 g fiber, 0 g sugar

- One serving David's Low-Fat Egg Salad (see Index): 91 calories, 14 g protein, 3 g carbohydrate, 2 g fat, 1 g saturated fat, 1 g fiber, 0 g sugar
- One serving Scrambled Egg Whites with Shiitake Mushrooms and Turkey Bacon (see Index): 130 calories, 16 g protein, 2 g carbohydrate, 6 g fat, 1 g saturated fat, 0 g fiber, 1 g sugar
- One serving Scrambled Egg Whites with Ground Turkey and Chopped Tomato (see Index): 92 calories, 18 g protein, 3 g carbohydrate, 1 g fat, 0 g saturated fat, .5 g fiber, 2 g sugar
- Frittata with Broccoli Rabe, Sun-Dried Tomatoes, and Parmesan (see Index): 151 calories, 16 g protein, 7 g carbohydrate, 7 g fat, 3 g saturated fat, 1 g fiber, 2 g sugar
- Turkey Bacon, Spinach, and Egg White Frittata (see Index): 72 calories, 10 g protein, 2 g carbohydrate, 3 g fat, 1 g saturated fat, 0 g fiber, 1 g sugar
- Turkey Bacon, Sweet Potato, and Green Onion Frittata (see Index): 96 calories, 9 g protein, 9 g carbohydrate, 2 g fat, 1 g saturated fat, 2 g fiber, 4 g sugar
- One serving Tuna Salad with Whole-Grain Mustard and Water Chestnuts (see Index): 113 calories, 22 g protein, 3 g carbohydrate, 1 g fat, 0 g saturated fat, 1 g fiber, 1 g sugar

Still Healthy

- One-quarter cup of any type of nuts or seeds (such as pumpkin seeds): 187 calories, 8 g protein, 6 g carbohydrate, 16 g fat, 3 g saturated fat, 1 g fiber, 0 g sugar
- One-half cup edamame in the shell, lightly salted: 100 calories, 8 g protein, 9 g carbohydrate, 3 g fat, 0 g saturated fat, 4 g fiber, 1 g sugar
- One celery stick with one tablespoon almond butter (preferred) or natural peanut butter: 109 calories, 3 g protein, 6 g carbohydrate, 9 g fat, 1 g saturated fat, 2 g fiber, 1 g sugar
- One celery stalk stuffed with one-half cup No-Fat Hummus (see Index): 124 calories, 7 g protein, 23 g carbohydrate, 2 g fat, 0 g saturated fat, 6 g fiber, 3 g sugar
- One orange: 80 calories, 1 g protein, 21 g carbohydrate, 0 g fat, 0 g saturated fat, 7 g fiber, 14 g sugar

- One apple: 80 calories, 0 g protein, 22 g carbohydrate, 0 g fat, 0 g saturated fat, 5 g fiber, 16 g sugar
- One-half cup mixed berries: 35 calories, .5 g protein, 8 g carbohydrate, 0 g fat, 0 g saturated fat, 2 g fiber, 5 g sugar
- Half an apple, sliced and smeared with one tablespoon almond butter (preferred) or natural peanut butter: 140 calories, 2 g protein, 14 g carbohydrate, 9 g fat, 1 g saturated fat, 4 g fiber, 9 g sugar
- One-quarter cup nonfat cottage cheese mixed with one-quarter cup mixed berries: 58 calories, 7 g protein, 7 g carbohydrate, 0 g fat, 0 g saturated fat, 1 g fiber, 5 g sugar
- One small (four ounces) microwaved sweet potato with skin: 103 calories, 2 g protein, 24 g carbohydrate, 0 g fat, 0 g saturated fat, 4 g fiber, 10 g sugar
- Five Kashi TLC 7 Grain crackers dipped in one-half cup No-Fat Hummus (see Index): 157 calories, 7 g protein, 27 g carbohydrate, 3 g fat, 0 g saturated fat, 6 g fiber, 3 g sugar
- Five Kashi TLC 7 Grain crackers dipped in one-quarter cup (four tablespoons) Roasted Red Pepper and Almond Dip (see Index): 146 calories, 4 g protein, 12 g carbohydrate, 10 g fat, 1 g saturated fat, 4 g fiber, 4 g sugar
- Five Kashi TLC 7 Grain crackers dipped in one-half cup Sweet Potato Spread (see Index): 140 calories, 4 g protein, 27 g carbohydrate, 2 g fat, 0 g saturated fat, 5 g fiber, 7 g sugar
- Whole wheat pita wedges (one-half pita) dipped in one-quarter cup Roasted Red Pepper and Almond Dip (see Index): 163 calories, 5 g protein, 17 g carbohydrate, 10 g fat, 1 g saturated fat, 5 g fiber, 3 g sugar
- Whole wheat pita wedges (one-half pita) dipped in one-half cup No-Fat Hummus (see Index): 174 calories, 8 g protein, 32 g carbohydrate, 3 g fat, 0 g saturated fat, 7 g fiber, 2 g sugar
- Whole wheat pita wedges (one-half pita) dipped in one-half cup Sweet Potato Spread (see Index): 157 calories, 5 g protein, 32 g carbohydrate, 2 g fat, 0 g saturated fat, 6 g fiber, 6 g sugar
- One Wasa Multigrain Crispbread smeared with one-half cup No-Fat Hummus (see Index): 149 calories, 7 g protein, 29 g carbohydrate, 2 g fat, 0 g saturated fat, 7 g fiber, 2 g sugar

- One Wasa Multigrain Crispbread smeared with one-quarter cup Roasted Red Pepper and Almond Dip (see Index): 138 calories, 4 g protein, 14 g carbohydrate, 9 g fat, 1 g saturated fat, 5 g fiber, 3 g sugar
- One Wasa Multigrain Crispbread smeared with one tablespoon almond butter: 135 calories, 3 g protein, 12 g carbohydrate, 9 g fat, 1 g saturated fat, 3 g fiber, 1 g sugar
- Cucumbers/carrots/celery dipped in one-half cup No-Fat Hummus (see Index): 134 calories, 7 g protein, 26 g carbohydrate, 2 g fat, 0 g saturated fat, 7 g fiber, 3 g sugar
- Cucumbers dipped in one-half cup Sweet Potato Spread (see Index): 105 calories, 3 g protein, 22 g carbohydrate, 1 g fat, 0 g saturated fat, 4 g fiber, 7 g sugar
- Two slices roasted deli turkey breast: 45 calories, 10 g protein, 1 g carbohydrate, 0 g fat, 0 g saturated fat, 0 g fiber, 0 g sugar

To Satisfy Your Craving

- One-third cup Kashi Cinnamon Harvest cereal, dry: 63 calories, 1 g protein, 15 g carbohydrate, 0 g fat, 0 g saturated fat, 2 g fiber, 3 g sugar
- One small (eight ounces) skim-milk cappuccino, no sugar: 55 calories, 5 g protein, 7 g carbohydrate, 0 g fat, 0 g saturated fat, 0 g fiber, 7 g sugar
- One Kashi TLC frozen whole-grain waffle, toasted, with one-quarter cup fresh or frozen strawberries: 97 calories, 4 g protein, 20 g carbohydrate, 2 g fat, 0 g saturated fat, 4 g fiber, 4 g sugar
- One small (eight ounces) plain, nonfat yogurt: 100 calories, 10 g protein, 19 g carbohydrate, 0 g fat, 0 g saturated fat, 0 g fiber, 13 g sugar
- Pop Secret Light Butter Premium Microwave Popcorn (five cups popped): 125 calories, 3 g protein, 20 g carbohydrate, 5 g fat, 1 g saturated fat, 4 g fiber, 0 g sugar
- 13 Guiltless Gourmet Spicy Black Bean tortilla chips dipped in two tablespoons salsa: 90 calories, 3 g protein, 18 g carbohydrate, 1 g fat, 0 g saturated fat, 2 g fiber, 1 g sugar
- 14 100% Whole Grain Wheat Thins: 123 calories, 2 g protein, 18 g carbohydrate, 5 g fat, 1 g saturated fat, 2 g fiber, 3 g sugar

- Five Health Valley Low Fat Whole Wheat Crackers: 50 calories, 2 g protein, 8 g carbohydrate, 1 g fat, 0 g saturated fat, 2 g fiber, 1 g sugar
- Two Wasa Multigrain Crispbreads: 70 calories, 2 g protein, 18 g carbohydrate, 0 g fat, 0 g saturated fat, 4 g fiber, 0 g sugar
- 19 Cascadian Farms Organic French Fries with one tablespoon ketchup: 152 calories, 2 g protein, 26 g carbohydrate, 4 g fat, 1 g saturated fat, 2 g fiber, 4 g sugar
- One small package (one-ounce bag) baked potato chips: 110 calories, 2 g protein, 23 g carbohydrate, 2 g fat, 0 g saturated fat, 2 g fiber, 2 g sugar
- One ounce Snyder's of Hanover Sourdough Hard Pretzels (or the equivalent of another brand): 100 calories, 3 g protein, 23 g carbohydrate, 0 g fat, 0 g saturated fat, 1 g fiber, 0 g sugar
- One small (eight ounces) hot chocolate made with nonfat milk: 152 calories, 9 g protein, 30 g carbohydrate, 1 g fat, 1 g saturated fat, 1 g fiber, 27 g sugar
- Two Oreos: 107 calories, 1 g protein, 15 g carbohydrate, 5 g fat, 1 g saturated fat, 1 g fiber, 9 g sugar
- Half a small slice (two ounces) of unfrosted chocolate cake: 165 calories, 3 g protein, 27 g carbohydrate, 6 g fat, 3 g saturated fat, 1 g fiber, 18 g sugar
- Half a jelly doughnut: 120 calories, 2 g protein, 16 g carbohydrate, 5 g fat, 1 g saturated fat, .5 g fiber, 6 g sugar
- One small (six-ounce container) fruit yogurt: 170 calories, 5 g protein, 33 g carbohydrate, 2 g fat, 1 g saturated fat, 0 g fiber, 27 g sugar
- Two chocolate miniatures: 90 calories, 2 g protein, 10 g carbohydrate, 5 g fat, 3 g saturated fat, 0 g fiber, 9 g sugar

DAVID'S SUGGESTED CHEAT MEALS

During phase 3, you're allowed to have a cheat meal once a week. During this meal you can eat whatever you want. This will help keep your motivation strong for the rest of the week, reduce cravings, and prevent bingeing. If you find yourself craving a particularly naughty food, reserve it for your cheat meal. Once your cheat meal rolls around, eat guiltlessly. Research shows that the body will turn up the metabolism and burn off excess calories during occasional indulgences. So you can safely cheat once a week without seeing ill effects on your waistline. That said, cheating any more than one meal a week could have disastrous consequences.

You do, however, want to avoid unconscious bingeing. No matter what you eat during phase 3, eat it mindfully. Taste it. Savor it. Don't allow yourself to mindlessly reach into the bag of chips while you talk on the phone or watch TV. You'll end up eating more than you planned for and not enjoying the experience. In short, you waste your cheat meal. If you're going to cheat, enjoy what you're cheating with—taste and savor it rather than gobble it down in a New York minute.

I've listed my favorite cheat meals here.

- One chicken burrito with a side of black beans and salsa (if possible, ask for a whole wheat burrito) is a favorite cheat meal. There's also nothing like a good serving of fresh guacamole with lots of jalapeño peppers and cilantro.
- Barbecue beef ribs and macaroni and cheese at New York's Blue Smoke is another favorite meal. Blue Smoke is also home to the best roasted peanuts in New York.
- When the urge for pizza takes over, I'll have one slice (no meat toppings or extra cheese) with a side salad; bonus points for veggie toppings. I choose wood-burning-oven pizza, as it tends to have less oil and a much thinner crust and is a little smaller than those traditional, doughy, oily pies that we (especially all you fellow suburbanites) grew up with.
- When my sweet tooth takes over, I head over to one of Danny Meyer's restaurants—Eleven Madison Park—for the *best* chocolate soufflé I have ever tasted. The tricky thing is that Danny's team knows me very well and doesn't expect me to order dessert. When I do, I often get a little playful abuse. It's all in a day's work for this fitness/wellness guru.

No matter what you choose for your cheat meal, remember that you do not have to finish the entire plate of food. Eat consciously, and listen to the signals your stomach sends to your brain. If you're like me, then perhaps one or two bites of chocolate soufflé or pecan pie will do.

PHASE 3 MENUS

Day 29

Breakfast: David's Energy Boost, David's Protein (Meal-Replacement) Shake, *or* Breakfast Shake (either see Index for David's recipes, or see Chapter 3 for guidelines on choosing an appropriate shake)

Snack: selection from approved snack list

Lunch: Grilled Chicken and Bean Salad (see Index)

Snack: Two to three hard-boiled eggs (only the whites)

Dinner: Sun-Dried Tomato–Crusted Baked Halibut (see Index) with one cup steamed broccoli; one white wine spritzer (three ounces white wine with three ounces seltzer)

Total: 833 calories, 107 g protein, 57 g carbohydrate, 12 g fat, 4 g saturated fat, 18 g fiber, 14 g sugar

Day 30

Breakfast: David's Energy Boost, David's Protein (Meal-Replacement) Shake, *or* Breakfast Shake (either see Index for David's recipes, or see Chapter 3 for guidelines on choosing an appropriate shake)

Snack: selection from approved snack list

Lunch: Tuna and Quinoa Salad (see Index)

Snack: 10 raw almonds

Dinner: Turkey Meat Loaf (see Index), mixed-greens salad (topped with any veggies of your choice), and one cup sautéed spinach

Total: 903 calories, 85 g protein, 60 g carbohydrate, 38 g fat, 6 g saturated fat, 19 g fiber, 16 g sugar

Day 31

Breakfast: David's Energy Boost, David's Protein (Meal-Replacement) Shake, *or* Breakfast Shake (either see Index for David's recipes, or see Chapter 3 for guidelines on choosing an appropriate shake)

Snack: selection from approved snack list

Lunch: Chopped Salad with Roasted Chicken, Tomatoes (see Index)

Snack: One can tuna

Dinner: Almond Lentil Loaf (see Index), Cauliflower Mushroom Mash (see Index), and mixed-greens salad; one white wine spritzer (three ounces white wine with three ounces seltzer)

Total: 899 calories, 96 g protein, 74 g carbohydrate, 20 g fat, 4 g saturated fat, 25 g fiber, 19 g sugar

Day 32

Breakfast: David's Energy Boost, David's Protein (Meal-Replacement) Shake, *or* Breakfast Shake (either see Index for David's recipes, or see Chapter 3 for guidelines on choosing an appropriate shake)

Snack: selection from approved snack list

Lunch: Leftover Almond Lentil Loaf (see Index) with mixed-greens salad

Snack: Scrambled Egg Whites with Ground Turkey and Chopped Tomato (see Index)

Dinner: Turkey Meat Loaf (see Index), mixed-greens salad (topped with any veggies of your choice), and one cup sautéed spinach

Total: 955 calories, 92 g protein, 83 g carbohydrate, 31 g fat, 6 g saturated fat, 28 g fiber, 24 g sugar

Day 33

Breakfast: David's Energy Boost, David's Protein (Meal-Replacement) Shake, *or* Breakfast Shake (either see Index for David's recipes, or see Chapter 3 for guidelines on choosing an appropriate shake)

Snack: selection from approved snack list

Lunch: Poached Chicken Breast (see Index) with mixed-greens salad (topped with chopped veggies of your choice)

Snack: Two to three hard-boiled egg whites

Dinner: cheat meal

Total: 560 calories, 91 g protein, 23 g carbohydrate, 10 g fat, 4 g saturated fat, 9 g fiber, 6 g sugar (analysis does not include dinner)

Day 34

Breakfast: David Kirsch's Power Pancakes (see Index) topped with one-quarter cup berries

Snack: selection from approved snack list

Lunch: Warm Salmon and Lentil Salad (see Index)

Snack: Sesame Chicken Fingers (see Index)

Dinner: Guiltless Barbecue Burger (see Index), Cauliflower Mushroom Mash (see Index), and mixed-greens salad

Total: 1,058 calories, 124 g protein, 88 g carbohydrate, 25 g fat, 9 g saturated fat, 28 g fiber, 24 g sugar

Day 35

Breakfast: Frittata with Broccoli Rabe, Sun-Dried Tomatoes, and Parmesan (see Index)

Snack: selection from approved snack list

Lunch: Baked Falafel with Yogurt-Mint Dressing (see Index) with mixed-greens salad

Snack: David's Low-Fat Egg Salad (see Index)

Dinner: Chicken Satay (see Index), one cup sautéed spinach, and mixed-greens salad

Total: 997 calories, 104 g protein, 87 g carbohydrate, 29 g fat, 7 g saturated fat, 28 g fiber, 22 g sugar

Day 36

Breakfast: David's Energy Boost, David's Protein (Meal-Replacement) Shake, *or* Breakfast Shake (either see Index for David's recipes, or see Chapter 3 for guidelines on choosing an appropriate shake)

Snack: selection from approved snack list

Lunch: Leftover Baked Falafel with Yogurt-Mint Dressing (see Index) over mixed-greens salad

Snack: Salmon Cakes (see Index)

Dinner: Shiitake Chicken Paillard (see Index) with one cup steamed broccoli and mixed-greens salad

Total: 984 calories, 116 g protein, 90 g carbohydrate, 20 g fat, 4 g saturated fat, 30 g fiber, 32 g sugar

Day 37

Breakfast: David's Energy Boost, David's Protein (Meal-Replacement) Shake, *or* Breakfast Shake (either see Index for David's recipes, or see Chapter 3 for guidelines on choosing an appropriate shake)

Snack: selection from approved snack list

Lunch: Grilled Chicken and Bean Salad with mixed-greens salad

Snack: Two to three hard-boiled egg whites

Dinner: Thai Shrimp Sauté (see Index) with one cup steamed broccoli and mixed-greens salad

Total: 907 calories, 104 g protein, 86 g carbohydrate, 17 g fat, 4 g saturated fat, 29 g fiber, 22 g sugar

Day 38

Breakfast: David's Energy Boost, David's Protein (Meal-Replacement) Shake, *or* Breakfast Shake (either see Index for David's recipes, or see Chapter 3 for guidelines on choosing an appropriate shake)

Snack: selection from approved snack list

Lunch: Poached Chicken Breast (see Index) with microwaved sweet potato

Snack: 10 raw almonds

Dinner: Asian Pepper Chicken (see Index) with Asian Broccoli Stir-Fry (see Index) and one-half cup frozen edamame (cooked according to package instructions)

Total: 1,002 calories, 131 g protein, 63 g carbohydrate, 24 g fat, 5 g saturated fat, 20 g fiber, 20 g sugar

Day 39

Breakfast: David's Energy Boost, David's Protein (Meal-Replacement) Shake, *or* Breakfast Shake (either see Index for David's recipes, or see Chapter 3 for guidelines on choosing an appropriate shake)

Snack: selection from approved snack list

Lunch: Almond Lentil Loaf (see Index) with mixed-greens salad

Snack: Sesame Chicken Fingers (see Index)

Dinner: Herb-Crusted Turkey Breast (see Index) with one cup sautéed spinach and mixed-greens salad

Total: 1,038 calories, 123 g protein, 71 g carbohydrate, 30 g fat, 4 g saturated fat, 27 g fiber, 14 g sugar

Day 40

Breakfast: David's Energy Boost, David's Protein (Meal-Replacement) Shake, *or* Breakfast Shake (either see Index for David's recipes, or see Chapter 3 for guidelines on choosing an appropriate shake)

Snack: selection from approved snack list

Lunch: Warm Salmon and Lentil Salad (see Index) with mixed-greens salad

Snack: Mexican Turkey Burger with Jalapeño Peppers and Mexican Salsa (see Index)

Dinner: cheat meal with one glass of wine

Total: 754 calories, 77 g protein, 55 g carbohydrate, 16 g fat, 4 g saturated fat, 20 g fiber, 13 g sugar (analysis does not include dinner)

Day 41

Breakfast: David Kirsch's Power Pancakes (see Index)

Snack: selection from approved snack list

Lunch: Thai Shrimp Sauté (see Index), one cup steamed broccoli, and mixed-greens salad

Snack: 10 raw almonds

Dinner: Guiltless Barbecue Burger (see Index) with Cauliflower Hash (see Index) and mixed-greens salad

Total: 881 calories, 103 g protein, 78 g carbohydrate, 22 g fat, 7 g saturated fat, 22 g fiber, 22 g sugar

Day 42

Breakfast: Turkey Bacon, Spinach, and Egg White Frittata (see Index)

Snack: selection from approved snack list

Lunch: Thai Ginger Sirloin Salad (see Index), one cup steamed broccoli, and Quinoa Salad (see Index)

Snack: Two to three hard-boiled egg whites

Dinner: Herb-Crusted Turkey Breast (see Index), one cup steamed asparagus, and mixed-greens salad; one white wine spritzer (three ounces white wine with three ounces seltzer)

Total: 1,088 calories, 117 g protein, 85 g carbohydrate, 24 g fat, 6 g saturated fat, 19 g fiber, 20 g sugar

Day 43

Breakfast: David's Energy Boost, David's Protein (Meal-Replacement) Shake, *or* Breakfast Shake (either see Index for David's recipes, or see Chapter 3 for guidelines on choosing an appropriate shake)

Snack: selection from approved snack list

Lunch: Grilled Chicken and Bean Salad (see Index)

Snack: David's Low-Fat Egg Salad (see Index)

Dinner: Sun-Dried Tomato–Crusted Baked Halibut (see Index) with one cup steamed broccoli and mixed greens

Total: 871 calories, 113 g protein, 69 g carbohydrate, 14 g fat, 5 g saturated fat, 23 g fiber, 17 g sugar

Day 44

Breakfast: David's Energy Boost, David's Protein (Meal-Replacement) Shake, *or* Breakfast Shake (either see Index for David's recipes, or see Chapter 3 for guidelines on choosing an appropriate shake)

Snack: selection from approved snack list

Lunch: Red Peppers Stuffed with Quinoa (see Index), Poached Chicken Breast (see Index), and mixed-greens salad

Snack: One can tuna

Dinner: Shrimp Marinara (see Index) with mixed-greens salad (topped with any veggies of your choice)

Total: 1,020 calories, 138 g protein, 77 g carbohydrate, 18 g fat, 5 g saturated fat, 21 g fiber, 27 g sugar

Day 45

Breakfast: David's Energy Boost, David's Protein (Meal-Replacement) Shake, *or* Breakfast Shake (either see Index for David's recipes, or see Chapter 3 for guidelines on choosing an appropriate shake)

Snack: selection from approved snack list

Lunch: Almond Lentil Loaf (see Index), one cup of steamed broccoli, and mixed-greens salad

Snack: Spicy Wasabi Salmon Burger (see Index)

Dinner: cheat meal

Total: 751 calories, 74 g protein, 64 g carbohydrate, 24 g fat, 4 g saturated fat, 22 g fiber, 13 g sugar (analysis does not include dinner)

Day 46

Breakfast: David's Energy Boost, David's Protein (Meal-Replacement) Shake, *or* Breakfast Shake (either see Index for David's recipes, or see Chapter 3 for guidelines on choosing an appropriate shake)

Snack: selection from approved snack list

Lunch: Shrimp and Whole Wheat Pasta with Arugula Dressing (see Index) with mixed-greens salad (topped with chopped veggies of your choice)

Snack: Sesame Chicken Fingers (see Index)

Dinner: Asian Pepper Chicken (see Index) with Asian Broccoli Stir-Fry (see Index)

Total: 930 calories, 116 g protein, 71 g carbohydrate, 19 g fat, 4 g saturated fat, 23 g fiber, 16 g sugar

Day 47

Breakfast: David's Energy Boost, David's Protein (Meal-Replacement) Shake, *or* Breakfast Shake (either see Index for David's recipes, or see Chapter 3 for guidelines on choosing an appropriate shake)

Snack: selection from approved snack list

Lunch: Ginger-Glazed Halibut (see Index) with Couscous Salad (see Index) and one-half cup frozen edamame (cooked according to package instructions)

Snack: Two to three hard-boiled egg whites

Dinner: Guiltless Barbecue Burger (see Index) with Cauliflower Hash (see Index) and mixed-greens salad

Total: 867 calories, 110 g protein, 76 g carbohydrate, 13 g fat, 3 g saturated fat, 18 g fiber, 18 g sugar

Day 48

Breakfast: David Kirsch's Power Pancakes (see Index)

Snack: selection from approved snack list

Lunch: Baked Falafel with Yogurt-Mint Dressing (see Index) with mixed-greens salad

Snack: 10 raw almonds

Dinner: Herb-Crusted Turkey Breast (see Index), one cup steamed asparagus, and mixed-greens salad; one white wine spritzer (three ounces white wine with three ounces seltzer)

Total: 942 calories, 104 g protein, 90 g carbohydrate, 14 g fat, 5 g saturated fat, 26 g fiber, 25 g sugar

Day 49

Breakfast: Frittata with Broccoli Rabe, Sun-Dried Tomatoes, and Parmesan (see Index)

Snack: selection from approved snack list

Lunch: Leftover Baked Falafel with Yogurt-Mint Dressing (see Index) over mixed-greens salad

Snack: Wild Salmon Burger (see Index)

Dinner: Turkey Meat Loaf (see Index) with mixed-greens salad and Cauliflower Hash (see Index)

Total: 948 calories, 90 g protein, 90 g carbohydrate, 28 g fat, 7 g saturated fat, 24 g fiber, 28 g sugar

Day 50

Breakfast: David's Energy Boost, David's Protein (Meal-Replacement) Shake, *or* Breakfast Shake (either see Index for David's recipes, or see Chapter 3 for guidelines on choosing an appropriate shake)

Snack: selection from approved snack list

Lunch: Turkey Chili (see Index) with mixed-greens salad

Snack: Tuna Salad with Whole-Grain Mustard and Water Chestnuts (see Index)

Dinner: Poached Chicken Breast (see Index) with Roasted Brussels Sprouts (see Index) and mixed-greens salad

Total: 959 calories, 131 g protein, 59 g carbohydrate, 21 g fat, 7 g saturated fat, 21 g fiber, 20 g sugar

Day 51

Breakfast: David's Energy Boost, David's Protein (Meal-Replacement) Shake, *or* Breakfast Shake (either see Index for David's recipes, or see Chapter 3 for guidelines on choosing an appropriate shake)

Snack: selection from approved snack list

Lunch: Red Peppers Stuffed with Quinoa (see Index) and mixed-greens salad

Snack: David's Low-Fat Egg Salad (see Index)

Dinner: Thai Shrimp Sauté (see Index) with mixed-greens salad; one glass white wine

Total: 875 calories, 78 g protein, 81 g carbohydrate, 18 g fat, 3 g saturated fat, 23 g fiber, 25 g sugar

Day 52

Breakfast: David's Energy Boost, David's Protein (Meal-Replacement) Shake, *or* Breakfast Shake (either see Index for David's recipes, or see Chapter 3 for guidelines on choosing an appropriate shake)

Snack: selection from approved snack list

Lunch: Herb-Crusted Turkey Breast (see Index) with one cup steamed broccoli and mixed-greens salad

Snack: Frittata with Broccoli Rabe, Sun-Dried Tomatoes, and Parmesan (see Index)

Dinner: cheat meal

Total: 655 calories, 94 g protein, 40 g carbohydrate, 14 g fat, 5 g saturated fat, 15 g fiber, 10 g sugar (analysis does not include dinner)

Day 53

Breakfast: David's Energy Boost, David's Protein (Meal-Replacement) Shake, *or* Breakfast Shake (either see Index for David's recipes, or see Chapter 3 for guidelines on choosing an appropriate shake)

Snack: selection from approved snack list

Lunch: Grilled Chicken and Bean Salad (see Index)

Snack: two to three hard-boiled egg whites

Dinner: Guiltless Barbecue Burger (see Index), Cauliflower Mushroom Mash (see Index), and mixed-greens salad

Total: 822 calories, 107 g protein, 72 g carbohydrate, 11 g fat, 4 g saturated fat, 23 g fiber, 21 g sugar

Day 54

Breakfast: David's Energy Boost, David's Protein (Meal-Replacement) Shake, *or* Breakfast Shake (either see Index for David's recipes, or see Chapter 3 for guidelines on choosing an appropriate shake)

Snack: selection from approved snack list

Lunch: Sesame Buckwheat Noodles with Low-Fat Peanut Sauce (see Index), mixed-greens salad, and one cup steamed broccoli

Snack: 10 raw almonds

Dinner: Branzino (Sea Bass) Puttanesca (see Index) with mixed-greens salad; two chocolate miniatures

Total: 1,077 calories, 86 g protein, 106 g carbohydrate, 32 g fat, 7 g saturated fat, 26 g fiber, 29 g sugar

Day 55

Breakfast: David Kirsch's Power Pancakes (see Index)

Snack: selection from approved snack list

Lunch: Baked Falafel with Yogurt-Mint Dressing (see Index) with mixed-greens salad

Snack: Sesame Chicken Fingers (see Index)

Dinner: Wild Salmon Burger (see Index) with Cauliflower Hash (see Index) and mixed-greens salad

Total: 975 calories, 105 g protein, 92 g carbohydrate, 21 g fat, 7 g saturated fat, 25 g fiber, 24 g sugar

Day 56

Breakfast: Turkey Bacon, Spinach, and Egg White Frittata (see Index)

Snack: selection from approved snack list

Lunch: Herb-Crusted Turkey Breast (see Index), Sweet Potato and Almond Salad with Mustard Vinaigrette (see Index), and mixed-greens salad

Snack: Wild Salmon Burger (see Index)

Dinner: Poached Chicken Breast (see Index) with Cauliflower Mushroom Mash (see Index) and mixed-greens salad

Total: 1,099 calories, 148 g protein, 74 g carbohydrate, 23 g fat, 4 g saturated fat, 19 g fiber, 17 g sugar

Congratulations! You are now eight weeks into a way of eating that will span the rest of your life. By now you are seeing stunning results. I'm confident that you have nurtured the skills needed to go the distance. You can branch out from here in many different directions—and I encourage you to do just that. Create your own Ultimate New York Diet recipes and snacks. Mix and match menu items as you see fit. If you loved one recipe, cook it often. I hope you didn't find any recipes that you hated, but if that's the case, definitely don't make those again.

You control what comes next. In the coming chapters you'll find the advice that you need to navigate the common challenges that tend to crop up once you go off a formal meal plan and begin really *living* the diet. You'll gain advice for eating out, surviving cocktail parties, and more. So read on and stick with me. You've made it through eight weeks. There's nothing you can't accomplish!

The Ultimate New York Recipes

When I started my food company, One of a Kind Food, in the late 1990s, I was determined to eliminate the excuse of "I don't have time to prepare a healthful meal." I believed then and I still believe that you can make almost anything healthfully. I love going into restaurants, taking delicious-sounding entrées, and re-creating them without the butter, sauce, or almost everything else fattening. If you start with fresh, clean, organic (if possible) foods, you can easily bring out their flavors without drowning them in butter, oil, salt, and fat-laden sauces.

Today, One of a Kind Food delivers hundreds of prepared meals—individual and full day—all over the metropolitan New York area. You need not, however, pay for and order meals through the Madison Square Club in order to succeed on this plan. Throughout the following pages, you'll find my most popular recipes—the ones that my clients request over and over again. In fact, some such as the Turkey Chili and the Turkey Bacon, Spinach, and Egg White Frittata have been same-day shipped to Las Vegas, Nevada (well worth the trip!).

You may eat the recipes in the phase 1 section at any point on the plan. If a recipe is listed under the phase 2 or phase 3 section, it's still healthful but may contain quinoa, fruit, or another healthy ingredient that I suggest you keep off your plate during the first two weeks of the plan.

Through the process of preparing these easy, delicious, and nutritious meals, you will learn to be "less frightened" in the kitchen. In the recipes contained in the following pages, I have adapted and created from scratch meals that are short on effort but long on flavor. They look great, taste delicious, and are good for your health and waistline. These recipes will teach you how to cook with herbs and spices instead of fats, cheese, and sauces, a skill that allows you to appreciate the foods you are eating and spare yourself hundreds of calories and grams of unnecessary fat.

Phase 1 Recipes

The phase 1 recipes are simple, delicious, and nutritious. They will give you the fuel needed to energize you throughout the day.

BREAKFASTS

David's Protein (Meal-Replacement) Shake

This quick and easy shake will serve as your breakfast throughout phase 1. If you desire, you can also have it for dinner.

10 ounces noncarbonated mineral water

5 ice cubes

1 scoop vanilla-flavored whey protein powder*

In a blender, combine the water, ice cubes, and protein powder. Blend on high speed for 45 seconds. Serve immediately.

Makes 1 serving.

*Per serving using generic protein powder: 90 calories, 18 g protein, 2 g carbohydrate, 1.5 g fat, .5 g saturated fat, 0 g fiber, 2 g sugar

*Per serving using 1 packet David Kirsch's Vanilla Protein Powder: 180 calories, 25 g protein, 10 g carbohydrate, 3.5 g fat, 1.5 g saturated fat, 5 g fiber, 3 g sugar

Scrambled Egg Whites with Ground Turkey and Chopped Tomato

This hearty "stick-to-your-ribs" meal is one of Linda Evangelista's favorites. It will fuel your morning in a low-fat, energetic way.

Nonfat vegetable cooking spray

2 ounces ground turkey breast

Pinch of ground coriander

Pinch of cayenne

¼ cup chopped fresh tomato

3 egg whites

1 tablespoon water

Salt

Pepper

Coat a 9-inch nonstick skillet with cooking spray. Heat over medium-high heat. In a small bowl, mix the ground turkey breast with the coriander and cayenne. Place the turkey mixture into the skillet, and brown for about 1 minute. Add the chopped tomato and continue to brown, stirring frequently. Cook for about 3 minutes or until thoroughly cooked through. Remove the turkey and tomatoes from pan.

In a small bowl, whisk together egg whites and water. Season to taste with the salt and pepper.

Add the egg mixture to the skillet and cook for about 1 minute or until the edges begin to set.

Place the eggs, turkey, and tomatoes on a serving platter and serve immediately.

Makes 1 serving. Per serving: 92 calories, 18 g protein, 3 g carbohydrate, 1 g fat, 0 g saturated fat, .5 g fiber, 2 g sugar

Scrambled Egg Whites with Shiitake Mushrooms and Turkey Bacon

At the Madison Square Club, plain scrambled egg whites will never do. We've livened up this breakfast platter by adding sautéed shiitake mushrooms and turkey bacon.

Nonfat vegetable cooking spray

2 strips turkey bacon

1 shiitake mushroom cap, julienned

3 egg whites

1 tablespoon water

Freshly ground black pepper

¼ teaspoon chopped fresh parsley for garnish

Coat a 9-inch nonstick skillet with cooking spray. Heat over medium-high heat. Add the turkey bacon to the pan, and heat until cooked through and crispy, about 1 to 2 minutes per side. Remove the bacon and set aside.

Place the mushroom in the same skillet, and sauté until slightly browned, about 1 to 2 minutes. Remove from heat and set aside.

In a small bowl, whisk together the egg whites and water. Season to taste with the pepper. Place the eggs in the nonstick skillet, and stir until cooked through, about 1 minute or until the edges begin to set. Do not overcook.

Arrange the eggs and the mushrooms on a plate, sprinkle with parsley, and add the turkey bacon on the side.

Makes 1 serving. Per serving: 130 calories, 16 g protein, 2 g carbohydrate, 6 g fat, 1 g saturated fat, 0 g fiber, 1 g sugar

ENTRÉES

Asian Pepper Chicken

The asparagus (a great natural diuretic), onion, and mushrooms dress up this Ultimate New York Diet staple.

Nonfat olive oil cooking spray

6 ounces skinless, boneless, chicken breast, cut into ½-inch strips

2 asparagus spears, trimmed and cut into 1-inch pieces

¼ small red onion, sliced

2 shiitake mushrooms, cleaned and sliced

½ teaspoon crushed red pepper flakes

½ tablespoon freshly ground black pepper

½ cup water

Coat a large nonstick skillet with cooking spray and heat over medium-high heat. Place the chicken in the skillet. Cook 1 to 3 minutes per side, stirring frequently until cooked through. Transfer the meat into a bowl, and cover it to keep it warm. Respray the skillet with the cooking spray. Add the rest of the ingredients except water, and cook 5 to 10 minutes, stirring with a wooden spoon until the vegetables are tender and hot throughout. Add the chicken and water to the skillet, stirring until the chicken and vegetables are hot.

Makes 1 serving. Per serving: 217 calories, 36 g protein, 8 g carbohydrate, 4 g fat, 1 g saturated fat, 2 g fiber, 2 g sugar

Branzino (Sea Bass) Puttanesca

Thoughts of Capri abound with this fresh and tasty entrée.

½ teaspoon olive oil

1 clove garlic, chopped

1 cup all-natural chopped tomato

¼ cup white wine

Salt

Pepper

1 tablespoon chopped black olives

½ teaspoon capers

1 6-ounce branzino fillet

Heat olive oil in a deep skillet over medium-high heat. Add garlic and sauté 30 seconds. Add tomato and wine; add salt and pepper to taste. Bring mixture to a boil, then simmer for 10 minutes, until saucelike in consistency. Stir in olives and capers. Place branzino on top of mixture, and cover skillet. Simmer 10 minutes, until fish is opaque.

Makes 1 serving. Per serving: 277 calories, 33 g protein, 10 g carbohydrate, 7 g fat, 1 g saturated fat, 2 g fiber, 5 g sugar

Herb-Crusted Turkey Breast

Always make more of this recipe than you need, and use leftovers on salad or for a quick, lean snack.

2 tablespoons chopped fresh thyme

2 tablespoons Dijon mustard

1 tablespoon chopped fresh oregano

1 teaspoon chopped fresh rosemary

½ teaspoon freshly ground black pepper

1 whole turkey breast (4 to 5 pounds)

Preheat oven to 350°F. In a small bowl, combine the thyme, mustard, oregano, rosemary, and pepper. Place the turkey breast in a roasting pan, skin side up. Spread the herb mixture evenly over the top. Bake for 1¼ to 1½ hours, until the juices run clear and a thermometer inserted into the thickest portion registers 170°F. Remove and discard the skin.

Makes 6 servings. Per serving: 212 calories, 46 g protein, 1 g carbohydrate, 2 g fat, 0 g saturated fat, 0 g fiber, 0 g sugar

Horseradish-Encrusted Salmon

This deliciously crispy fish takes just a minute or two to prepare. Serve it for dinner after a busy day at work, when you're too tired to spend a lot of time slicing and dicing.

1 6-ounce wild salmon fillet, skinned

Salt

Pepper

1 tablespoon white horseradish

1 tablespoon fresh lemon juice

Nonfat olive oil cooking spray

Preheat oven to 375°F. Season salmon with salt and pepper to taste on both sides. Blend the horseradish and lemon juice in a small dish. Coat an ovenproof casserole dish with cooking spray, and place salmon on top. Spread the horseradish mixture over the fillet. Bake 20 minutes. Raise heat to a broil, and cook for 2 additional minutes, until the crust is golden.

Makes 1 serving. Per serving: 253 calories, 34 g protein, 3 g carbohydrate, 11 g fat, 2 g saturated fat, 1 g fiber, 2 g sugar

Mexican Turkey Burger with Jalapeño Peppers and Mexican Salsa

The turkey burger, a staple in my kitchen, goes south of the border with this recipe. The addition of the jalapeños and salsa spices up this popular dish.

Mexican Salsa

½ cup chopped tomato

1 tablespoon chopped scallion, white part only

½ tablespoon chopped fresh cilantro

1 teaspoon white wine vinegar

Turkey Burger

4 ounces ground turkey breast

1 tablespoon chopped scallion, white part only

½ teaspoon seeded and minced jalapeño pepper

½ teaspoon minced garlic

¾ teaspoon chili powder

¼ teaspoon ground cumin

Pinch of salt

In a medium mixing bowl, combine all salsa ingredients. Mix well, cover, and refrigerate. You can make this part of the recipe ahead of time. It keeps well for 2 to 3 days.

In a medium mixing bowl, combine the turkey, scallion, jalapeño pepper, garlic, chili powder, cumin, and salt, and mix thoroughly. Shape the mixture into a patty.

Grill the turkey burger for 4 to 5 minutes on each side until cooked through.

To serve, top with salsa.

Makes 1 serving. Per serving: 129 calories, 22 g protein, 7 g carbohydrate, 2 g fat, 0 g saturated fat, 2 g fiber, 3 g sugar

Poached Chicken Breast

This simple recipe yields wonderfully tender and juicy chicken. Make a few extra breasts to use on salads or as leftovers.

2 cups bottled water

2 cups low-fat, low-sodium chicken broth

2 tablespoons tricolor peppercorns

8 ounces boneless, skinless chicken breast

Pour the water and chicken broth into a stockpot or deep sauté pan. Bring to a gentle boil. Add the peppercorns and chicken, making sure the chicken is completely covered by liquid. (Add more water or broth as needed.) Reduce the heat to a simmer. Cook for about 12 minutes, until the chicken is fork-tender and the center is no longer pink. Avoid overcooking, which will dry out the chicken.

Makes 1 serving. Per serving: 273 calories, 52 g protein, 1 g carbohydrate, 6 g fat, 2 g saturated fat, 0 g fiber, 0 g sugar

Salmon Cakes

Heart-healthy salmon is pretty adaptable and quite tasty, as you will see in this recipe.

1 egg white
4 ounces wild salmon fillet, ground
1 teaspoon chopped fresh parsley
1 teaspoon white wine vinegar
½ teaspoon Worcestershire sauce
¼ teaspoon red pepper flakes
Nonfat vegetable cooking spray

In a large bowl, beat the egg white until thick. In another bowl, combine the salmon, parsley, vinegar, Worcestershire sauce, and red pepper flakes. Carefully fold the egg white into salmon mixture.

Coat a medium nonstick skillet with cooking spray, and heat over medium heat. Spoon the mixture onto the skillet, forming a salmon cake about 4 inches wide and 1 inch thick. Cook over medium heat for 3 minutes, for medium rare. Turn and cook for an additional 2 minutes for medium rare.

Makes 1 serving. Per serving: 183 calories, 26 g protein, 1 g carbohydrate, 7 g fat, 1 g saturated fat, 0 g fiber, 1 g sugar

Sesame Chicken Fingers

This easy dish goes over well at parties. It's also great as a light meal served with broccoli. I particularly enjoy it with David's Low-Fat Peanut Sauce (see Index), which is included with the phase 2 and 3 recipes.

¼ teaspoon light soy sauce

¼ teaspoon Dijon mustard

1 teaspoon water

1 teaspoon turmeric

1 4-ounce boneless, skinless chicken breast sliced into 4 strips

1 tablespoon toasted black and white sesame seeds

In a small bowl, mix the soy sauce, mustard, water, and turmeric. Marinate the chicken in the mixture up to 1 hour. Coat the chicken with sesame seeds.

Preheat oven to 350°F. Place the chicken on a nonstick baking pan. Bake 12 to 15 minutes or until chicken strips are cooked through.

Makes 1 serving. Per serving: 195 calories, 26 g protein, 2 g carbohydrate, 8 g fat, 1 g saturated fat, 2 g fiber, 0 g sugar

Sesame-Encrusted Tuna

Tuna tastes delicious when seared and served raw in the middle. Do not overcook it, or you risk drying out the fish.

1 6-ounce ahi tuna fillet

¼ cup of Ginger Soy Dressing (see Index)

1 tablespoon sesame seeds

¼ teaspoon wasabi mustard

Nonfat olive oil cooking spray

Place the tuna fillet in a shallow dish, pour the dressing over it, and turn to cover it with the dressing. Refrigerate 30 minutes. Mix the sesame seeds and wasabi mustard in a small bowl. Coat the tuna on both sides with the mustard–sesame seed mixture. Coat a nonstick skillet with cooking spray, and heat over medium-high heat. Sear the tuna 3 minutes on each side or until medium rare.

Makes 1 serving. Per serving: 309 calories, 43 g protein, 9 g carbohydrate, 11 g fat, 1 g saturated fat, 0 g fiber, 4 g sugar

Shiitake Chicken Paillard

Mushrooms and garlic add some additional healthy, immune-building nutrients to this tasty dish.

1 6-ounce boneless, skinless chicken breast

Salt

Pepper

Nonfat cooking spray

¾ cup (2 ounces) sliced shiitake mushrooms

1 clove garlic, minced

2 tablespoons red wine vinegar

¼ cup low-fat, low-sodium chicken stock

1 teaspoon chopped fresh thyme

Place the chicken between sheets of plastic, and pound with a meat mallet to ⅛-inch thickness. Season both sides of the chicken with salt and pepper to taste. Heat a large nonstick skillet over medium-high heat, and coat with cooking spray. Place the chicken on one side of the heated pan. Place the mushrooms and garlic on the other side. Cook the chicken for 2 minutes, until browned. Turn and cook for 3 minutes, until the chicken is no longer pink. While the chicken is cooking, cook the mushrooms and garlic for 3 to 4 minutes, until lightly browned. Remove the chicken and the mushroom-garlic mixture to a serving plate.

Add red wine vinegar, stock, and thyme to the pan. Bring to a boil over high heat. Reduce the heat to medium-low, and simmer for 30 seconds, until slightly thickened. Pour over the chicken, and serve immediately.

Makes 1 serving. Per serving: 221 calories, 38 g protein, 8 g carbohydrate, 4 g fat, 1 g saturated fat, 1 g fiber, 0 g sugar

Shrimp Marinara

When the thought of one more chicken dish is too much to bear, try this tasty shrimp recipe.

1 teaspoon olive oil

1 clove garlic, finely chopped

1 teaspoon chopped red bell pepper

⅛ teaspoon dried oregano

⅛ teaspoon dried marjoram

2 cups chopped all-natural tomato (with juice)

¾ pound shrimp, peeled and deveined

Heat the oil in a medium skillet over medium-high heat. Add the garlic, pepper, oregano, and marjoram, stirring frequently until the garlic is lightly golden. Add the tomato with juice, and bring to a slow boil, reducing the heat if necessary. Cook for 20 minutes, until the mixture reaches a saucelike consistency. Add the shrimp, and cook until opaque, about 4 minutes. Serve immediately.

Makes 2 servings. Per serving: 189 calories, 29 g protein, 9 g carbohydrate, 4 g fat, 1 g saturated fat, 2 g fiber, 5 g sugar

Southwestern Pepper Chicken

The Tabasco and jalapeño pepper add a kick to this dish to wake up both your taste buds *and* your metabolism.

1 boneless, skinless chicken breast, sliced in ½-inch slices

2 dashes Tabasco

1 teaspoon minced fresh jalapeño pepper

Salt

Pepper

Nonfat cooking spray

1 red bell pepper, seeded and sliced in ½-inch strips

1 cup all-natural stewed tomato

In a small bowl, season the chicken with the Tabasco, jalapeño pepper, and salt and pepper to taste. Coat a large, nonstick skillet with cooking spray, and heat over medium-high heat. Add the chicken, and stir-fry for 4 minutes, or until cooked through and no longer pink. Remove the chicken from the skillet and set aside. Add the red bell pepper, and stir-fry for 2 to 3 minutes, or until tender. Add the tomato, and bring to a boil. Cook for 2 minutes, stirring occasionally. Return chicken to the skillet, and cook until thoroughly heated.

Makes 1 serving. Per serving: 210 calories, 30 g protein, 19 g carbohydrate, 2 g fat, 0 g saturated fat, 2 g fiber, 9 g sugar

Spicy Wasabi Salmon Burger

This is one of my favorite burgers. It's great as a lunch served with spinach or as an afternoon snack.

1 teaspoon water

1 teaspoon wasabi powder

½ teaspoon Dijon mustard

4 ounces wild salmon fillet, cut into ½-inch cubes

1 egg white, lightly beaten

½ tablespoon low-sodium soy sauce

1 teaspoon black sesame seeds

In a medium bowl, mix water with wasabi powder, and whisk until blended. Add Dijon mustard, salmon, egg white, soy sauce, and sesame seeds, and stir until mixed well. Form into a burger, and grill 2 to 3 minutes per side (or until desired doneness).

Makes 1 serving. Per serving: 205 calories, 28 g protein, 3 g carbohydrate, 9 g fat, 1 g saturated fat, 1 g fiber, 0 g sugar

Sun-Dried Tomato–Crusted Baked Halibut

This simply prepared, light fish tastes great over a bed of sautéed spinach.

2 6-ounce halibut fillets

Nonfat cooking spray

2 tablespoons chopped sun-dried tomato, rinsed and drained

1 cup water

Preheat the oven to 225°F. Coat the fish lightly with cooking spray. Spread 1 tablespoon sun-dried tomato onto each fillet. Place the fillets in a glass dish with water, and bake for 20 minutes or until the fish is opaque.

Makes 2 servings. Per serving: 196 calories, 36 g protein, 2 g carbohydrate, 4 g fat, 1 g saturated fat, 0 g fiber, 1 g sugar

Turkey Chili

Double this recipe, making a big pot of the stuff at the beginning of the week. Whenever you are rushed and don't have time to prepare a more elaborate lunch or dinner, serve up some leftovers. The chili always tastes better the second time around.

Nonfat cooking spray

1 pound lean ground turkey

Salt

Pepper

1 cup peeled and grated carrot (omit during phase 1)

⅔ cup chopped onion

⅔ cup chopped celery

1 clove garlic, minced

2 teaspoons chili powder

1 teaspoon paprika

1 teaspoon ground cumin

⅛ teaspoon ground cayenne

1 14½-ounce can chopped plum tomato in juice

½ cup low-fat, low-sodium chicken broth

1 bay leaf

Heat a 3-quart nonstick saucepan over high heat and coat with cooking spray. Add the turkey, and season to taste with salt and pepper. Cook for 2 to 3 minutes, breaking up the turkey into pieces, until browned. Remove to a bowl, and cover with foil to keep warm.

Reduce the heat to low, and add the carrot, onion, celery, and garlic. Cook for 3 to 5 minutes, until the vegetables begin to soften. Add the chili powder, paprika, cumin, and cayenne. Cook, stirring, for 1 minute. Increase the heat to medium, and add the tomato, stock, and bay leaf. Bring to a boil over high heat. Reduce the heat to medium-low, and simmer for 15 minutes, covered.

Add the browned turkey, and simmer for 5 minutes more. Remove and discard the bay leaf before serving.

Makes 4 servings. Per serving: 240 calories, 23 g protein, 15 g carbohydrate, 10 g fat, 3 g saturated fat, 4 g fiber, 8 g sugar

Turkey Meat Loaf

This dish is wonderful with steamed spinach or Cauliflower Hash (see Index) and tastes great the next day as leftovers.

Nonfat cooking spray
½ cup chopped onion
¼ cup chopped celery
¼ cup chopped carrot (omit during phase 1)
½ teaspoon paprika
½ teaspoon salt
⅛ teaspoon ground cayenne
⅛ teaspoon freshly ground black pepper
8 ounces lean ground turkey
1 egg white
¾ cup diced canned plum tomato in juice

Preheat oven to 350°F. Heat a medium nonstick skillet over medium heat, and coat with cooking spray. Add the onion, celery, and carrot. Cook for 3 minutes, until softened. Stir in the paprika, salt, cayenne, and black pepper. Cook for 1 minute. Remove to a medium bowl, and let cook for 2 minutes.

Add the turkey, egg white, and tomato to the bowl. Mix until just blended. Shape into a loaf, and place in an ovenproof baking dish or loaf pan. Bake for 30 to 40 minutes until loaf is no longer pink in the center and a thermometer inserted registers 165°F.

Makes 2 servings. Per serving: 232 calories, 23 g protein, 12 g carbohydrate, 10 g fat, 3 g saturated fat, 2 g fiber, 8 g sugar

Wild Salmon Burger

Top this burger with salsa or serve it plain, for either a meal or a snack.

½ pound wild salmon fillet, chopped

1 tablespoon Dijon mustard

Dash Tabasco

1 egg white, beaten

1 teaspoon drained capers

1 teaspoon fresh lemon juice

1 teaspoon chopped fresh dill

1 teaspoon white horseradish

Salt and pepper, to taste

Nonfat vegetable cooking spray

In a large bowl combine all of the ingredients except the cooking spray. Mix well and form into two patties. Spray a nonstick skillet with cooking spray, and place over medium heat. Add patties, and cook 3 to 4 minutes per side, until browned.

Makes 2 servings. Per serving: 179 calories, 26 g protein, 2 g carbohydrate, 7 g fat, 1 g saturated fat, 0 g fiber, 0 g sugar

SIDE DISHES

Asian Broccoli Stir-Fry

Use this delicious side dish—a calcium powerhouse—alongside any lean protein. It goes great with everything.

Nonfat olive oil cooking spray

2 cups broccoli florets, washed

1 clove garlic, minced

1 teaspoon grated gingerroot

¼ cup bottled water

2 teaspoons low-sodium soy sauce

⅛ teaspoon sesame oil

Heat a large nonstick skillet over high heat and coat with cooking spray. Add the broccoli and cook for 2 minutes, stirring. Add the garlic and ginger, and cook for 1 minute. Add the water, soy sauce, and sesame oil. Cover and cook for 2 to 3 minutes, until the broccoli is tender-crisp.

Makes 1 serving. Per serving: 59 calories, 5 g protein, 9 g carbohydrate, 1 g fat, 0 g saturated fat, 4 g fiber, 3 g sugar

Cauliflower Hash

You can mix this recipe with cubed grilled chicken or turkey breast to create a complete entrée. It also goes well over steamed spinach.

Nonfat cooking spray

¼ cup chopped shallots

1 cup steamed cauliflower florets

⅓ cup chopped celery

⅓ cup sliced roasted red peppers (store-bought, or see Index for recipe)

1 teaspoon chopped fresh thyme

Salt

Pepper

Heat a medium nonstick skillet over medium heat, and coat with cooking spray. Add the shallots and cook for 1 to 2 minutes, until softened. Add the cauliflower and celery. Cook 3 to 5 minutes, until the vegetables begin to brown. Add the roasted red peppers and thyme. Cook for 2 minutes more. Season to taste with salt and pepper.

Makes 2 servings. Per serving: 41 calories, 2 g protein, 9 g carbohydrate, 0 g fat, 0 g saturated fat, 2 g fiber, 2 g sugar

Cauliflower Mushroom Mash

This dish looks, feels, and tastes almost like mashed potatoes—without the fast-digesting carbs, excessive calories, and guilt.

Nonfat cooking spray

½ cup sliced mushrooms

1 tablespoon chopped shallots

1 cup steamed cauliflower florets

1 teaspoon whole-grain mustard

1 tablespoon chopped fresh parsley

Freshly ground black pepper

Heat a small nonstick skillet over high heat, and coat with cooking spray. Add the mushrooms and shallots, and cook for 2 to 3 minutes. Transfer to a food processor and let cool slightly. Add the cauliflower and mustard to the food processor, and puree until smooth. If the mixture is too thick, add 1 to 2 tablespoons water. Stir in the chopped parsley and pepper to taste.

Makes 1 serving. Per serving: 58 calories, 4 g protein, 10 g carbohydrate, 1 g fat, 0 g saturated fat, 5 g fiber, 3 g sugar

Roasted Brussels Sprouts

This is one of my (and my sister Elise's) favorite vegetables. It goes wonderfully with Herb-Crusted Turkey Breast (see Index).

1 cup halved brussels sprouts
1 teaspoon lemon juice*
1 teaspoon minced chives
Salt
Pepper

Preheat the oven to 400°F. Place the brussels sprouts on a large piece of foil. Sprinkle with the lemon juice, chives, and salt and pepper to taste. Fold up foil to enclose the ingredients, and place on a baking sheet. Bake for 30 minutes, until the brussels sprouts are cooked through and lightly browned. Remove from the foil packet immediately and serve.

*Use lemon juice only during phases 2 and 3 of the plan. Omit this ingredient for phase 1.

Makes 1 serving. Per serving: 39 calories, 3 g protein, 8 g carbohydrate, 0 g fat, 0 g saturated fat, 3 g fiber, 2 g sugar

Roasted Red Peppers

For quick and easy cooking, you can usually find roasted peppers at most grocery stores these days. If you cannot, here's how to make them at home.

3 red bell peppers

Preheat the broiler. Cut off the tops of the peppers. Remove the core and seeds from each. Cut the peppers lengthwise into quarters. Lay the pieces skin side up on a baking pan. Broil until the skin is charred. Remove from the heat. When cool enough to handle, remove and discard the skin using a paring knife. Use immediately, or freeze in an airtight plastic bag for up to 3 weeks.

Makes 3 servings. Per serving: 44 calories, 1 g protein, 11 g carbohydrate, 0 g fat, 0 g saturated fat, 3 g fiber, 4 g sugar

Roasted Vegetable Caponata

This versatile Mediterranean favorite is perfect as a side dish or as the featured main course for all of you vegetarians out there.

1 medium eggplant

Nonfat cooking spray

½ cup chopped Vidalia onion

½ cup chopped fennel bulb

¼ cup chopped celery

1 clove garlic, minced

⅓ cup sliced roasted red peppers (store-bought, or see Index for recipe)

4 canned plum tomatoes, chopped

½ cup juice from canned tomatoes

½ cup bottled water

1 tablespoon coarsely chopped fresh parsley

4 fresh basil leaves

2 teaspoons baby capers (optional)

Preheat the oven to 400°F. Wrap the eggplant in foil, and bake for 50 to 60 minutes, until tender when pricked with a fork. Cut the eggplant in half, and scoop out 1 cup roasted eggplant from the center. Set aside.

Heat a medium nonstick skillet over medium heat, and coat with cooking spray. Add the onion, and cook for 3 to 4 minutes, until onion begins to soften. Add the fennel, celery, and garlic, and cook for 3 minutes. Add the eggplant, roasted red peppers, plum tomatoes, juice, water, parsley, and basil. Simmer 15 to 20 minutes, until the liquid is absorbed and the vegetables are soft. Remove the basil leaves and add the capers. Remove from heat, and cool to room temperature. Cover and refrigerate for up to 2 weeks. Serve at room temperature.

Makes 2 servings. Per serving: 86 calories, 3 g protein, 20 g carbohydrate, 1 g fat, 0 g saturated fat, 5 g fiber, 10 g sugar

SALADS

Chopped Salad with Roasted Chicken, Tomatoes

Whenever you're in a rush, look to this great lean salad for lunch or dinner.

    1 cup of baby spinach, stems removed
    1 cup mixed field greens, chopped
    1 cup halved cherry tomato
    1 scallion, thinly sliced
    2 tablespoons David's Red Wine Vinaigrette (see Index)
    1 boneless, skinless chicken breast, cooked and sliced into 1-inch strips

Wash the spinach and the field greens. Dry thoroughly. In a medium bowl, place the greens, tomato, and scallion. Toss with vinaigrette to coat the greens. Arrange the chicken on top.

Makes 1 serving. Per serving: 200 calories, 29 g protein, 13 g carbohydrate, 4 g fat, 1 g saturated fat, 4 g fiber, 5 g sugar

Chopped Salad with Salmon

Similar to the chopped salad with chicken, this version swaps heart-healthy wild salmon for chicken and adds walnuts for some crunch, fiber, and vitamin E.

1 cup baby spinach, stems removed

1 cup mixed field greens, chopped

1 cup halved cherry tomato

1 scallion, thinly sliced

2 tablespoons David's Red Wine Vinaigrette (see Index)

1 3.5-ounce can wild salmon

2 teaspoons chopped walnuts

Wash the spinach and the field greens. Dry thoroughly. In a medium bowl, place the greens, tomato, and scallion. Toss with vinaigrette to coat the greens. Arrange the salmon on top of the salad greens and top with walnuts.

Makes 1 serving. Per serving: 211 calories, 25 g protein, 16 g carbohydrate, 7 g fat, 0 g saturated fat, 4 g fiber, 5 g sugar

David's Low-Fat Egg Salad

This is the perfect to-go breakfast or midmorning snack. When more time is available, serve on a bed of mesclun salad.

3 hard-boiled egg whites, coarsely chopped

¼ cup chopped celery

1 teaspoon Dijon mustard

1 tablespoon chopped fresh parsley

1 slice well-cooked (crispy) turkey bacon, coarsely chopped

In a small bowl, mix all ingredients.

Makes 1 serving. Per serving: 91 calories, 14 g protein, 3 g carbohydrate, 2 g fat, 1 g saturated fat, 1 g fiber, 0 g sugar

Roasted Turkey Basil Salad

The fresh, clean-tasting basil is the perfect complement to roasted turkey.

2 tablespoons chopped fresh basil

1 tablespoon chopped fresh parsley

6 ounces sliced roasted turkey breast

2½ cups romaine lettuce leaves, cleaned and torn into pieces

2 tablespoons David's Red Wine Vinaigrette (see Index)

Place the basil and parsley in a medium bowl. Mash into a chunky paste with the back of a spoon, adding a few drops of water if necessary. Add the turkey, and toss to coat. Line a serving plate with the lettuce. Arrange the turkey on top of the lettuce. Drizzle with the vinaigrette just before serving.

Makes 1 serving. Per serving: 262 calories, 53 g protein, 7 g carbohydrate, 2 g fat, 0 g saturated fat, 3 g fiber, 2 g sugar

DRESSINGS

David's Red Wine Vinaigrette

This dressing is the perfect flavor enhancer for the most ordinary salads. When you move on to phase 2, you can "dress up" this dressing with some honey and swap the red wine vinegar for balsamic. For phase 1, however, you may use this recipe or 1 teaspoon of oil with vinegar on your salads.

¼ cup red wine vinegar

2 tablespoons bottled water

1 tablespoon lemon juice

1 teaspoon chopped fresh thyme

1 teaspoon chopped fresh dill

1 teaspoon chopped fresh parsley

Fresh ground black pepper

In a small bowl or glass jar, combine the vinegar, water, lemon juice, and herbs and season to taste with the pepper. Whisk or shake until mixed. Use immediately, or refrigerate for up to 1 week.

Makes 8 servings. Per serving: 3 calories, 0 g protein, 1 g carbohydrate, 0 g fat, 0 g saturated fat, 0 g fiber, 0 g sugar

Ginger Soy Dressing

This versatile dressing goes great with fish and chicken as well as over most salads. During phase 1 of the plan, omit the honey from this recipe.

2 tablespoons rice wine vinegar

2 tablespoons bottled water

1 tablespoon low-sodium soy sauce

1 teaspoon sesame oil

1 teaspoon honey*

1 teaspoon grated fresh gingerroot

1 teaspoon toasted sesame seeds

In a small bowl or glass jar, combine the vinegar, water, soy sauce, oil, honey, ginger, and sesame seeds. Whisk or shake until mixed. Use immediately, or refrigerate for up to 1 week.

*Do not use honey during phase 1.

Makes 5 servings. Per serving: 21 calories, 0 g protein, 2 g carbohydrate, 1 g fat, 0 g saturated fat, 0 g fiber, 1 g sugar

Phases 2 and 3 Recipes

In these phases you will see the introduction of certain select carbs such as quinoa, lentils, and sweet potatoes. The ease and simplicity of phase 1 is continued in these tasty, albeit a little more indulgent, recipes.

BREAKFASTS

Breakfast Shake

If you'd like a more substantial "smoothie" in the morning, try this dose of fresh fruit in your morning shake.

    8 ounces noncarbonated mineral water
    5 ice cubes
    ½ cup frozen mixed berries
    1 scoop vanilla- or chocolate-flavored whey protein powder*

In a blender, combine the water, ice cubes, berries, and protein powder. Blend on high speed for 45 seconds. Serve immediately.

Makes 1 serving.

*Per serving using generic protein powder (vanilla): 125 calories, 19 g protein, 10 g carbohydrate, 1.5 g fat, .5 g saturated fat, 2 g fiber, 7 g sugar

*Per serving using generic protein powder (chocolate): 135 calories, 18 g protein, 10 g carbohydrate, 2.5 g fat, 1 g saturated fat, 2 g fiber, 7 g sugar

*Per serving using David Kirsch's Vanilla Protein Powder: 215 calories, 26 g protein, 18 g carbohydrate, 3.5 g fat, 1.5 g saturated fat, 7 g fiber, 8 g sugar

David Kirsch's Power Pancakes

Usually pancakes consist of white flour, sugar, and milk, which all weigh you down and make you feel like taking a nap after breakfast. My power pancakes, on the other hand, are rich in protein and whole grains. They're a great way to start the day after a grueling weekend-morning workout.

½ cup cooked steel-cut oatmeal

2 egg whites

½ cup water

¼ teaspoon cinnamon

1 scoop whey protein powder*

Nonfat cooking spray

1 tablespoon nonfat plain yogurt (optional)**

¼ cup sliced fresh strawberries (optional)**

In a large bowl, combine the oatmeal, egg whites, water, cinnamon, and protein powder. Heat a medium, nonstick skillet over medium-high heat, and coat with cooking spray. Place two heaping tablespoons of batter on the skillet. Cook 3 minutes, or until puffy and dry around the edges. Turn and cook on the other side, until golden brown. Serve with yogurt or strawberries.

Makes 1 serving.

*Per serving using generic protein powder (vanilla): 200 calories, 28 g protein, 16 g carbohydrate, 3 g fat, .5 g saturated fat, 2 g fiber, 4 g sugar

*Per serving using David Kirsch's Vanilla Protein Powder: 290 calories, 35 g protein, 24 g carbohydrate, 5 g fat, 2 g saturated fat, 7 g fiber, 5 g sugar

**Optional ingredients are not included in the nutritional analysis.

David's Energy Boost

I am not a big coffee advocate, but I do suggest this "healthy" coffee alternative for those days when you need a little extra "kick in the pants."

6 ounces very strong coffee

2 ounces fat-free milk

5 ice cubes

1 scoop chocolate- or vanilla-flavored whey protein powder*

In a blender, combine the coffee, milk, ice cubes, and protein powder. Blend on high speed for 45 seconds. Serve immediately.

Makes 1 serving.

*Per serving using generic protein powder (vanilla): 113 calories, 20 g protein, 5 g carbohydrate, 1.5 g fat, .5 g saturated fat, 0 g fiber, 5 g sugar

*Per serving using generic protein powder (chocolate): 123 calories, 19 g protein, 5 g carbohydrate, 2.5 g fat, 1 g saturated fat, 0 g fiber, 5 g sugar

*Per serving using David Kirsch's Protein Powder: 203 calories, 27 g protein, 13 g carbohydrate, 3.5 g fat, 1.5 g saturated fat, 5 g fiber, 6 g sugar

Frittata with Broccoli Rabe, Sun-Dried Tomatoes, and Parmesan

Picture yourself in Tuscany at dawn while you eat this Italian-inspired breakfast treat.

Nonfat vegetable cooking spray

8 ounces broccoli rabe, washed, trimmed, and cut into 1-inch pieces

1 medium garlic clove, minced or pressed through garlic press

11 egg whites

1 whole egg

⅛ teaspoon red pepper flakes

3 ounces oil-packed sun-dried tomatoes, drained and chopped coarse

¼ cup fat-free milk (or water)

Salt

Pepper

3 ounces freshly grated Parmigiano-Reggiano

Coat a medium nonstick skillet with cooking spray. Sauté the broccoli rabe until tender. Add the garlic and sauté 2 to 3 minutes. Set aside. In a large bowl, whisk together the egg whites, whole egg, red pepper flakes, tomato, and milk (or water). Mix in the salt and pepper to taste. Pour the egg mixture into the skillet with the broccoli and garlic, cover, and cook 10 minutes, until the top is set. Sprinkle the grated cheese on top. Preheat the broiler. Place the skillet under the broiler for 3 minutes, until the frittata is golden brown.

Makes 6 servings. Per serving: 151 calories, 16 g protein, 7 g carbohydrate, 7 g fat, 3 g saturated fat, 1 g fiber, 2 g sugar

Turkey Bacon, Spinach, and Egg White Frittata

This rich-tasting dish sets you back only a fraction of calories.

Nonfat cooking spray

1 cup fresh spinach, stems removed

11 egg whites

1 whole egg

¼ cup fat-free milk (or water)

4 strips of turkey bacon, cooked and crumbled

Salt

Pepper

Heat a large ovenproof skillet over medium-high heat, and coat with cooking spray. Sauté the spinach 2 to 3 minutes, and set aside. In a large bowl, whisk together the egg whites, whole egg, and milk (or water). Mix in the spinach, crumbled turkey bacon, and salt and pepper to taste. Preheat the broiler. Pour the egg mixture into the skillet, cover, and cook 10 minutes, until the top is set. Place the skillet under the broiler for 3 minutes, until the frittata is golden brown.

Makes 6 servings. Per serving: 72 calories, 10 g protein, 2 g carbohydrate, 3 g fat, 1 g saturated fat, 0 g fiber, 1 g sugar

Turkey Bacon, Sweet Potato, and Green Onion Frittata

Because of the sweet potato, save this dish for phase 2 and beyond. It's a great high-protein and high-fiber way to start your morning.

Nonfat vegetable cooking spray

1 large sweet potato, peeled and cut into ½-inch cubes

1 cup chopped green onion

11 egg whites

1 whole egg

¼ cup fat-free milk (or water)

4 strips of turkey bacon, cooked and crumbled

Salt

Pepper

Coat a medium ovenproof skillet with cooking spray. Sauté the potato for 15 to 20 minutes, until tender. Add the green onion, and sauté 2 to 3 minutes. Set aside. In a large bowl, whisk together the egg whites, whole egg, and milk (or water). Mix in the crumbled turkey bacon and salt and pepper to taste. Preheat the broiler. Pour the egg mixture into the skillet with the potato and onion, cover, and cook 10 minutes, until the top is set. Place the skillet under the broiler for 3 minutes, until the frittata is golden brown.

Makes 6 servings. Per serving: 96 calories, 9 g protein, 9 g carbohydrate, 2 g fat, 1 g saturated fat, 2 g fiber, 4 g sugar

ENTRÉES

Almond Lentil Loaf

Who needs the fat and calories of your traditional meat loaf when you can make this delicious, lean alternative?

3 cups water

1 cup dry lentils

1 teaspoon olive oil

½ cup chopped onion

1 clove garlic, minced

⅔ cup chopped carrot

⅓ cup chopped celery

2 egg whites, lightly beaten

1 tablespoon whole wheat flour

¾ cup chopped unsalted raw almonds

1 teaspoon dried thyme

In a medium saucepan, bring the water to a boil. Add the lentils, cover, and simmer until the lentils are soft, about 45 minutes. Set aside. Heat the oil in a nonstick skillet over medium-high heat. Add the onion and garlic, stirring frequently until the onion is translucent. Add the carrot and celery. Reduce heat to low and cover, cooking until the carrot is tender, about 10 to 15 minutes. Let cool.

Preheat the oven to 350°F. In a large bowl, mix together the lentils, vegetable mixture, and remaining ingredients. Spoon the mixture into an oiled loaf pan. Bake until firm, about 45 minutes. Serve warm.

Makes 6 servings. Per serving: 254 calories, 15 g protein, 29 g carbohydrate, 10 g fat, 1 g saturated fat, 7 g fiber, 5 g sugar

Chicken Satay

This is a great dish to serve at parties. Your guests will never know they are eating healthful fare.

6 ounces boneless, skinless chicken breast

½ teaspoon curry powder

¼ teaspoon ground cayenne

⅛ teaspoon freshly ground black pepper

3 tablespoons David's Low-Fat Peanut Sauce (see Index)

Slice the chicken into six pieces and place in a small bowl. Add the curry powder, cayenne, and black pepper. Toss to coat. Cover and refrigerate for 1 to 2 hours to marinate.

Preheat the broiler or grill. Thread the chicken onto skewers, and broil or grill 4 inches from the heat for 2 to 3 minutes per side, until no longer pink. Serve with peanut sauce.

Makes 1 serving. Per serving: 312 calories, 46 g protein, 7 g carbohydrate, 11 g fat, 3 g saturated fat, 2 g fiber, 2 g sugar

Baked Falafel with Yogurt-Mint Dressing

Falafel is usually loaded with oil. Because it's baked instead of fried, this version is as lean as it is delicious.

Falafel

½ cup dried chickpeas

¼ cup chopped green onion

¼ cup minced fresh parsley

½ teaspoon baking powder

½ teaspoon ground coriander

½ teaspoon ground cumin

¼ teaspoon dried basil

¼ teaspoon dried thyme

¼ teaspoon hot pepper sauce

⅛ teaspoon salt

⅛ teaspoon freshly ground black pepper

⅛ teaspoon ground red pepper

2 large egg whites

1 garlic clove, chopped

Nonfat vegetable cooking spray

Relish

1 cup chopped, seeded plum tomato

½ cup chopped, seeded Kirby cucumber

1 tablespoon chopped green onion

1 teaspoon chopped fresh parsley

1 teaspoon fresh lemon juice

½ serrano chili, minced

Yogurt Dressing

½ cup nonfat plain yogurt

⅛ teaspoon salt

1 teaspoon chopped fresh mint leaves

1 garlic clove, finely minced

Place chickpeas in a large pot, and cover with water. Let stand overnight. Drain the chickpeas and discard the water.

Preheat oven to 350°F. Combine chickpeas and all of the falafel ingredients except the garlic, egg whites, and cooking spray in a food processor, and pulse until finely chopped. Place mixture in a medium bowl and add the garlic. Add the egg whites, and stir well. Let stand for 15 minutes. Divide the mixture into eight equal portions, shaping each into a ½-inch patty. Place the patties on a baking sheet coated with cooking spray. Bake at 350°F for 10 minutes or until lightly browned.

To prepare the relish, combine all of the relish ingredients.

To prepare the dressing, combine all of the dressing ingredients, and whisk until blended well.

Makes 2 servings. Per serving: 246 calories, 17 g protein, 41 g carbohydrate, 3 g fat, 0 g saturated fat, 11 g fiber, 12 g sugar

Ginger-Glazed Halibut

Ginger adds a sweet, Asian flavor to this lean protein dish.

Nonfat cooking spray

¾ tablespoon ginger preserves

½ teaspoon Dijon mustard

½ teaspoon reduced-sodium soy sauce

½ teaspoon freshly grated ginger

Coarsely ground black pepper

1½-pound halibut fillet

Preheat the broiler. Coat the broiler rack with cooking spray. In a small bowl, combine ginger preserves, Dijon mustard, soy sauce, ginger, and pepper to taste until smooth. Place the fish on broiler rack. Using a pastry brush, spread the ginger mixture over the fish. Broil 10 minutes, or until the fish flakes when tested with a fork.

Makes 2 servings. Per serving: 148 calories, 24 g protein, 6 g carbohydrate, 3 g fat, 0 g saturated fat, 0 g fiber, 4 g sugar

Guiltless Barbecue Burger

Red meat need not come loaded with saturated fat. Buffalo meat tastes just as delicious as beef, but it comes much leaner. Because of its leanness, it cooks more quickly as well.

4 ounces lean ground buffalo meat

4 ounces lean ground turkey breast

1 tablespoon Worcestershire sauce

2 tablespoons Dijon mustard

2 tablespoons low-sugar, low-sodium barbecue sauce

2 egg whites, lightly beaten

Nonfat vegetable cooking spray

Mix all of the ingredients except the cooking spray in a large bowl. Form the mixture into two patties. Spray a barbecue grill or nonstick skillet with cooking spray, and heat to medium-high heat. Place the patties on grill or skillet, and cook about 8 minutes per side (for medium), until cooked through.

Makes 2 servings. Per serving: 185 calories, 33 g protein, 8 g carbohydrate, 3 g fat, 1 g saturated fat, .5 g fiber, 4 g sugar

Sesame Buckwheat Noodles with Low-Fat Peanut Sauce

Serve this easy dish along with some steamed shrimp or cubed chicken breast for a complete meal.

4 ounces sesame buckwheat noodles
3 tablespoons David's Low-Fat Peanut Sauce (see Index)

Cook the buckwheat noodles according to package directions. Drain and mix with the peanut sauce. Serve immediately.

Makes 2 servings. Per serving: 291 calories, 13 g protein, 41 g carbohydrate, 9 g fat, 1 g saturated fat, 5 g fiber, 3 g sugar

Shrimp and Whole Wheat Pasta with Arugula Dressing

Whole wheat pasta has a slightly different texture than the typical variety made from refined flour. It cooks a little more quickly, so follow package directions carefully.

1 cup cooked 100 percent organic whole wheat pasta shells (½ cup uncooked pasta)
¼ pound cooked, cleaned shrimp, cut into bite-sized pieces
½ cup frozen peas, thawed
½ Kirby cucumber, peeled and diced
¼ red pepper, diced
1 scallion, thinly sliced
Yogurt-Arugula Dressing (see Index)

Mix pasta, shrimp, peas, cucumber, pepper, and scallion together in a large bowl. Mix in Yogurt-Arugula Dressing. Serve immediately.

Makes 2 servings. Per serving: 222 calories, 21 g protein, 31 g carbohydrate, 2 g fat, 0 g saturated fat, 6 g fiber, 5 g sugar

Thai Shrimp Sauté

What a nice tasty reward with calcium-rich broccoli and heart-healthy garlic. This dish is delicious and nutritious.

Nonfat olive oil cooking spray

6 ounces large shrimp, peeled and deveined

1 cup broccoli florets

½ cup sliced red bell pepper (½-inch strips)

½ cup sugar snap peas, cleaned and halved

1 teaspoon chili garlic sauce

⅓ cup David's Low-Fat Peanut Sauce (see Index)

Coat a large nonstick skillet with cooking spray, and heat over medium-high heat. Place shrimp in skillet, stirring frequently, 1 to 3 minutes until opaque. Place the shrimp in a bowl, and cover to keep warm. Respray the skillet, and place the vegetables and the chili garlic sauce in the skillet, stirring with a wooden spoon frequently until cooked through and tender, about 5 to 10 minutes. Add the shrimp and the peanut sauce to the vegetable mixture, and stir until shrimp and vegetables are evenly coated and warm.

Makes 2 servings. Per serving: 216 calories, 27 g protein, 10 g carbohydrate, 9 g fat, 1 g saturated fat, 3 g fiber, 3 g sugar

SIDE DISHES

Red Peppers Stuffed with Quinoa

This is two MVPs in one dish. Vitamin C–rich red pepper combined with all of the essential amino acids and nutrient-rich quinoa is a sure hit.

¼ cup quinoa
1 cup bottled water
2 red bell peppers
½ green apple, cored and chopped
1 tablespoon freshly squeezed lemon juice
1½ tablespoons chopped fresh parsley
1½ tablespoons chopped fresh mint
1 garlic clove, crushed
1 cup all-natural chopped tomatoes
3 scallions, thinly sliced
½ teaspoon olive oil
Sea salt
Freshly ground black pepper

Rinse and drain the quinoa in a fine-mesh strainer under running tap water until the water drains clear. Bring the water to a boil in a small saucepan. Add the quinoa, and cook for 15 minutes over medium-low heat, until all of the water is absorbed. Set aside.

Halve the peppers lengthwise, and scrape out and discard the seeds and membranes. Leave the stems intact so the peppers hold their shape. Place the peppers skin side down in an ovenproof dish.

In a medium bowl, mix the apple and lemon juice. Add the quinoa, herbs, garlic, tomato, scallion, and oil. Season with sea salt and pepper to taste, and mix well.

Preheat the oven to 350°F. Divide the quinoa mixture between the halved peppers. Pour a small amount of water in the dish around the peppers, and cook for 20 minutes, until the quinoa filling is hot.

Makes 2 servings. Per serving: 174 calories, 6 g protein, 35 g carbohydrate, 3 g fat, 0 g saturated fat, 6 g fiber, 13 g sugar

SALADS

Couscous Salad

Use this along with lean protein main dishes in phases 2 and 3 of the plan.

½ cup cooked couscous

1½ tablespoons nonfat plain yogurt

1 tablespoon chopped bell pepper

1 tablespoon diced tomato

1 tablespoon minced scallion

1 teaspoon chopped fresh parsley

¼ teaspoon grated lemon zest

Freshly ground black pepper

In a medium bowl, combine the couscous, yogurt, bell pepper, tomato, scallion, parsley, and lemon zest. Season to taste with black pepper. Serve immediately, or refrigerate for up to 1 day.

Makes 1 serving. Per serving: 106 calories, 4 g protein, 22 g carbohydrate, 0 g fat, 0 g saturated fat, 2 g fiber, 2 g sugar

Grilled Chicken and Bean Salad

To speed up the preparation time for this great lunch salad, poach extra chicken breast at the beginning of the week. Use some of it for a lunch or dinner, saving the rest for this salad.

1 cup canned chickpeas, rinsed and drained

1 cup canned kidney beans, rinsed and drained

1 small red onion, chopped

8 ounces grilled or poached boneless, skinless chicken breast,
  cut into bite-sized pieces

½ cup Dijon Vinaigrette (see Index)

In a medium bowl, combine the chickpeas, beans, onion, and cooked chicken. Add the vinaigrette, and toss to combine. Cover, and refrigerate overnight to blend flavors. Just before serving, spoon the salad mixture into a bowl with a slotted spoon.

Makes 3 servings. Per serving: 292 calories, 31 g protein, 32 g carbohydrate, 3 g fat, 1 g saturated fat, 8 g fiber, 8 g sugar

Quinoa Salad

Use this salad as a great whole-grain accompaniment to a lean protein lunch during phase 2 or phase 3 of the plan.

½ cup quinoa
1 cup bottled water
¼ cup diced cucumber
¼ cup peeled, seeded, and diced tomato
3 orange segments, chopped coarse
2 tablespoons chopped celery
2 tablespoons Citrus Cilantro Dressing (see Index)
Fresh cilantro leaves for garnish

Rinse and drain the quinoa in a fine-mesh strainer under running tap water until the water drains clear. Bring the water to a boil in a small saucepan. Add the quinoa, and cook for 15 minutes over medium-low heat, until all of the water is absorbed.

Meanwhile, in a medium bowl, combine the cucumber, tomato, orange segments, celery, and dressing. Add the quinoa, and toss to mix. Refrigerate until cold. Garnish with cilantro leaves, and serve chilled.

Makes 2 servings. Per serving: 179 calories, 6 g protein, 33 g carbohydrate, 3 g fat, 0 g saturated fat, 3 g fiber, 3 g sugar

Sweet Potato and Almond Salad with Mustard Vinaigrette

As a young lawyer/bodybuilder, I used to carry a couple of hot sweet potatoes in my suit pockets. The richness of beta-carotene and the benefits of vitamin E and fiber are the nutritional rewards of this tasty side dish.

1½ pounds sweet potatoes (1 to 2 medium potatoes)

1 teaspoon Dijon mustard

1 teaspoon whole-grain mustard

2 teaspoons white wine vinegar

⅛ teaspoon salt

1 teaspoon olive oil

1 celery stalk, thinly sliced

2 tablespoons slivered raw almonds

2 scallions, thinly sliced

Peel and halve potatoes lengthwise, and then cut them into 1-inch squares. Steam the potatoes over boiling water 10 to 12 minutes, until just tender.

In a medium bowl, whisk together the mustards, vinegar, and salt. Add the oil slowly, whisking until emulsified. Add the potatoes, celery, and almonds, and gently toss to combine. Cool to room temperature, and add the scallions.

Makes 3 servings. Per serving: 191 calories, 4 g protein, 36 g carbohydrate, 4 g fat, 0 g saturated fat, 6 g fiber, 7 g sugar

Thai Ginger Sirloin Salad

This salad tastes delicious hot or cold. When chilled, the steak is not as spicy, so use ½ teaspoon red pepper flakes. If serving it warm, use only ¼ teaspoon. You can use extra mesclun greens if baby bok choy is not available.

6 ounces sirloin steak, trimmed of fat

1 teaspoon grated fresh gingerroot

1 clove garlic, minced

¼–½ teaspoon red pepper flakes

Juice of ½ lime

Nonfat cooking spray

1 head baby bok choy cabbage, sliced (about 1 cup)

1 cup mesclun greens, washed and dried

1 tablespoon grated carrot

¼ cup bean sprouts

3 tablespoons Ginger Soy Dressing (see Index)

Cut the sirloin into ½-inch slices, and place them in a small bowl. Add the ginger, garlic, and pepper flakes. Squeeze the lime juice over the meat. Toss to coat. Let marinate at room temperate for 10 to 15 minutes.

Meanwhile, heat a medium nonstick skillet over medium-high heat, and coat with cooking spray. Add the bok choy, and cook for 1 to 2 minutes, until the leaves are just wilted but the cabbage is still crunchy. Remove to a serving plate.

Wipe out the skillet, and coat with cooking spray. Heat over high heat. Place the sirloin slices in the pan, and sear for 30 seconds per side for rare or 50 seconds per side for well done. Set aside.

Line a serving plate with the bok choy, mesclun greens, carrot, and bean sprouts. Arrange the steak over the salad. Serve immediately, or refrigerate for up to 6 hours and serve chilled. Drizzle with dressing just before serving.

Makes 1 serving. Per serving: 363 calories, 33 g protein, 18 g carbohydrate, 15 g fat, 5 g saturated fat, 3 g fiber, 9 g sugar

Tuna and Quinoa Salad

Make this simple phase 2 dish the night before for a healthful lunch loaded with fiber and lean protein.

½ cup cooked quinoa

1 6-ounce can chunk light tuna packed in water, rinsed, drained, and flaked

¼ cup cherry tomato

¼ cup finely chopped Italian parsley

⅛ cup chopped walnuts

1 tablespoon fresh lemon juice

½ tablespoon extra-virgin olive oil

¼ teaspoon kosher salt

Pinch of coarsely ground black pepper

In a large bowl, combine all ingredients, and mix gently to combine.

Makes 2 servings. Per serving: 281 calories, 26 g protein, 18 g carbohydrate, 12 g fat, 1 g saturated fat, 2 g fiber, 1 g sugar

Tuna Salad with Whole-Grain Mustard and Water Chestnuts

Who needs mayonnaise? Certainly not you! This recipe is full of flavor but low on fat.

1 can light tuna packed in spring water

1 teaspoon whole-grain mustard

1 teaspoon nonfat plain yogurt

3 water chestnuts, coarsely chopped

1 celery stalk, coarsely chopped

1 teaspoon freshly squeezed lemon juice

In a small mixing bowl, combine all of the ingredients.

Makes 2 servings. Per serving: 113 calories, 22 g protein, 3 g carbohydrate, 1 g fat, 0 g saturated fat, 1 g fiber, 1 g sugar

Warm Salmon and Lentil Salad

Make this delicious salad the night before for a protein- and fiber-packed lunch that will keep you going all afternoon long.

Nonstick cooking spray

½ cup chopped red bell pepper

¼ cup chopped shallots

1 can sockeye (or another variety of wild) salmon, rinsed clean and drained

1 cup cooked lentils

Salt

Freshly ground black pepper

Coat a nonstick skillet with cooking spray, and heat over medium-high heat. Sauté peppers and shallots for 2 to 3 minutes. Add salmon, and heat thoroughly, 3 to 5 minutes. Remove from heat, and add lentils to salmon mixture, stirring gently to combine. Add salt and pepper to taste.

Makes 2 servings. Per serving: 288 calories, 27 g protein, 26 g carbohydrate, 10 g fat, 2 g saturated fat, 9 g fiber, 4 g sugar

SAUCES, DIPS, AND DRESSINGS

Balsamic Vinaigrette

In phase 1, substitute the balsamic vinegar with red wine vinegar and omit the honey.

¼ cup balsamic vinegar

2 tablespoons bottled water

1 tablespoon lemon juice

1 teaspoon honey

1 teaspoon chopped fresh thyme

1 teaspoon chopped fresh dill

1 teaspoon chopped fresh parsley

Freshly ground black pepper

In a small bowl or glass jar, combine the vinegar, water, lemon juice, honey, and herbs. Season to taste with the pepper. Whisk or shake until mixed. Use immediately, or refrigerate for up to 1 week.

Makes 8 servings. Per serving: 9 calories, 0 g protein, 2 g carbohydrate, 0 g fat, 0 g saturated fat, 0 g fiber, 2 g sugar

Citrus Cilantro Dressing

Because of the orange juice, this dressing is a no-no until phase 2 of the plan. That said, it's much better for you than many conventional, store-bought dressings.

2 tablespoons fresh orange juice

1 tablespoon bottled water

2 teaspoons fresh lime juice

2 teaspoons fresh lemon juice

1 teaspoon whole-grain mustard

½ teaspoon grated orange zest

½ teaspoon chopped cilantro

½ teaspoon olive oil (optional)

In a small bowl or glass jar, combine the orange juice, water, lime juice, lemon juice, mustard, orange zest, cilantro, and oil. Whisk or shake until mixed. Use immediately or refrigerate for up to 1 week.

Makes 5 servings. Per serving: 6 calories, 0 g protein, 1 g carbohydrate, 0 g fat, 0 g saturated fat, 0 g fiber, 1 g sugar

David's Healthy Seafood Sauce

Who needs mayonnaise and fat-packed tartar sauce when you have this great-tasting nonfat topping for fish?

½ cup nonfat plain yogurt

1 tablespoon rinsed and drained capers

1 tablespoon rinsed, drained, and chopped sweet dill pickle

1 teaspoon rinsed, drained, and chopped cornichon

1 tablespoon fresh lemon juice

1 tablespoon chopped fresh dill

2 tablespoons Dijon mustard

2 tablespoons prepared white horseradish

Salt and pepper, to taste

Mix all the ingredients in a medium bowl, cover, and chill until ready to use.

Makes 2 servings. Per serving: 57 calories, 6 g protein, 12 g carbohydrate, 0 g fat, 0 g saturated fat, 1 g fiber, 5 g sugar

David's Low-Fat Peanut Sauce

This low-fat, low-sugar sauce tastes delicious on Poached Chicken Breast (see Index), on whole wheat pasta, and as a dip with fresh vegetables.

¼ cup unsweetened peanut butter

¼ cup bottled water

2 tablespoons fresh lime juice

1 tablespoon low-sodium soy sauce

½ teaspoon grated lime zest

½ teaspoon minced garlic

½ teaspoon grated fresh gingerroot

½ teaspoon Thai chili paste

In a small bowl or food processor, combine all ingredients. Mix until smooth. Use immediately, refrigerating extra sauce for up to 3 days.

Makes 10 servings. Per serving: 40 calories, 2 g protein, 2 g carbohydrate, 3 g fat, .5 g saturated fat, 0 g fiber, 0 g sugar

Dijon Vinaigrette

This dressing is the perfect flavor enhancer for the most ordinary salads. In phase 1, substitute the balsamic vinegar with red wine vinegar and omit the honey.

¼ cup balsamic vinegar
2 tablespoons bottled water
1 tablespoon lemon juice
1 teaspoon Dijon mustard
1 teaspoon honey
Freshly ground black pepper

In a small bowl or glass jar, combine the vinegar, water, lemon juice, mustard, and honey. Season to taste with the pepper. Whisk or shake until mixed. Use immediately, or refrigerate for up to 1 week.

Makes 8 servings. Per serving: 9 calories, 0 g protein, 2 g carbohydrate, 0 g fat, 0 g saturated fat, 0 g fiber, 2 g sugar

No-Fat Hummus

Serve this as a snack with celery, whole-grain crackers, or cucumber slices during phase 2 or phase 3 of the plan. For more zip, add more cayenne or a few drops of hot pepper sauce.

1½ cups cooked or canned chickpeas, rinsed and drained

¼ cup nonfat plain yogurt

1 tablespoon chopped parsley

1 tablespoon minced garlic

¼ teaspoon ground cumin

¼ teaspoon ground cayenne

¼ cup fresh-squeezed lemon juice

In a food processor, combine all ingredients. Process until well blended. Use immediately, or refrigerate up to 3 hours.

Makes 2 servings. Per serving: 227 calories, 12 g protein, 40 g carbohydrate, 3 g fat, 0 g saturated fat, 10 g fiber, 4 g sugar

Roasted Red Pepper and Almond Dip

Serve this delicious dip with celery, sliced cucumber, or whole wheat crackers for a great midmorning snack.

Nonfat vegetable cooking spray

1 large garlic clove, smashed

½ teaspoon crushed red pepper flakes

3 roasted red bell peppers, halved, membranes removed

½ cup organic raw almonds, coarsely chopped

1 tablespoon olive oil

Salt

Pepper

Coat a medium nonstick skillet with cooking spray. Add the garlic and red pepper flakes, and cook over low heat for 10 minutes.

Place cooled roasted red peppers in a food processor, and pulse until coarsley chopped. Add the almonds, garlic, and red pepper flakes. Pulse just until coarsely ground. Slowly add the oil, and pulse one or two more times. Season with salt and pepper to taste.

Makes 3 servings. Per serving: 227 calories, 7 g protein, 15 g carbohydrate, 17 g fat, 2 g saturated fat, 6 g fiber, 8 g sugar

Sweet Potato Spread

Serve this dish either at room temperature or chilled. It's a great snack with cucumber slices or (if you're feeling naughty and you're not in phase 1 of the diet) whole wheat pita wedges.

Nonfat vegetable cooking spray

3 large sweet potatoes (about 2 pounds), peeled and cut into 1-inch cubes

1 small yellow onion, chopped

1 cup canned chickpeas, rinsed and drained

¾ teaspoon salt

¼ teaspoon curry powder

¼ teaspoon ground cumin

2 tablespoons water

Preheat oven to 400°F. Coat a shallow roasting pan with cooking spray. Add potatoes, cover with foil, and cook for 15 minutes. Uncover, and roast until tender, about 30 minutes. Set aside.

Meanwhile, sauté the onion in a medium nonstick skillet over medium heat until soft (2 to 3 minutes). Add the chickpeas and sauté, stirring frequently for another 1 to 2 minutes. Set aside. Add the onion mixture to a food processor, pureeing until smooth. Add the potatoes, salt, curry powder, and cumin, and pulse until well blended. Add the water as needed, until the mixture is sufficiently smooth.

Makes 4 servings. Per serving: 193 calories, 6 g protein, 41 g carbohydrate, 1 g fat, 0 g saturated fat, 7 g fiber, 11 g sugar

Yogurt-Arugula Dressing

This is perfect as a dip or a salad dressing, and you'll love the peppery taste of the baby arugula.

⅛ cup nonfat plain yogurt

1 teaspoon fresh lemon juice

¼ cup firmly packed baby arugula leaves, stems removed

Pinch of dried oregano

Pinch of dried marjoram

Salt and pepper, to taste

In a food processor, combine all of the ingredients, and blend until smooth.

Makes 2 servings. Per serving: 9 calories, 1 g protein, 2 g carbohydrate, 0 g fat, 0 g saturated fat, 0 g fiber, 1 g sugar

Embracing Everything New York

I'm writing this chapter just a few days after Thanksgiving. I did enjoy a nice piece of pecan pie, my homemade corn bread stuffing, and some delicious red wine. Life is too short to forgo these finer culinary moments. That being said, I am a Capricorn and love order and discipline in my life. I look, feel, and think better when I eat well and drink alcohol minimally.

After the days—such as Thanksgiving—when I do indulge, I run harder, cycle farther, or row longer than usual. I drink more water and eat foods that help clean the pollutants out of my system. I fully embrace the concept of the "pay-and-play" mentality. I offset the occasional cheeseburger and fries with my protein shakes, vitamin drinks, and egg white frittatas.

Throughout this chapter, you'll find my solutions for having it all without suffering the consequences. You'll learn how to enjoy everything the New York lifestyle has to offer—the fast pace, the great food, the fantastic parties—without also experiencing the usual side effects of this lifestyle—stress, hangovers, and extra fat around the middle.

Surviving New York Nightlife

Alcohol is on the A, B, C, D, E, and F list for good reason. Pure alcohol contains about seven calories per gram, which makes it nearly twice as fattening as carbohydrates or protein (which both contain about four calories per gram). If you're having a mixed drink, don't forget the calories in the juice, soft drink, and sugary mixer. Those elements plus alcohol usually add up to more calories than the typical slice of chocolate cake. That said, you can safely drink in phase 3 of the Ultimate New York Diet if you follow these smarter drinking strategies.

1. EAT BEFORE YOU DRINK—ALWAYS

Not long ago, I broke this rule and paid the price. It was Halloween, and I didn't follow my own advice. I went to a party that served only alcohol. I hadn't eaten before and did not take bottled water with me. I was thirsty, so I had a few drinks. I'd like to say that I was forced to drink, but I'm in control of my life and my choices, so I won't go that far. Later, I found myself at a late-night restaurant, eating turkey burgers and fries. I was desperate to soak up the alcohol. I probably drank about four bottles of Fiji water before I went to bed. Unfortunately, eating and drinking water did not prevent me from suffering a very painful and somewhat embarrassing hangover. Suffice it to say, the next morning, I paid the price. When I woke up with a pounding headache, I laughed at myself. "You should know better," I thought. "What was I thinking?" You're never too old to learn a lesson. Here, candy corn and vodka cranberries were definitely not a good mixture.

When you have food in your stomach, it slows the absorption of alcohol into your bloodstream. Yes, OK, I'll admit it, this is a literal buzzkill, but it helps your morning after to remain headache free. It also protects your organs from the damage caused by alcohol toxicity.

Before you head out the door to the bar or cocktail party, have a protein shake and multivitamin drink. The shake will coat your stomach, slowing the absorption of alcohol into your system. The multivitamin/mineral supplement will supply your body with antioxidants to neutralize the free radicals that alcohol will create—especially if you overdo it. Follow up with a glass of water to prehydrate your system. Alcohol induces urination—which explains why most drinkers spend a lot of time in the bathroom. To prevent dehydration—which, in itself, can cause hangover-like symptoms—you'll want to drink a lot of water at the start of and throughout the evening. Follow every drink with at least two drinks of water. This will continue to hydrate your body, and you will lessen the amount of alcohol you consume.

Now, if you want to take things a step further to prevent a morning-after hangover, you can try the following advice as well. I had a friend many years ago who liked to have a cocktail or two. Before going out she would swallow two tablespoons of olive oil to coat her stomach. She swore by this method and never admitted to waking up with a hangover.

2. KNOW WHAT'S IN YOUR DRINK

To cash in on the low-carb lifestyle, many spirits advertisers market their fare as "zero carb." Although this claim isn't exactly an outright lie, it is misleading. Hard liquor is distilled and thus contains no carbohydrates. That said, the "zero carb" campaign for vodka and whiskey is similar to bragging that a candy bar is "cholesterol free." It's still fattening, nonetheless.

Instead of the number of carbs, choose your alcohol based on the number of calories. A five-ounce glass of wine typically contains 110 calories, 5 grams of carbohydrates, and about 13 grams of alcohol. In my mind, it's the best choice. Not only has wine been linked with heart health (a benefit that stems from the phytochemicals present in grapes), it also is generally absorbed more slowly than mixed drinks (because most are mixed with carbonated water or soda) and shots of alcohol. Opt for a dry variety of wine, as sweeter wines generally contain more sugar, which equals more calories. For example, a glass of dry wine has about 120 calories, and a glass of sweet dessert wine has a whopping 270 calories. Mixing some club soda into your wine to create a spritzer will reduce calories even more.

Your next best selection is champagne. With only about 100 calories per glass, champagne is as light on calories as it is on texture. That said, the carbonation causes your body to process the alcohol more quickly, which can result in a killer hangover if you're not careful.

After that comes beer. Light beers, of course, have fewer calories than regular beer. These beers, however, generally are also light on taste. If you are a beer connoisseur, then opt for the beer you crave, but try to limit yourself to just one. And savor it.

The absolute worst option is a mixed drink. You have the calories not only from the alcohol itself but from the mixer as well. If you simply have to have a drink with a pretty umbrella in it, then at least swap high-calorie mixers (juice, soda) for low- or no-calorie mixers (iced black or green tea or club soda).

When choosing mixed drinks, also consider the size that the bar or restaurant generally serves up. The larger the drink, the higher the calorie content. Most bars serve up margaritas the size of swimming pools, which is why these drinks can easily total more than 400 calories. For this reason, martinis and cosmopolitans—which come in smaller glasses—generally make better choices than margaritas.

Use the following chart to make smarter drink choices. All cocktails in the chart are made with a one-and-one-half-ounce serving of distilled spirits (unless otherwise noted):

Shot of alcohol (80 proof)	1.5 oz.	100 calories
Beer	12 oz.	150 calories
Wine, red	6 oz.	128 calories
Wine, white	6 oz.	120 calories
Wine, rosé	6 oz.	128 calories
Wine, sweet dessert	6 oz.	270 calories
Champagne	4 oz.	105 calories
Margarita	5 oz.	550 calories
Mudslide	4.5 oz.	417 calories
Long Island iced tea	8 oz.	380 calories
Piña colada	6 oz.	293 calories
Mike's Hard Lemonade	12 oz.	240 calories
Bacardi Silver	12 oz.	225 calories

3. DRINK MODERATELY

Personally, I recommend you drink no more than once or twice a week. That said, I'm also realistic. I know some of you simply have to have your wine with dinner, and no matter what I tell you, you will never give that up.

In that case, try to at least hold yourself to the government's *Dietary Guidelines for Americans* recommendation for safe, moderate drinking, which is no more than one drink a day for women and no more than two daily for men. One drink equals 12 ounces of beer, 5 ounces of wine, 1.5 ounces of 80-proof distilled spirits, or 10 ounces of wine cooler.

Why the limit? Other than the obvious effects on your waistline, drinking more than that limit can raise your risk for various diseases. Although some research shows moderate drinking (one to two drinks a day) lowers risk for heart disease and can certainly help you relax at the end of the day, going above that limit may pose adverse health effects such as liver disease and breast cancer.

4. CHASE EACH DRINK WITH WATER

OK, I just admonished you to drink moderately, which, for women, means stopping at one. Again, I'm a realist. I know there will be some nights—such as New Year's Eve or your birthday or even Halloween—when you will throw caution to the wind. On those nights, try to drink a glass or two of water between each alcoholic drink. The water will help to keep you hydrated and will also slow down your drinking pace. Before you go to sleep, have another glass of water to avoid waking with a dehydration-induced headache.

5. CLEANSE YOUR SYSTEM THE MORNING AFTER

When you drink, you bathe your brain in ethanol. Your brain cells quickly adapt to this state, so, when you stop drinking and blood and brain alcohol levels drop, your brain cells go into *alcohol withdrawal*. Withdrawal symptoms include headache, nausea, dry mouth, swollen eyes, sweaty skin, and an upset stomach. These signs worsen as blood alcohol levels fall, peaking when blood alcohol levels reach zero.

Depending on how many and what types of drinks you've had the night before, the last thing you'll want to do is get out of bed. All I can say is buck up. Get up. Drink more water, have a protein shake, take a vitamin/mineral supplement, and get your butt outside for a power walk.

Exercise at a brisk pace to induce sweating. (I understand if you want to avoid jumping jacks and other jerky motions; I'm not a sadist.) The exercise will help your body detoxify itself from the alcohol and burn off the excess calories that you ate. If you really overdid it, you'll smell the alcohol seeping from your sweat glands. In that case, keep moving until you no longer smell like last night's martini.

Then have breakfast. You'll crave greasy fare. Instead of the burger and fries, however, opt for a turkey or buffalo burger or turkey chili. This will comfort your belly and mind without the fat and calories of the foods you crave. If you can stomach it, try to include some veggies in each meal. They will help to neutralize the acid that built up in your body the night before. I know food may be the last thing on your mind, but after hydrating with water and exercising, it is really important to get quality protein and carbohydrate calories back into your body.

Waking Up in a New York Minute

In Manhattan it seems as if every block has one or more coffee houses—all with New Yorkers waiting in line for their daily dose of caffeine, milk, and sugar.

Anyone who knows me knows that I'm not a big believer in caffeine. It discourages your intestines from absorbing water, which induces dehydration. It also tends to rev you up in a stressful way. A cup of coffee definitely makes you more alert, but it also makes you more jittery, anger prone, and easily frustrated.

So, should you give up coffee, Red Bull, and other highly caffeinated drinks? Yes, it's probably a good idea. Can you occasionally indulge in a cup of coffee? Of course. This leads back to my saying: "If some is good, more is not better." The occasional espresso won't harm you, but if you feel as if you need the "grande latte" from Starbucks a few times a day, you have a problem.

David's Cocktail Party Survival Guide

Whether you've been invited to a cocktail party or you are hosting your own, you can take proactive steps to ensure you indulge without going overboard. If you are hosting your own—great—you are in charge of the menu and can serve healthful foods that fit into the Ultimate New York Diet. If you are attending someone else's party, be a considerate guest. Call ahead and ask if you can help out by bringing some food along. Here you'll find my favorite cocktail party hors d'oeuvres.

- A bowl of mixed nuts (preferably raw almonds and walnuts)
- Steamed edamame, lightly salted
- Sashimi (purchased from a reputable Japanese restaurant that serves sushi-grade fish)
- Raw vegetables (cauliflower, broccoli, cucumber, celery, snap peas) and whole wheat pita wedges served with the following dips: Roasted Red Pepper and Almond Dip (see Index), No-Fat Hummus (see Index), pureed edamame with cilantro, and Sweet Potato Spread (see Index)

For drinks, offer (or bring) plenty of bottled water. That will help you and your guests stay hydrated between sips of wine and beer.

First, let's talk about weaning yourself off the stuff. I've done this many times throughout my life, so I can speak from experience. If you're also a multiple-cup-a-day coffee drinker, you'll need to deal with the headaches and nausea that may come from caffeine withdrawal. What does that tell you about the drug caffeine that we ingest as if it were water? To cut back, you'll need to find a substitute for the experience of drinking coffee as well as a substitute for the stimulation it provides. In terms of the experience, consider switching to green tea. It supplies much less caffeine (about 40 milligrams compared to coffee's 120). It also is good for you, helping to reduce your risk of heart disease and cancer. It revs up the metabolism, helping your body burn fat. Finally, you can put it in the same mug from which you usually drink your coffee, simulating the experience.

In addition to green tea, consider taking some supplements, such as the ones mentioned in Chapter 3 under "Energy Boosters." Follow up by getting plenty of sleep and reducing your daily stress (see next section), as stress can sap your energy levels.

Now, let's talk about that occasional cup of coffee. If that's all you have—black coffee—you're in the clear. In today's coffee house world, however, that's rarely the case. Usually, coffee drinks are loaded with milk and sugar, two Ultimate New York Diet no-nos. To reduce some of the damage, consider the following:

- Stick with a small rather than a medium or a large.
- Order a cappuccino instead of a latte or au lait. Because the former is made with more foam, it contains less milk than the latter.
- Always order a skinny (nonfat milk) versus a regular.
- Nix the flavor shot. It's pure sugar. If you simply can't bring yourself to do so, at least ask the barista to use only half as much syrup as usual.
- Find a coffee house that uses coffee soon after grinding the beans and doesn't let it sit out in a pot all day long. Coffee left to sit on a burner not only tastes horrible, it's also incredibly acidic, which can actually slow the metabolism.
- Try drinking naturally water-processed decaffeinated coffee instead of the regular cup of joe. That, however is not a license for you to have an unlimited number of cups of the decaf variety.

Soothing Away City Stress

Many of my clients use their lofts and apartments for just one thing: sleep. They wake early in the morning, leave early, and don't stop until they fall back into bed later in the evening. Whether they are corporate CEOs or full-time parents, they keep full schedules with one appointment after another. For them, the New York minute ticks by ever so quickly. Their schedules don't allow them a minute to spare.

This type of fast-paced lifestyle can leave you feeling either exhilarated and on top of your game or frenzied and dull. It can either infuse your life with meaning and confidence or leave you with all of the negative side effects of stress, including insomnia, poor health, and a dull appearance.

Why am I talking about stress in a diet book? When you are under stress, your body releases cortisol and other stress hormones that trigger sugar and fat cravings. Chronically high levels of these hormones cause weight gain, particularly in the tummy. I'm also interested in your wellness, and chronic stress has been linked to heart disease, cancer, diabetes, insomnia, and low energy levels, among other ailments.

The problem isn't stress per se. It's how you react to it. Are you the type of person who—when caught in traffic—sits and stews about your bad luck, or are you the type of person who makes lemonade out of lemons, using your time to plan for the rest of the day, make a few phone calls, or listen to a radio show that you never have time to hear? It's the latter type of person who thrives within the energy of New York. The former tends to get used up and spit out by the city.

Even if you are someone with the former mind-set, however, you can change. I know because I've seen this transformation take place among many of my clients. The Ultimate New York Diet will help support you in your stress-soothing efforts. When you feed yourself wholesome foods, you put less stress into your body. When you exercise regularly, you help get stress out of your body. Many of my clients have told me that their moods lifted after embarking on this program.

To further reduce stress, take the following actions.

- **Learn how to relax.** In order to feel relaxed during life's tense situations, you need to practice relaxation on a regular basis. Once a day spend five minutes doing some form of relaxation. Put on some headphones and listen to your favorite music. Sit quietly as you focus on the sensation of breathing. Don't underestimate the power of breathing and its ability to calm and soothe your body, mind, and spirit. Lie on the floor and systematically relax the muscles of your body, starting at your feet and working your way up to your head. Do what works for you.

- **Find positive ways to deal with bad situations.** You can't control your boss's behavior or whether the subway gets stuck in a tunnel, but you can control your reaction to such situations. Are you in a cab that's caught in traffic? Get out and walk. Just get an annoying e-mail from a coworker? Instead of wasting time by sitting and stewing, head to the stairwell and run up and down a flight of stairs until it's out of your system, or get down on the floor and do a quick set of push-ups. Just get home after a crazy day at the office? Instead of reaching for a martini, put on your sneakers and head out for a jog, sit quietly and meditate, or head to a yoga class.

  Music has always been an important part of my life. Aside from documenting moments in time (I know where I was or what I was doing the first time I heard that song!), I use music to quiet me down or liven me up, depending on the moment. There's nothing like turning on my favorite radio station, WKTU 103.5, and dancing around with my dog Houston first thing in the morning. It's better than the strongest cup of espresso! To de-stress, a little Ella Fitzgerald or Etta James helps quiet the savage beast within.

- **Create a daily ritual of self-love.** I know a few stay-at-home parents who take lots of time to dress their children but spend very little time on their own appearance. Your appearance matters. It goes a long way to helping you to feel confident and secure. It also helps you to focus on what you can control—your appearance—and not on what you can't control, such as traffic. So each morning, brush your teeth, style your hair, put on makeup, and get dressed in nice clothing—even if you don't plan to go outside.

- **Use multitasking wisely.** Cell phones, beepers, personal organizers, and other technological inventions can either reduce stress or create it, depending on how you use them. Your cell phone, for example, allows you to conduct that important business call from the cab that's stuck in traffic (or from the sidewalk as you walk to the office). In this way, you can use technology to reduce the stress of waiting as well as to get more done in a given day. That being said, it is important to remember that there are times when you should shut all of these devices down and reenergize your internal batteries. Movie theaters aside (we all know to silence our phones, pagers, and BlackBerries), we need to have our own quiet time—time when we are not so accessible. Being a bit of a BB addict (BlackBerry addict), this has been the hardest for me to cut back on, but I force myself to shut it down from time to time.

Handling Overindulgences of the Culinary Kind

In life there are many foods worth living without. Conversely, other foods put the living in life. I can easily give up cheese, milk, potato chips, and many of the other A, B, C, D, E, and Fs. I will never miss them, but I won't give up my chicken burrito or biscotti.

So I've learned to live with them. I choose to eat them. In making it a choice—rather than an accidental indiscretion—I'm able to work such indulgences into my day. When you consciously choose to indulge, you shed the guilt that leads to overeating and bingeing.

Everyone has his or her own unique indulgence. For my clients Sara Rotman and Sue Blake, it's the occasional coffee with milk. Usually they have green or herbal tea, but sometimes they choose the coffee. For Perry Wolfman, it's the once- or twice-weekly pasta meal.

In order to have your indulgence without suffering the fattening consequences, you must do the following:

- **Find your balancing point.** One of the cruelties of life is this basic fact: some people can indulge more than others. For some people, an ice cream cone is an indulgence, and that's the end of it. For others, it's an overindulgence that makes its way into their fat cells. If you follow phase 3 to the letter, you can rest assured that your every indulgence will remain just that—something you savor and not something you regret. Many of my clients, however, have gone beyond the rules of phase 3, experimenting with what foods they can add back in and how often. Although I encourage you to do this, you must do so carefully. Keep a diary of what you eat and your weight and, most important, clothing fit. If your pants start feeling tight, you're probably doing too much overindulging.

Heidi Klum

I've been working with Heidi for years, so long that I think of her as a close friend rather than a client. When she told me she planned on modeling at the Victoria's Secret Fashion Show just eight weeks after giving birth to her son, I knew our time together would test the effectiveness of the New York Diet to the limit. Heidi had two children very close together—just 15 months apart—which meant that she had been either pregnant or nursing—and not exercising intensely—for almost two years. I was simply amazed at how quickly she transformed her body for the show.

Q: **How did you feel about yourself and your body leading up to the show?**

A: After you give birth, you realize just how miraculous your body is. As a model, I'm used to thinking about how my body looks, but pregnancy and nursing helped me to see my body more for what it can do.

As I trained for the show, my energy, of course, was down. I was tired from being up every three hours at night (if I was lucky). In addition to my baby, I have a 17-month-old running around who wants to be entertained. So, I couldn't nap during the day. At night, I would go to bed at 10:00 exhausted. I'd be up a few times at night to nurse, and then I'd be up at 7:00 A.M. for the rest of the day.

Q: **The Victoria's Secret Fashion Show was eight weeks after you gave birth. Did you ever worry that you wouldn't have enough time to get into lingerie shape?**

A: The Victoria's Secret show is the most challenging appearance any model has. It's live, so you can't be retouched. Also, you're walking down the runway in lingerie, so everyone can see exactly how you look.

For me, having a deadline helps. If I didn't have that date, I would probably not train as hard. Still, my family comes first, so I didn't do anything to get into shape that would hinder my ability to nurse my son. I gave myself some leeway.

The first couple of weeks after giving birth, I didn't push myself too hard. I saved my energy for taking care of my baby and myself. Then, I eased back into working out with David, as I knew I had to get ready for the show. No one can expect someone to be totally pre-baby fabulous in no time flat, so I did what I could with David's help, and I felt fine. David and I have worked together for a long time, so he knows how far to take my training and what I need to do to get to a good place.

Q: **How did your diet change as you readied yourself for the show?**

A: I love fattening foods. I love burgers, gummi candy, french fries, chocolate, bread with butter, coffee with milk, and cheese. I don't eat those types of things a lot, but I do like to indulge. When I was pregnant, I drank a liter of milk a day. I love milk, and I like to drink it whole, not skim. Yet, I didn't blow up like a balloon when I was pregnant. I simply gave my body what it craved.

Leading up to the show, I didn't have any of those things. I started every day with one of David's protein shakes and often ended the day with one of his shakes, too. In between, I ate healthy, balanced meals every three or so hours and left behind the bananas, apples, corn, pastas, rice, and bread in order to trim down faster.

Q: **How did you feel when you stepped onto the runway for the first time since having a baby?**

A: It's always a scary thing—walking onto the runway in front of hundreds of people (millions if you count all the people who will watch the show on TV) in your lingerie! I felt great, though. I had worked hard leading up to the show, and I felt really confident. None of my looks were too skimpy, and I felt really comfortable in all of them. I felt great at the show, and I've felt great afterward. It takes time to get fully back to your prebaby body,

but that's normal, and I have no problem with that.

Q: **What lessons have you learned from training for the show that you will take with you?**

A: I'm not the most eager bunny when it comes to working out. If I could pay someone to do it for me, I gladly would. That said, I know that I need to put in the hard work myself. Modeling is my job, and training to look good is part of that job. I didn't push myself too hard or too fast. Taking care of my family is my biggest priority, and I like being fit and healthy for my life, not just for a single job.

HEIDI'S ADVICE FOR YOU: Load up your refrigerator with all the right foods. If you don't have the right things in the fridge, you'll end up grabbing a bag of chips. So stock up on good snacks, like hard-boiled egg whites, and get the tempting snacks out of your kitchen.

POSTSCRIPT: *Working with Heidi is always a special treat for me. She has become a great friend, and I admire how she was able to be present for her family first and still find enough energy for me and our workouts. I am extremely proud of her and her accomplishments. To everyone out there who thinks it can't be done, think again!*

David's Holiday Survival Guide

I recently did a segment with "Fox and Friends" during which I showed Americans how to eat healthily for Thanksgiving. You heard me correctly—healthy Thanksgiving dinner. There will be some of the old familiar favorites—roasted turkey, cranberry relish, and dessert—but there will be some key things missing. The foods you should not include in healthful holiday feasts include butter, sugar, and added fat. Your heart, waist, and arteries will be eternally grateful.

You can accomplish this with some easy swaps.

- For appetizers, instead of cheese and crackers or chips and dip, think low-fat hummus with vegetable wedges and shrimp with cocktail sauce.
- For the main attraction—the bird—think brine. To brine or not to brine has been one of those debates that has gone on among some of the best chefs in the world. After consulting two turkey aficionados—Martha Stewart and Danny Meyer—I've decided that brining is the way to go. The technique ensures that you end up with a moist, seasoned, tasty bird. In days of old, I have been known to melt a couple of sticks of butter and soak my cheesecloth and swath the bird in this fatty, artery-clogging mixture. Now, instead of the buttery cheesecloth, I slow roast, basting the bird with a mixture of turkey stock, white wine, carrots, celery, onion, parsnips, and apples. Last, to get that *Gourmet Magazine* cover shot of the perfectly browned turkey, I brush the turkey with olive oil with about 30 to 45 minutes of roasting to go.
- For side dishes, roasted brussels sprouts, green beans with lemon zest and almonds, and mashed sweet potatoes with cinnamon and balsamic

vinegar are all healthier options than some of the standard fare. There will be no marshmallows in your future. The sweet potatoes are sweet enough without them.

- Now, I've already confessed to having a small sliver of pecan pie for dessert. The healthier choice would definitely have been the dark chocolate and berries instead of pie and ice cream.
- I've also thought of a unique twist on an old favorite for the Christmas holidays:

David's Healthy Eggnog

This is a healthy twist on an old classic. It delivers all of the flavor of the classic nog without the calories, sugar, or fat.

1 packet (or scoop) of David Kirsch's Sound Mind Sound Body Meal
    Replacement Powder (vanilla)
8 ounces cold water
2 tablespoons nonfat milk
4 or 5 ice cubes
Pinch of freshly ground nutmeg
Pinch of cinnamon

Place the protein powder, water, milk, and ice in a blender, and blend until smooth and frothy, about 1 minute. Pour in a mug, and sprinkle with nutmeg and cinnamon.

Makes 2 servings. Per serving: 95 calories, 13 g protein, 6 g carbohydrate, 2 g fat, 1 g saturated fat, 3 g fiber, 3 g sugar

- **Know the deal that you are making with the devil.** Plenty of people indulge without guilt—and they get fat. They choose to eat fattening foods but do so out of ignorance. They have no clue as to how much that piece of cake is setting them back. So, yes, indulge, but do so mindfully. Know what you are eating and what it will cost you in terms of calories. To aid you in that effort, consider the following:

  Cheeseburger and fries = 88 minutes of aerobics
  Fish and chips = 68 minutes of jogging five miles per hour
  Three pancakes with butter and syrup = 104 minutes of walking
  Plain doughnut = 20 minutes of jogging five miles per hour
  Blueberry muffin (one and one-half ounce) = 23 minutes of swimming
  Cheddar cheese (one ounce) = 13 minutes of jogging five miles per hour
  Hot fudge sundae = 58 minutes of walking
  Ice cream cone = 41 minutes of jogging five miles per hour
  French dressing (two tablespoons) = 28 minutes of dancing
  Beer (12 ounces) = 17 minutes of jogging five miles per hour
  Bagel (three and one-half inches) = 25 minutes of aerobics

- **When you overindulge, take compensatory actions.** For example, if I meet friends at a restaurant and overdo it a little on the pasta (a very rare indulgence), I go for a long walk afterward. I walk until the mental and physical feeling of fullness dissipates, and I want you to do the same.

- **Savor every bite.** Indulgences tend to turn into overindulgences when you tune out from the eating process. Whenever you have something from the A, B, C, D, E, and F list, do so mindfully. Turn off the TV, refrain from talking, and even close your eyes. Focus on the taste, scent, and texture of your food. (This is good advice for all of the foods you eat, but especially true with indulgence foods.) When you eat this way, sweet foods taste sweeter, salty foods saltier, and crunchy foods crunchier. In the end, because you focus on and notice what you are eating, you'll feel sated sooner and, as a result, eat less.

Eating Out

In my previous book, I asked readers to refrain from eating out during the two-week meal plan, which followed the same basic structure as phase 1 of the Ultimate New York Diet. My point was (and still is) that cooking your own food is the surest way to guarantee that your food complies with your nutrition plan. When you eat out, not only are you hostage to the chef's will, but you also place yourself in hell's kitchen, surrounding yourself with the sights and smells of all things tempting. Finally, restaurants (particularly those in the United States) notoriously serve up gigantic food portions, leaving it up to you to practice self-control.

Since I wrote that book, however, I've heard from countless clients and book buyers who were able to make the plan work while eating out almost every single meal. It made me take a step back. After all, I do live in New York City, proclaimed "the restaurant capital of the world" by Fodor's. With roughly 6,000 restaurants in Manhattan alone—and on average 250 new restaurants opening each year—one could literally eat out every single meal for more than a year and not eat at the same restaurant twice. Add the fact that you can find any type of food—including Indonesian, Indian, Russian, Aegean, and Zambian and the many different types of

American food from barbecue to Southern—in New York. Once you add all of those variables together, you can understand why just about no one in New York cooks.

So, yes, I do still believe that the best-case scenario is doing it yourself. That said, I'm realistic. If you must eat out, be mindful of how and why you are eating, and you will be able to eat out intelligently and safely. This chapter will help guide your food choices.

How to Eat Out

In the following pages you'll find my personal tips—along with some of the strategies developed by my clients—to navigating restaurant fare. You'll learn how to order well and eat well without going overboard. The key to eating out and staying well stems from the following Eight Rules of Restaurant Eating.

RULE 1: DO YOUR HOMEWORK

After learning the A, B, C, D, E, and Fs of the plan, one of my clients, Richard Jones, at first ventured into the world of restaurant eating with trepidation. He didn't have much of a choice about eating out. As a corporate president and CEO, he entertained many clients at business dinners and traveled for work. He had to find a way to balance eating out with eating according to the rules of the Ultimate New York Diet. He told me recently that eating out wasn't as difficult as he had assumed it would be. "I've learned that it's not that difficult to eat healthfully at any restaurant in the world. Almost all restaurants are willing to accommodate simple requests. I survive by eating out or getting takeout. You can do this diet anywhere and everywhere," he said.

Like many of my clients, Richard is able to eat out so often because he's done his homework. He knows which restaurants will accommodate his meal requests and which ones will not. You need to do the same, both at home and away from home.

At home: find a few restaurants in your area that serve Ultimate New York Diet–type meals and that will accommodate special requests (such as dressing or sauce on the side). Don't be shy. I've had clients who have asked for all sorts of things and had their wishes granted. One of them, Kevin Sayers, talked a deli near his place of employment into scraping their grill before making him an egg white omelet stuffed with vegetables he personally picked from the restaurant's salad bar. His salad-bar egg creations were not on the menu, and clearing the grill of grease certainly took the chef time, but Kevin ate one of his self-created meals from this deli every day, so the management was only too happy to accommodate him.

Away from home: about a year ago I was working on a television project and ended up in a suburb outside of Columbus, Ohio. It had been years since I left the friendly confines of suburban Long Island, New York, and, in an instant, I was faced with a quandary. In this town outside of Columbus, there were three restaurant choices, with the best one being an Olive Garden. The other choices were McDonald's and some other fast-food establishment. I chose where to eat by weighing what each restaurant had to offer. To dine out away from home, do the same. For breakfast joints, look for places that allow you to substitute egg whites for whole eggs and turkey bacon or sausage for pork. Most places will offer either egg whites or egg substitutes these days. For lunch, look for salad and lean meat combinations served with a vinaigrette on the side. For dinner, think grilled chicken breast or fish with a side of steamed vegetables.

Whether at home or away from home, ask the host, hostess, maître d', or manager the following questions:

- Do you take special food-preparation requests?
- Can you prepare dishes without MSG, salt, sauces, butter, oil, and other toppings? I will go to the extreme and tell the server that I am very allergic to butter and will get very ill if it is used in preparing any of my meal (e.g., steak is often prepared with a big slab of butter on top. I make sure that my steak is grilled dry).
- Will you serve dressings and sauces on the side?
- Do you permit patrons to bring their own salad dressing?
- Will you blend and serve my protein shake? Many will, for a fee.
- Do you trim visible fat from meat and remove the skin from poultry before cooking?
- Will you broil, bake, steam, or poach rather than fry foods?

RULE 2: EAT BEFORE YOU EAT OUT

When you're hungry, all foods look and sound delicious. You may intend to order the grilled chicken breast with steamed broccoli rabe but be surprised to find yourself saying "prime rib with garlic mashed potatoes" when the waiter comes to take your order. That's why I suggest you have your first course at home. Always have a small protein shake, a protein bar, or a hard-boiled egg white to take the edge off. (By the way, this goes for grocery shopping as well. When you shop when you're hungry, you are much more likely to pile your cart high with ice cream, cheese, potato chips, and cookies.) A little food in your belly will make it less likely that you'll binge on caloric hors d'oeuvres.

RULE 3: SEND THE FREE FOOD BACK TO THE KITCHEN

Most restaurants decorate the center of the table with something from your A, B, C, D, E, and F list. Usually it's in the form of a crunchy, unconscious eating food. For example, if you're having Mexican, you'll find a heaping bowl of fried tortilla chips along with salsa. This is my downfall, so, if I am feeling particularly strict, I will have them send the basket of chips back to the kitchen.

Before the host guides you to your table, make your wishes known. Say, "I would prefer no bread," or whatever free fare they usually offer. Believe me, once you sit down and physically see the bread or crunchy fried wontons or cheese and crackers, it will be 10 times harder to make the same request.

RULE 4: SAVE ALCOHOL FOR YOUR MAIN COURSE

If you're in phase 1 of the plan, remember: no alcohol. In phase 2 or 3, however, you still want to keep drinking to a minimum for all the reasons you learned in Chapter 9. An alcoholic drink will lower your reserve if you have one before you order, so if you plan to drink, have your drink with your meal and not before—especially not before you order.

RULE 5: SKIP THE APPETIZER

If everyone else at the table is ordering one and you find that you just can't muster the willpower to "just say no," go for a mixed salad or a broth-based soup. The salad contains fiber that can dampen your appetite, helping you to eat less of your main course. Order oil and vinegar on the side, and ask for a wedge of lemon. Broth-based soups can also dampen the appetite. Make sure neither the salad nor the soup contains anything from your A, B, C, D, E, and F list. You might want to run down that list for the waiter or waitress because the menu may not list everything in the salad or soup. In particular, be wary of crackers, croutons, shredded cheese, beans, and pasta. It's much better to make sure those things don't end up on the plate or bowl in front of you. Few people have the willpower to pick off croutons and leave them on the side. Certain types of restaurants may have additional appetizer options that fit into the plan, such as sashimi (raw fish) or a vegetable. If you're eating in an Italian restaurant (one of my favorite foods), be wary of cold vegetable antipasti as they are often drowning in tons of olive oil and therefore will pack a ton of calories onto a seemingly innocent dish.

RULE 6: ORDER LEAN PROTEIN PLUS VEGGIES

Lean protein means grilled, broiled, or poached fish, chicken, turkey, or lean sirloin. Stay away from anything described as fried, basted, braised, au gratin, crispy, escalloped, panfried, sautéed, stewed, and pan-roasted. Also, don't be taken in by the phrase "light cream sauce." Yes, it might be light in texture, but it's almost certainly heavy in terms of fat and calories.

If your dish comes with a sauce or gravy, order it on the side as sauces are usually loaded with sugar, salt, cheese, butter, oil, or cream. Make sure your veggie is not on the A, B, C, D, E, and F list. That means no potatoes or carrots of any kind in phase 1 of the plan. Think broccoli, spinach, green beans, arugula, and bok choy. If the dish comes with a starch—such as rice, pasta, or potato—ask to substitute another vegetable instead.

RULE 7: TUNE INTO YOUR INNER SENSE OF HUNGER

It's easy to eat everything that's on your plate as you enjoy the conversation of friends and family. To prevent the sensation of feeling stuffed, try to portion your meal ahead of time. For meat, eat a piece no larger than the size of the palm of your hand. As soon as your plate hits the table,

Lose the Weight—and Keep It Off

If you read The Ultimate New York Body Plan *you may remember the stories of Sam Shahid, Kenna DuBose, and Michele Perritt. They had all lost stunning amounts of weight (up to 14 pounds) on my two-week plan. More spectacular, however, is that they all kept it off. It's now roughly three years since they all tackled the two-week plan. Here you'll find their secrets for lasting results.*

Kenna

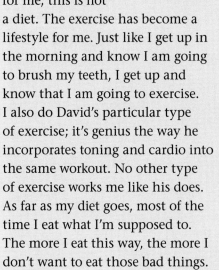

"I now look even better than I did two years ago, when David first profiled me for his book. I've been able to maintain these results—and even lose more weight—because, for me, this is not a diet. The exercise has become a lifestyle for me. Just like I get up in the morning and know I am going to brush my teeth, I get up and know that I am going to exercise. I also do David's particular type of exercise; it's genius the way he incorporates toning and cardio into the same workout. No other type of exercise works me like his does. As far as my diet goes, most of the time I eat what I'm supposed to. The more I eat this way, the more I don't want to eat those bad things.

For example, I used to love chocolate, and now I don't crave it at all. I used to eat chocolate chip cookies or M&M's every day, and now I don't remember the last time I had one. I think it's been about three years. More recently I began taking David's supplements. He has one called Hoodia. It really does curb the appetite. The rest of his supplements are wonderful, too. I like to take his chocolate shake with me to work. I mix it ahead of time, put it in the fridge, and have it for lunch or an afternoon snack."

KENNA'S SECRET TO SUCCESS: "I keep a calendar on my fridge at home. On it I mark down every day that I exercise, what type of exercise I do, and for how long. Each week, I tally up my exercise hours. It gives me a sense of pride as well as something physical to look at in order to stay on track."

Sam

"I got here because I suffered. I worked hard. I'm not going to go back. Also, I've purchased new clothes in smaller sizes, and that feels great. Plus, people keep telling me how great I look. That all works together to keep me committed. I've also learned how to give in to simple pleasures in moderation. One night over the summer, for example, I was dying for ice cream. So I indulged and had a couple of bites, and I loved it. I can't indulge like I used to before embarking on this plan. I can't eat candy every night and have five glasses of wine. That's common sense to me now. Now, when I indulge, it's a special treat. Once a week I have friends over, and we all have a martini before going out to dinner. That's my special night, and I look forward to it."

SAM'S SECRET TO SUCCESS: "I travel a lot for business. I always take my sneakers and shorts with me so I can run at least two miles a day. When I'm out of town, I'm out of bed every morning at 6:00 A.M. to exercise. Of course there are days when I would rather relax with some coffee and read the paper, but I exercise instead because I want this. You have to want it in order to consistently motivate yourself."

Michele

"The past year of my life has been a roller coaster because I lost my mother, brother, and uncle, all of whom were very close to me. Such life transitions can send you into a tailspin. For a couple of weeks after each setback, I can't say I stuck to the diet 100 percent. Other people were cooking for me, and I ate the pasta and sandwiches that they gave me. As a consequence, I gained about 10 pounds. I have a favorite pair of jeans, and I realized they were starting to feel tight. I didn't want to go out and buy bigger clothes, and I didn't want to lose the new slimmed-down physique that I had worked so hard to achieve, so I recommitted myself to the plan. Now, if I'm feeling too down to cook, I mix up one of David's protein shakes and a vitamin packet rather than grabbing easy comfort food. I also remind myself that I may be sad about my losses, but I am still here living, and I need to take care of me. Oh, and it wasn't long before my favorite jeans fit again, and I was back where I needed to be."

MICHELE'S SECRET TO SUCCESS: "Every day you wake up and don't know what's going to happen. You can't control life, but you can give yourself a fighting chance by keeping yourself physically healthy. Each morning I remind myself that I may not have a day to wake up to if I don't have my body and my health."

investigate the size of your portion, slice off any extra, and ask the waiter or waitress to put it in a take-out container.

During your meal, eat slowly and pay attention to your hunger. Your mother was right; you should *chew your food*. Studies have shown that people who chew their food longer eat less and are better able to digest and metabolize their foods efficiently than people who gulp their food quickly. Further, by taking longer to eat, you're giving your belly the chance to tell your brain that it is no longer hungry. There is generally a delay in your belly delivering this message to your brain, so chewing slower and longer is better. I also find it helps to wear a pair of unforgiving pants to give yourself a little feedback.

RULE 8: DON'T LOOK AT THE DESSERT MENU

Chances are, if you see the menu or dessert tray, you'll find something you just have to try. Don't be taken in by so-called low-fat offerings such as sorbets or fruit cobblers. They are generally loaded in sugar and calories.

Tips for Different Eateries

Later in this chapter, you'll find specific best and worst suggestions for national restaurant chains. That list will help you to navigate the McDonald's and Olive Gardens of the world.

But what if you find yourself in a chef-owned establishment? Not to worry. Here you'll find some basic suggestions for various types of restaurants. If you pair these with the tips I've already mentioned in the previous pages, you can't go wrong.

BREAKFAST DINERS

If you are in phase 1, stay away from just about everything on the menu, including the pancakes, waffles, and breakfast cereal. In phases 2 and 3, you might get away from some of these higher-carb items at certain types of breakfast spots that offer real whole-grain pancakes, for example, or steel-cut oats.

Usually your best option will be the eggs. Ask for egg whites (preferable) or egg substitute. Look for egg white omelets that are stuffed with vegetables (onion, tomato, bell pepper, spinach, asparagus, and so on). In lieu of an egg white omelet, try for hard-boiled egg whites, fried eggs, eggs over easy, or scrambled eggs (make sure the scrambled eggs are not mixed with milk or cream). If the restaurant offers lean turkey bacon or sausage, that's fair game. Ask the waiter to *not* bring the toast or fried potatoes that usually come with the eggs. Drink water with your meal instead of orange juice.

CAJUN

Cajun cuisine is spicy, which is great for weight loss. Research shows that spicy foods both rev up the metabolism and reduce appetite. That said, this type of cooking originated in southern France and took hold in south Louisiana, so most Cajun dishes center on fat and more fat as one of the main ingredients.

Steer clear of fried seafood and hush puppies. Also, avoid blackened entrées as they are usually dipped in butter or oil, covered with spices, and panfried. Ask for all sauces and gravies on the side.

Good choices include boiled crawfish or shrimp and boiled or grilled seafood.

CHINESE

Although it was once thought of as a healthful alternative to typical American fare, we now know that Chinese food is loaded with MSG, oil, and white rice (a refined carb). Ask the cook to use less oil when preparing stir-fry and other dishes. Because Chinese main dishes are usually twice the size of what a normal person should eat, always order fewer entrées than you have dining companions.

Choose entrées with chicken or shrimp and lots of vegetables. I usually order the steamed moo shoo chicken and shrimp with the hoisin sauce on the side and two pancakes. I consider that a cheat meal because of the pancakes, but the balance of most of the meal consists of Chinese cabbage and either chicken or shrimp.

Ask the waiter to not bring the rice that generally comes with the entrée. If you are bent on having rice, at least get the steamed variety (rather than fried), and see if you can get brown rice instead of white.

FAMILY-STYLE RESTAURANTS

These types of restaurants serve a little of everything, which is what makes them so popular for families. Avoid dishes that come with lots of cheese, sour cream, and mayonnaise. Instead of fried oysters, calamari, or fried fish or chicken, look for boiled spiced shrimp or baked, boiled, or grilled fish or chicken. Most of these restaurants generally serve great salads. Look for salads with lots of greens and veggies along with grilled chicken or fish. Get the dressing on the side.

Good options for family restaurants include peel-and-eat shrimp, broth-based soup (watch for the sodium content), or salad for an appetizer; veggie or chicken burger without the bun for a main course; grilled fish or chicken for a main course; and steamed vegetables or a tossed salad as a side dish.

FRENCH

Like Cajun fare, French food generally means many menu items will be high in fat, with butter as the staple item. Look for French restaurants that advertise themselves as "nouvelle cuisine," which is a new, lighter way of cooking. The portions at these types of French restaurants also tend to be smaller.

The key to French food is to keep it clean and simple. Mussels are great with white wine and garlic, and fish is fine if it's grilled clean with lemon and olive oil. Also consider steak frites (without the peppercorn cream sauce), salad niçoise (the olive oil, vinegar, and Dijon mustard on the side), or mixed-greens salad as an appetizer. Avoid anything "Francese," as this contains lots of butter.

GREEK/MIDDLE EASTERN

Look for fish (it should be on the menu in abundance). Stay away from all of the following during phase 1: fried calamari, dolmas, baba ganoush, tzatziki, couscous, moussaka, gyros, spanakopita, and dessert pastries. If you're in phase 2 or 3, then many of the items on the Greek menu will be good to eat. My favorites are the tzatziki, the baba ganoush, and the whole roasted fish. Also, see if the restaurant serves plaki, which is fish cooked in tomatoes, onions, and garlic.

JAPANESE

If you like sushi, then you can't do better than Japanese. Order sashimi (raw fish without the rice) with edamame (soybeans). Avoid foods that are deep-fried, battered, breaded, or fried. Ask to substitute shrimp, scallops, or chicken for beef dishes.

If you want to treat yourself, you can order hand-cut rolls that are rolled with seaweed or cucumber and have no rice. Some restaurants now offer sushi rolled with brown rice, which would be permitted in phases 2 and 3. Avoid salty dishes such as miso soup, soy sauces (even the low-sodium variety), and sake during phase 1, and eat these sparingly during phases 2 and 3.

INDIAN

Indian food tends to accent carbohydrates and spices and de-emphasize protein. Also, the food is usually prepared with ghee (clarified butter) or is fried or sautéed in sesame or coconut oil. This all makes it tough for you to follow the Ultimate New York Diet at an Indian restaurant, especially during phase 1.

Choose a chicken or seafood dish rather than beef or lamb for phase 1 of the plan. In phases 2 or 3, the lean beef or even the lamb would be a great choice. The tandoori chicken or fish is probably your best bet. Ask for dishes prepared without ghee. Order one protein and one vegetable dish to cut down the fat and calories. Definite taboo items include Samosas, pappadam, saag paneer, and pakora.

ITALIAN

In Italy, the Italians actually eat much less pasta than we do in America. Instead, they eat quite a bit of fish, and, as a result, most authentic Italian restaurants serve a great assortment of wonderfully cooked fish dishes. Many Italian restaurants serve delicious roasted red peppers as an appetizer, a dish that fits wonderfully into the Ultimate New York Diet.

Sardines are actually very healthy, being a great source of calcium, low in fat, and low in mercury (many of the better-known fish such as salmon and tuna can have much higher levels of mercury). If you don't go for the sardines, then try the branzino, a Mediterranean sea bass that is served grilled whole or filleted. A tasty and satisfying meal, it's low in fat and a good, quality source of protein. I love biscotti (Italian cookies usually served with Vin Santo—sweet Italian dessert wine). One or two biscotti at the end of my meal is the perfect punctuation and is definitely a smarter choice than the tiramisu (which means "pull me up").

MEXICAN

I'm a great fan of Mexican food, so I know only too well the temptations that arise from stepping foot into a Mexican establishment. Many Mexican entrées come with tortillas (a carb) and cheese (a dairy). Instead of typical Mexican fare such as burritos and enchiladas, look for chicken and fish entrées, such as chicken mole or Vera Cruz (a tomato-based sauce). Grilled fish is also a great option. Salsa, another staple in Mexican food, is low in fat and calories and great for seasoning and giving zip to otherwise-bland dishes. Just avoid the chips.

STEAK HOUSES

If you can talk yourself into it, consider ordering chicken or fish, as many steak houses do a great job preparing these dishes. That said, you go to a steak house because you want steak. In that case, choose the smallest, leanest cut available, which will generally be the petit filet mignon, round or flank, London broil, or sirloin. Avoid fatty cuts of meat such as the porterhouse. Ask to have any visible fat trimmed from your steak, and emphatically (but politely) instruct your waiter that the steak should be prepared without any butter before it reaches the table.

Order steamed vegetables or a mixed salad on the side. If you want to splurge, order sautéed spinach, as the olive oil is a much smarter choice than the creamed variety. In phases 2 and 3, the baked potato would be a treat, but nix the toppings. Also, portions in steak houses tend to be notoriously large. If you've been served one of those "mutant" one-pound baked potatoes, then cut it in half and either offer it to the person you're dining with or have the waiter take it back to the kitchen. Why tempt yourself?

VEGETARIAN FOOD

I love great vegetarian food, but I caution vegetarians who want to embark on the Ultimate New York Diet. I'm not saying that you need to eat meat to successfully complete the plan, but you must use caution as many vegetarian dishes are high in fat and calories and laden with lots of grams of carbohydrates. Many dishes are starch based, using potatoes, pasta, beans, rice, cheese, and soy protein as a substitute for meat.

I'm not a big fan of soy protein. It is not utilized by the body as readily as whey protein, and it can cause bloating as it spikes progesterone in the body (not something a woman wants unless she's perimenopausal).

Choose foods that are low in fat, calories, and sodium. Pay special attention to portion size, sauces, and soups with lots of sodium. In phases 2 or 3, even things like Nayonaise (pseudo mayonnaise) has got more grams of fat than you would expect.

David's Best and Worst List

The following is not an exhaustive list by any means, but I hope it will give you a better idea of what to order and what not to order at national chains that you might encounter around the country.

McDonald's

Among the best
- Side salad with low-fat balsamic vinaigrette
- Hamburger without the bun
- California Cobb salad with chicken
- Grilled Chicken Classic sandwich without the bun

Among the worst
- Double Quarter Pounder with cheese

Burger King

Among the best

Veggie burger without the bun or the mayo

Side garden salad with light Italian dressing

Tendergrill garden salad with light Italian dressing (hold the cheese)

Low-carb angus steak burger

Among the worst

Double Whopper with cheese

Wendy's

Among the best

Small chili

Caesar side salad without dressing

Mandarin chicken salad (skip the crispy noodles, almonds, and dressing)

Junior hamburger without the bun

Side salad with reduced-fat creamy ranch dressing

Among the worst

Big Bacon Classic

KFC

Among the best

Chicken breast without skin or breading

Side of green beans

Among the worst

Two extra-crispy chicken breasts

Boston Market

Among the best

Three-ounce hand-carved boneless rotisserie turkey

Steamed vegetable medley

Among the worst

Double-sauced angus meat loaf and beef gravy

Subway

Among the best

Grilled chicken breast and baby spinach salad with fat-free Italian dressing

Among the worst

Six-inch meatball marinara

Taco Bell

Among the best

Crunchy taco, fresco style

Among the worst

Fiesta taco salad

Chili's

Among the best

Grilled salmon with veggies (hold the garlic bread)

Among the worst

Country-fried steak

Perkins

Among the best

Denver omelet

Among the worst

Granny's country omelet

Bob Evans

Among the best
>Scrambled egg substitute with one light sausage link
>Slow-roasted turkey with side of broccoli florets

Among the worst
>Sunshine skillet

Olive Garden

Among the best
>Chicken Giardino

Among the worst
>Stuffed chicken marsala with garlic mashed potatoes

Outback Steakhouse

Among the best
>Victoria's center-cut filet (seven-ounce steak)
>North Atlantic salmon

Among the worst
>Melbourne porterhouse (20-ounce steak)

Pizza Hut

Among the best
>One slice green pepper, red onion, and diced red tomato Fit n' Delicious pizza
>Salad with light Italian dressing

Among the worst
>Pepperoni Lover's personal pan pizza

Applebee's

Among the best

Blackened chicken salad

Among the worst

Crispy Orange Skillet with rice, veggies, and noodles

Arby's

Among the best

Martha's Vineyard salad (hold the cheese)

Among the worst

Chicken fingers combo with curly fries with tangy southwest sauce

Don Pablo's

Among the best

Mahi Mahi low-carb fajitas

Among the worst

Conquistador combo

Ruby Tuesday

Among the best

White bean chicken chili, no sides
Caesar side salad

Among the worst

Hang off the Plate Ribs, spicy honey barbecue sauce, full rack

Appendix

CONVERTING TO METRICS

Volume Measurement Conversions

U.S.	Metric
¼ teaspoon	1.25 milliliters
½ teaspoon	2.5 milliliters
¾ teaspoon	3.75 milliliters
1 teaspoon	5 milliliters
1 tablespoon	15 milliliters
¼ cup	62.5 milliliters
½ cup	125 milliliters
¾ cup	187.5 milliliters
1 cup	250 milliliters

Weight Measurement Conversions

U.S.	Metric
1 ounce	28.4 g
8 ounces	227.5 g
16 ounces (1 pound)	455 g

Cooking Temperature Conversions

Fahrenheit   Fahrenheit established 0°F as the stabilized temperature when equal amounts of ice, water, and salt are mixed.

Celsius/Centigrade   In Celsius, 0°C and 100°C are arbitrarily placed at the melting and boiling points of water and standard to the metric system.

To convert temperatures in Fahrenheit to Celsius, use this formula:

$$C = (F - 32) \times 0.5555$$

So, for example, if you are baking at 350°F and want to know that temperature in Celsius, use this calculation:

$$C = (350 - 32) \times 0.5555 = 176.65°C$$

Bibliography

Adam, T. C., and M. S. Westerterp-Plantenga. "Glucagon-like peptide-1 release and satiety after a nutrient challenge in normal-weight and obese subjects." *British Journal of Nutrition* 93, no. 6 (June 2005): 845–51.

Alvarado, R., S. Contreras, N. Segovia-Riquelme, and J. Mardones. "Effects of serotonin uptake blockers and of 5-hydroxytryptophan on the voluntary consumption of ethanol, water and solid food by UChA and UChB rats." *Alcohol: An International Biomedical Journal* 7, no. 4 (July–August 1990): 315–19.

Arora, S. K., and S. I. McFarlane. "The case for low carbohydrate diets in diabetes management." *Nutrition and Metabolism (London)* 14, no. 2 (July 2005): 16.

Astrup, A. "Atkins and other low-carbohydrate diets: Hoax or an effective tool for weight loss?" *Lancet* 364, no. 9,437 (September 4–10, 2004): 897–99.

Bell, S. J. "A functional food product for the management of weight." *Critical Reviews in Food Science and Nutrition* 42, no. 2 (March 2002): 163–78.

Birdstall, T. C. "5-Hydroxytryptophan: A clinically-effective serotonin precursor." *Alternative Medicine Review* 3, no. 4 (August 1998): 271–80.

Bolton, R. P. "The role of dietary fiber in satiety, glucose, and insulin: Studies with fruit and fruit juice." *American Journal of Clinical Nutrition* 32, no. 2 (February 1981): 211–17.

Butki, B. D., J. Baumstark, and S. Driver. "Effects of a carbohydrate-restricted diet on affective responses to acute exercise among physically active participants." *Perceptual and Motor Skills* 96, no. 2 (April 2003): 607–15.

Dansinger, M. L., J. A. Gleason, J. L. Griffith, H. P. Selker, and E. J. Schaefer. "Comparison of the Atkins, Ornish, Weight Watchers, and Zone diets for weight loss and heart disease risk reduction: A randomized trial." *Journal of the American Medical Association* 293, no. 1 (January 5, 2005): 43–53.

Dhuley, J. N. "Anti-oxidant effects of cinnamon (*Cinnamomum verum*) bark and greater cardamom (*Amomum subulatum*) seeds in rats fed high fat diet." *Indian Journal of Experimental Biology* 37, no. 3 (March 1999): 238–42.

Docherty, J. P., D. A. Sack, M. Roffman, M. Finch, and J. R. Komorowski. "A double-blind, placebo-controlled, exploratory trial of chromium picolinate in atypical depression: Effect on carbohydrate craving." *Journal of Psychiatry Practice* 11, no. 5 (September 2005): 302–14.

Ernouf, D., M. Daoust, D. Poulain, and G. Narcisse. "Triptosine, an L-5-hydroxytryptophan derivative, reduces alcohol consumption in alcohol-preferring rats." *Alcohol and Alcoholism* 27, no. 3 (May 1992): 273–76.

Evans, E., and D. S. Miller. "Bulking agents in the treatment of obesity." *Nutrition and Metabolism* 18, no. 4 (1975): 199–203.

Foster, G. D., H. R. Wyatt, J. O. Hill, B. G. McGuckin, C. Brill, B. S. Mohammed, P. O. Szapary, D. J. Rader, J. S. Edman, and S. Klein. "A randomized trial of a low-carbohydrate diet for obesity." *New England Journal of Medicine* 348, no. 21 (May 22, 2003): 2082–90.

Fuhr, J. P., H. He, N. Goldfarb, and D. B. Nash. "Use of chromium picolinate and biotin in the management of type 2 diabetes: An economic analysis." *Disease Management* 8, no. 4 (August 2005): 265–75.

Grieger, J. A., J. B. Keogh, M. Noakes, P. R. Foster, and P. M. Clifton. "The effect of dietary saturated fat on endothelial function." *Asia Pacific Journal of Clinical Nutrition* 13, Suppl. (2004): S48.

Han, L. K., Y. N. Zheng, M. Yoshikawa, H. Okuda, and Y. Kimura. "Anti-obesity effects of chikusetsusaponins isolated from Panax japonicus rhizomes." *BioMed Central Complementary and Alternative Medicine* 5, no. 1 (April 6, 2005): 9.

Hsu, C. C., M. C. Ho, L. C. Lin, B. Su, and M. C. Hsu. "American ginseng supplementation attenuates creatine kinase level induced by submaximal exercise in human beings." *World Journal of Gastroenterology* 11, no. 4 (September 2005): 5327–31.

Johnson, C. S., S. L. Tjonn, and P. D. Swan. "High-protein, low-fat diets are effective for weight loss and favorably alter biomarkers in healthy adults." *Journal of Nutrition* 134, no. 3 (March 2004): 586–91.

Kemps, E., and M. Tiggemann. "Working memory performance and preoccupying thoughts in female dieters: Evidence for a selective central executive impairment." *British Journal of Clinical Psychology* 44, part 3 (September 2005): 357–66.

Kim, S. H., S. H. Hyun, and S. Y. Choung. "Anti-diabetic effect of cinnamon extract on blood glucose in db/db mice." *Journal of Ethnopharmacology* 104, no. 1–2 (October 3, 2005): 119–23.

Kovacs, E. M., M. S. Westerterp-Plantenga, W. H. Saris, K. J. Melanson, I. Goossens, P. Geurten, and F. Brouns. "The effect of addition of modified guar gum to a low-energy semisolid meal on appetite and body weight loss." *International Journal of Obesity Related Metabolic Disorders* 25, no. 3 (March 2001): 307–15.

———. "The effect of guar gum addition to a semisolid meal on appetite related to blood glucose, in dieting men." *European Journal of Clinical Nutrition* 56, no. 8 (August 2002): 771–78.

Layman, D. K., E. Evans, J. I. Baum, J. Seyler, D. J. Erickson, and R. A. Boileau. "Dietary protein and exercise have additive effects on body composition during weight loss in adult women." *Journal of Nutrition* 135, no. 8 (August 2005): 1903–10.

Lejeune, M., E. M. R. Kovacs, M. S. Westerterp-Plantenga. "Additional protein intake limits weight regain after weight loss in humans." *British Journal of Nutrition* 93 (2005): 281–89.

Liu, T. P., I. M. Liu, and J. T. Cheng. "Improvement of insulin resistance by panax ginseng in fructose-rich chow-fed rats." *Hormone and Metabolic Research* 37, no. 3 (March 2005): 146–51.

MacLean, D. B., and L. G. Luo. "Increased ATP content/production in the hypothalamus may be a signal for energy-sensing of satiety: Studies of the anorectic mechanism of a plant steroidal glycoside." *Brain Research* 1020, nos. 1–2 (September 10, 2004): 1–11.

McAuley, K. A., C. M. Hopkins, K. J. Smith, R. T. McLay, S. M. Williams, R. W. Taylor, and J. I. Mann. "Comparison of high-fat and high-protein diets with a high-carbohydrate diet in insulin-resistant obese women." *Diabetologia* 48, no. 1 (January 2005): 8–16. Epub December 23, 2004.

———. "Long-term effects of popular dietary approaches on weight loss and features of insulin resistance." *International Journal of Obesity (London)* 30, no. 2 (2006): 342–49.

Mita, Y., K. Ishihara, Y. Fukuchi, Y. Fukuya, and K. Yasumoto. "Supplementation with chromium picolinate recovers renal cr concentration and improves carbohydrate metabolism and renal function in type 2 diabetic mice." *Biological Trace Element Research* 105, nos. 1–3 (Summer 2005): 229–48.

Nicklos-Richardson, S. M., M. D. Coleman, J. J. Volpe, and K. W. Hosig. "Perceived hunger is lower and weight loss is greater in overweight premenopausal women consuming a low-carbohydrate/high-protein vs. high-carbohydrate/low-fat diet." *Journal of the American Dietetic Association* 105, no. 9 (September 2005): 1433–37.

Park, M. Y., K. S. Lee, and M. K. Sung. "Effects of dietary mulberry, Korean red ginseng, and banaba on glucose homeostasis in relation to PPAR-alpha, PPAR-gamma, and LPL mRNA expressions." *Life Sciences* 77, no. 26 (November 12, 2005): 3344–54.

Rabinovitz, H., A. Friedensohn, A. Leibovitz, G. Gabay, C. Rocas, and B. Habot. "Effect of chromium supplementation on blood glucose and lipid levels in type 2 diabetes mellitus elderly patients." *International Journal for Vitamin and Nutrition Research* 74, no. 3 (May 2004): 178–82.

Reay, J. L., D. O. Kennedy, and A. B. Scholey. "Single doses of Panax ginseng (G115) reduce blood glucose levels and improve cognitive performance during sustained mental activity." *Journal of Psychopharmacology* 19, no. 4 (July 2005): 357–65.

Slavin, J. L. "Dietary fiber and body weight." *Nutrition* 21, no. 3 (March 2005): 411–18.

Sullivan, A. C. "Caloric compensatory responses to diets containing either nonabsorbable carbohydrate or lipid by obese and lean Zucker rats." *American Journal of Clinical Nutrition* 31, no. 10, Suppl. (October 1978): S261–S266.

Suzuki, Y., T. Unno, M. Ushitani, K. Hayashi, and T. Kakuda. "Antiobesity activity of extracts from *Lagerstroemia speciosa L.* leaves on female KK-Ay mice." *Journal of Nutritional Science and Vitaminology (Tokyo)* 45, no. 6 (December 1999): 791–95.

Truby, H. "A randomised controlled trial of 4 different commercial weight loss programmes in the UK in obese adults: Body composition changes over 6 months." *Asia Pacific Journal of Clinical Nutrition* 13, Suppl. (August 2004): S146.

Yang, X., K. Palanichamy, A. C. Ontko, M. N. Rao, C. X. Fang, J. Ren, and N. Sreejayan. "A newly synthetic chromium complex—chromium(phenylalanine)3 improves insulin responsiveness and reduces whole body glucose tolerance." *FEBS Letters* 579, no. 6 (February 28, 2005): 1458–64.

Resources

Throughout the pages of this book, I've mentioned many products—from stability balls to supplements—for you to buy for best results on the program. What follows is my advice on what to look for and where to purchase each.

Fitness Equipment

My approach to fitness is unique in that I believe you can get a very effective workout with a relatively few, inexpensive pieces of equipment.

STABILITY BALLS

You'll find many brands, colors, and sizes of stability balls. Top brands include Resist-a-Ball, Duraball, Gymnic, Sissel, Gymnastik, and Fitball. Purchase a burst-resistant ball in a color you like that fits your body. (See sizing chart in Chapter 4.) You can purchase stability balls from most sporting goods stores such as the Sports Authority and Dick's Sporting Goods. You can also find them online from the following stores:

bodytrends.com

dickssportinggoods.com

lifestylesport.com

sissel-online.com

resistaball.com

gymball.com

thesportsauthority.com

MEDICINE BALLS

As with stability balls, you'll find many colors, weights, and types of medicine balls (sometimes called "heavy balls"). Choose a ball that weighs between 2 and 10 pounds, or 1 and 4 kilograms. You can purchase medicine balls from most sporting goods stores such as the Sports Authority and Dick's Sporting Goods. You can also find them online from the following stores:

davidkirsch.com (davidkirsch.co.uk)

madisonsquareclub.com

theultimatenewyorkbodyplan.com

sissel-online.com

bodytrends.com

dickssportinggoods.com

jumpusa.com

lifestylesport.com

thesportsauthority.com

warehousefitness.com

DUMBBELLS

Your dumbbells should weigh between two and five pounds. You can purchase dumbbells from most sporting goods stores such as the Sports Authority and Dick's Sporting Goods. I sell a personally branded gym-in-a-bag that includes a set of hand weights, medicine ball, gym bag, and a fitness video. It's great for people who travel. You can find it on davidkirsch.com (davidkirsch.co.uk). You can also find dumbbells from the following online stores:

theultimatenewyorkbodyplan.com

dickssportinggoods.com

thesportsauthority.com

megafitness.com

warehousefitness.com

bodytrends.com

Nutritional Supplements

I am a strong believer in nutritional supplementation. Here are some of the criteria most important to me when choosing the proper supplements and when to take them.

PROTEIN POWDERS, SHAKES, AND BARS

Look for a protein powder or shake with no more than five net carbs and 25 grams of protein. Avoid shakes that contain artificial sweeteners, such as aspartame, and opt for powders and shakes made from whey protein over soy, egg, and other types of protein. Also, stay away from shakes that contain maltodextrin and high-fructose corn syrup. As for protein bars, I recommend just one brand—Bio Chem Ultimate Lo Carb—available at many nutrition supplement stores and the websites listed below. You can find protein powders, bars, and shakes at health food stores, supplement stores such as GNC and Vitamin Shoppe, and most grocery stores. If you'd like to try my personal brand, go to davidkirsch.com (davidkirsch.co.uk). You can also shop online at the following locations:

affordablesupplements.com

amazon.com/health

wowsupplements.com

shopping.com

OTHER SUPPLEMENTS

I recommended numerous supplements in Chapter 3. You can purchase my personal brand in convenient blends with the optimal dosages at davidkirsch.com (davidkirsch.co.uk). I recommend, at the very least, you use my Protein Powder and Vitamin/Mineral Super Juice. For optimal results, pair those supplements with Hoodia, Afternoon Energy, and my PM Appetite Suppressant. You can also shop for nutritional supplements at the following online stores:

vitaminlife.com

affordablesupplements.com

vitacost.com

drugstore.com

vitaminshoppe.com

Optional Items

The key to these items is comfort and assistance with the work that needs to be done on your body.

CLOTHING

You need not purchase special clothing for this plan, but you should wear clothes that feel comfortable and allow you to move with ease. If you're the type of person who tends to break a sweat, look for performance fabrics made from synthetic materials such as CoolMax and SUPPLEX, which wick sweat away from your skin. You can find fitness clothing from sporting goods stores such as the Sports Authority and most department stores. For women, Title 9 Sports offers a wide selection of sports clothing (title9sports.com).

EXERCISE MATS

An exercise mat provides a nonslip surface and a buffer between your body and the floor. You can easily roll up most types and store them behind your couch or in a closet. Look for a mat you find both comfortable and aesthetically pleasing. Make sure it is long and wide enough to cover the floor when you are lying down. You can find exercise mats at sporting goods stores such as the Sports Authority and Dick's Sporting Goods, most department stores, and the following online stores:

dickssportinggoods.com

bodytrends.com

matsuperstore.com

matsmatsmats.com

thera-band.com

thesportsauthority.com

FITNESS BOOKS AND VIDEOS

Sound Mind, Sound Body (Rodale Press, 2001), available at Barnes & Noble, B&N.com, Amazon.com, and davidkirsch.com (davidkirsch.co.uk)

The Ultimate New York Body Plan (McGraw-Hill, 2005), available at Barnes & Noble, B&N.com, Amazon.com, and davidkirsch.com (davidkirsch.co.uk)

David Kirsch's Ultimate Fitness Boot Camp, available on Amazon.com and davidkirsch.com (davidkirsch.co.uk)

David Kirsch's One on One Training Series, available on Amazon.com and davidkirsch.com (davidkirsch.co.uk)

The Ultimate New York Body Plan Video, available on Amazon.com and davidkirsch.com (davidkirsch.co.uk)

Index

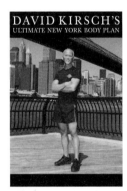

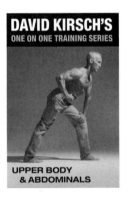